11911
971, 2011092 RAE

FROM PROTEST
→ TO POWER ←

*Personal Reflections
on a Life in Politics*

BOB RAE

THE ONTARIO HISTORICAL SOCIETY

VIKING

VIKING
Published by the Penguin Group
Penguin Books Canada Ltd, 10 Alcorn Avenue, Toronto, Ontario,
Canada M4V 3B2
Penguin Books Ltd, 27 Wrights Lane, London W8 5TZ, England
Viking Penguin, a division of Penguin Books USA Inc., 375 Hudson Street,
New York, New York 10014, U.S.A.
Penguin Books Australia Ltd, Ringwood, Victoria, Australia
Penguin Books (NZ) Ltd, 182–190 Wairau Road, Auckland 10,
New Zealand

Penguin Books Ltd, Registered Offices: Harmondsworth,
Middlesex, England

First published 1996
1 3 5 7 9 10 8 6 4 2

Copyright © Bob Rae, 1996

All rights reserved. Without limiting the rights under copyright
reserved above, no part of this publication may be reproduced, stored in
or introduced into a retrieval system, or transmitted in any form or
by any means (electronic, mechanical, photocopying, recording or
otherwise), without the prior written permission of both the copyright
owner and the above publisher of this book.

Printed and bound in Canada on acid free paper

Canadian Cataloguing in Publication Data

Rae, Bob, 1948-
From protest to power : personal reflections on a life in politics

ISBN 0-670-86842-6

1. Rae, Bob, 1948–   . 2. Prime ministers - Ontario - Biography.
3. Ontario - Politics and government - 1990-   . I. Title.

FC3077.1.R34A3 1996   971.3'04'092   C95-933394-0
F1058.R3A3 1996

The poem by Douglas Le Pan quoted on page 295
is from *Macalister, or, Dying in the Dark*
(Kingston: Quarry Press, 1995).
It is reprinted with permission.

To my wife, Arlene, and our children,
Judith, Lisa, and Eleanor

to my parents, Lois and Saul

to my brother John, sister-in-law Phyllis,
my sister, Jennifer, my sister-in-law Ginny

and in memory of my brother David,
my grandmothers Mildred and Nell,
and Al and Hannah Perly
who have all shown me the way

ACKNOWLEDGMENTS

I have many people to thank. My wife Arlene has surrounded me with love and support throughout our lives together. She read this book in its many drafts, and made it better at every turn. She has aptly described our recent life this way, "I don't see you that much more often now, but when I do you're in a better mood." Like most children, my three daughters Judith, Lisa, and Eleanor have had the good sense not to be preoccupied with the ups and downs of my career. Yet their love and good spirits have been an inspiration this past year, as for the past fifteen. Judith read the whole manuscript and made good suggestions.

My parents Saul and Lois have always given freely of their affection and their views. This project has been no exception. My sister, Jennifer, my brother John and my sister-in-law Phyllis, my sister-in-law Ginny, and Arlene's sister, Jeannie Conn, and her husband, Gary, have been enormously supportive of this project, and of my life, and to them I say thank you once again.

Rob Prichard, the president of the University of Toronto, and John Fraser, the master of Massey College, offered me the time and space to teach and write after our government lost the election in June of 1995. I am grateful to them both, and to the junior and senior fellows of Massey, for their generosity and encouragement throughout this project. My students have helped me in ways they do not necessarily know—I have learned much from them, and from my colleagues Peter Lindsay and Anil Verma.

My editors, Cynthia Good and Mary Adachi, pushed and prodded me into doing better. With the able help of Larissa McWhinney they deserve credit for the improvements, and no blame for its mistakes. Lori Ledingham pushed the manuscript to the printer with a gentle insistence. Pat Curley provided me with research and secretarial help when I badly needed assistance; Sonia Zanardi has provided a remarkable combination of steadiness and good humour for which I am grateful every day. My agent Michael Levine gave me good advice, which I usually accepted. He is now my fellow conspirator in the law. My partners and associates at Goodman Phillips and Vineberg have accepted me in their midst with a generosity that I continue to treasure. I hope that none of them are unduly embarrassed by the contents of this book.

I prevailed on several friends to read parts of this book at different stages. They managed to perform the difficult feat of providing both encouragement and tough editorial admonition. David Agnew, Andrée Crépeau, Michael Ignatieff, Graham Fraser, Eddie Goodman, Jonathan Hausman, Ross McClellan, Jeff Rose, Margaret Tatham and Barbara Uteck deserve medals for their forbearance.

The New Democratic Party has been my political family for more than twenty years, and it is hard to know how to acknowledge adequately the debt I owe so many people. My predecessor as M.P. for Broadview, John Gilbert, and his wife, Nora, were my original mentors. Ed Broadbent was my leader in the caucus I joined in 1978 and I owe him deep thanks for his example and friendship. My political colleagues in the provincial party, led by the deputy leader, Floyd Laughren, stuck with me even during the most difficult moments. This has made a huge difference in my life. I received a good part of my early political education from my friends in the labour movement.

Valerie Lawson and Tony Romano were my political eyes and ears in my constituency offices, and Sheila Kirouac worked for me during my entire public career. She has been a tremendous source of support. Arlene Wortsman joined me as an executive assistant in Ottawa. She remains a great friend. Marilyn Roycroft, Anita Shilton, and Hugh Mackenzie gave me great help during the earliest days of my leadership, followed by Robin Sears and Chuck Rachlis in the "accord years" and after. Sharon Vance travelled with me on every election campaign, and was a superb source of ironic inspiration. She has my unqualified thanks.

During my premiership I had the loyal and effective help of Lynn Spink, Richard McLellan, Ana Lopes and Grace Edward Galabuzzi, my executive assistants; Melody Morrison, David Mackenzie, and Dennis Young were invaluable as strategists and principal secretaries right up to my decision to leave political life. These are truly the unsung heroes of politics, as are the organizers like Gordon Brigden, Penny Dickens, Patty Park, Michael Lewis, Jack Murray, Brian Harling, André Foucault, and Jill Marzetti, who have served me and the party with such distinction.

Peter Mosher, Rob Mitchell, Dean Williams, Laurie Stephens, Norm Simon, John Piper, Sine Mackinnon, Cim Nunn, and Murray Weppler guided me through the maze of the modern media. They often received brickbats from the Press Gallery for their efforts, which they suffered with remarkable good humour. Peter Mosher was my first "travelling companion" on the highways, byways, and back concessions of Ontario, succeeded by Vasco Dos Santos in opposition, and a wider group after I became premier, which included Lynn Spink, Ana Lopes, Greg Paliouras, Jim Cook, Robert McGillvray, and my friends in the O.P.P. Peter Mosher's hand waving gently in a circle at the back of a hall, indicating that if I spoke any longer I'd be heading for the last round-up, was succeeded by Vasco's multilingual advice on every conceivable topic. They made late-night car rides across Ontario highways unforgettable.

David Agnew, Melody Morrison, Ross McClellan and Michael Mendelson served me and the government of Ontario with great distinction. Their friendship and support made my own public service possible, and more often than not enjoyable. Countless other public servants, whose careers I would not like to shorten by naming, have made a great contribution to the public good. They also became my friends. I cannot thank them enough for what our association has meant to me. I am a lucky man to know such fine people and to have them as companions and colleagues.

Naturally I cannot ascribe to anyone else responsibility either for what I did during my career or for how I have chosen to describe these events. For these, and for all sins of omission and commission, I take my full measure of blame and credit.

Bob Rae

Toronto and Portland, Ontario

July 1996

Contents

FROM PROTEST TO POWER

A DOSE OF REALITY AT
HONEY HARBOUR

September had always been the traditional month in politics for taking stock. In Ottawa and Queen's Park caucus had used the time before the opening of the parliamentary session to review plans, break bread, listen to music and gossip. Maybe even relax. Opposition retreats were usually fun. They always ended with a list of priorities and a ritual press conference denouncing the government of the day for its sins.

September 1991 was different. The government whose performance we were assessing was our own. The premier under the microscope was me. I always said I wanted to be premier in the worst way. A year after I took office, it was clear my wish had been granted.

At the Delawanna Inn, a rambling resort on the southern shore of Georgian Bay, our government came of age.

Ironically, Bill Davis was there to greet us. His cottage was on an island nearby, and he made a point of dropping in just as the bus arrived from Toronto.

"Welcome, Robert, to a part of Ontario that seems to survive whatever political formation of the day happens to have a majority, however temporary."

And then, with a chuckle and a suck on his pipe, he was gone.

                          ← →

Nothing had really prepared us for the first year of government. By the late summer of 1991 we were obviously in trouble. Ontario's recession was getting worse, much deeper and more intractable than we had thought possible. Two cabinet ministers had left their jobs earlier in the spring. I had shuffled the cabinet that summer, dropping two more ministers, and promoting others. There was the perception that the team was inexperienced and accident-prone.

The job had also taken its personal toll on me. I was working incredible hours, sleeping poorly, and carrying too much of the load. In early July, I'd had difficulty breathing, and Arlene insisted that I go to the doctor. I went to the little clinic in Portland, and the doctor sent me to Smiths Falls for X-rays. The verdict came back that I had pneumonia in both lungs. I was treated as an outpatient for two weeks, pretending on each visit that I was at the hospital to do a "walk around." The nurses would whisk me into the emergency room for a half-hour Ventolin treatment, and back out I would go.

I was left with residual asthma, which meant I had to carry a puffer around. My hair was suddenly whiter. "Boy wonder" no longer, I had to dig deeper to find the stamina I needed to do the job.

Other events combined to strengthen the wake-up call. Negotiations over the paper-mill in Kapuskasing had collapsed, and hundreds of citizens had descended on Queen's Park in early July. Algoma Steel was on the brink of bankruptcy, threatening thousands of jobs in the Sault. The feds were bumbling the de Havilland file, and trying to force a sale to the French competitor Aerospatiale, which would have destroyed the company.

Opinion favouring sovereignty in Quebec was running at well over 50 per cent, as the Rejection of Quebec through the Failure of the Meech Lake Accord was added to the mythological litany that fuelled nationalism in Quebec.

My first meeting with Prime Minister Brian Mulroney at

Harrington Lake earlier that summer above all convinced me that the unity file was bound to become a major preoccupation. The public in Ontario was sick of it, and the recession had made everyone even less tolerant of the issue, but it was there and had to be faced.

As a government we were doing too much. Ministers had an activist agenda, and together with their political staffs were especially eager to push ahead on every front. Sometimes we would read of each other's well-meaning intervention in the morning newspaper. Some would cheer. I would usually wince, for while I knew that this would bring solace to the hearts of some, for many others it would only indicate that the government was heading off in all directions at once.

I decided that we needed to narrow the agenda. Earlier promises and priorities would have to be dropped. I shared this feeling first with David Agnew, my friend and principal secretary. No one was closer to me politically, and I relied on him more than on anyone else during my entire political career. His extraordinary abilities as an organizer, his great good humour and wit, and his incredible capacity for work made him indispensable. He was rightly seen as the chief architect of our victory in 1990 and was the logical choice as my principal secretary, though only thirty-three when we formed the government.

David was even harder than me on how far we were losing our way, and what needed to be done to get us back on track. He never shared my enthusiasm for matters constitutional, though he came to accept it as part of my vision for the country and for the government. He saw more quickly than I did the need for a major turn in government policy on the economy, and more than anyone deserves the credit for insisting on greater discipline, from me and from the whole cabinet.

This did not, of course, always make him popular with my colleagues, because many were so keen to pursue what they saw as the government's best agenda. Already in that first year there were dramatic conflicts between spenders and savers, between advocates and managers. David shared my view that we needed to mend our ways, and mend them quickly. This was the subject of our July phone call.

I had shared my concerns with David many times. My problem was I couldn't see my way clear to a solution.

"Drop car insurance. The more we look at it the less sense it makes."

"The party will go nuts."

"The public doesn't care about this issue, and the public is what matters. You can carry the party."

"It's certainly bold enough. But what a broken promise."

"It will be a symbol of our maturity."

We were reinforcing each other's sense of what had to be done. We agreed to keep talking it through. But having his support and encouragement made a huge difference.

As we met, the news was full of change around the world. Statscan announced that Ontario had accounted for almost three-quarters of all the job losses in the recession. The Public Service Alliance of Canada announced its first ever general strike against the federal government. Lithuania, Latvia, and Estonia severed their ties with Moscow, marking the end of the Soviet Union. The African National Congress denounced F.W. de Klerk's constitutional proposals as minority rule in disguise. Investors snapped up a huge Ontario Eurobond float. Pierre Trudeau was a father again, which produced the cartoon of a fellow seventy-year-old in a restaurant pointing to Trudeau's meal and telling the waiter, "I'll have whatever he's having."

← →

The first couple of sessions with the whole caucus were devoted to a presentation by our pollster from the election campaign, David Gotthilf, and by Peter Donegan, who ran all the focus group discussions for us before, during, and after the election. Gotthilf had told me before the election that the "NDP universe" had a ceiling of about 30 per cent and that should be our target. Always good humoured, about two weeks before election day he let me know that our universe of those who were real, potential supporters had just expanded to 40 per cent. This, and countless other experiences, always made me sceptical about the "science" of polling.

Gotthilf was a man of imagination and intelligence. I lost an important adviser and friend when he died tragically of a heart attack at age thirty-five on December 22, 1993.

The message from Gotthilf and Donegan was very tough: the gains we had made in support for our party before the 1990 election, and after, had been largely dissipated. We were being jointly blamed with the Tories for the recession. We had failed to deliver on change. Our agenda was all over the map. The areas of our perceived greatest focus—better labour laws and public auto insurance—were at the bottom of the list of public priorities.

It was a lousy report card, made only marginally more palatable by the news that I personally scored quite well, and the other parties were not ranked much better. On hearing this news, the caucus members responded with their own sense of unease. Throughout our time in government, the caucus was the best focus group I had. They were new to politics, and new to political responsibility. They were a truly diverse group, always candid, sometimes angry, and yet through all our setbacks and difficulties extraordinarily loyal and stalwart.

Nothing had really prepared them for the experience of getting elected, and then having to face such a difficult moment in Ontario public life.

They were not an ideological group, which is what made them such a valuable reference point. How they felt about an issue was not necessarily the product of great intellectual reflection. But that in itself made it more worthwhile. Ideology and party policy I could get on order from sections of the party. Facts and figures, and fifty reasons why something wouldn't work I could get, regularly, from the bureaucracy. Political feel and judgment I got from the caucus, once I learned enough to consult and to listen.

Listen I did that weekend, after presenting them with the same dilemma I had given to cabinet. As matters stood, we were being told by the public that they wanted us to focus on jobs and the economy, and not much else. In turn, we had constructed an agenda that was far too complicated, with the public ownership of all car insurance heading the list. A strong majority of caucus wanted to drop the issue from the agenda. Their reasons were less complex than mine: they hadn't seen all the reports, but they did know that a mass lay-off carried out by our government in the middle of the worst recession since the 1930s didn't make sense. The estimates were that lay-offs of between 10,000 and 15,000 would follow a public takeover of the insurance business. If our message on jobs was going to get through, we had to focus our efforts on that, and avoid as much as possible the controversies that got in the way.

There were strong dissenters. In the cabinet, Howard Hampton from Rainy River felt the Manitoba example was compelling, and the politics of a U-turn unpalatable. Those members who had knocked on doors and plant-gated on this issue in the 1980s weren't happy to change course. But the overwhelming majority were, by almost three to one. Julie Davis, then party president and secretary-treasurer of the Ontario Federation of Labour, put it most bluntly,

"We weren't elected government to put 10,000 women on lay-off, not in the middle of this recession."

The press, of course, were all around the Delawanna Inn, and heard second-hand reports of what was afoot. "Rae Flip Flops" was one early headline. Peter Kormos left the meeting before the discussion was over, and shared his disgruntlement with whoever would listen.

I made the announcement on the Saturday morning at the end of the caucus discussion that we were not going to proceed with public auto insurance. "This is a day of reckoning. We have to come to terms with being a government." The public reaction was, to put it mildly, muted. Our telephone lines didn't light up, and the mail certainly didn't come pouring in from an angry general public. But that didn't end the matter, and the decision had a significance for all of us that I didn't fully appreciate at the time.

While the leadership of the party and the trade union movement accepted the decision with initial good grace, some people were very unhappy. Kormos used the decision to go permanently off-side, and took one other caucus member, Mark Morrow, with him. He continued to attract media attention as a focus for dissent and general unhappiness. Mel Swart, who had nominated me for the leadership in 1982 and had always been one of my strongest backers, never forgave me for the decision on car insurance. He took it upon himself to launch a campaign for my removal from office. This proved more difficult to handle than Kormos's attacks, since Mel had a large following in the party and had become something of an icon.

So it was that within parts of the party and labour movement, the decision on car insurance was to feed the myth of betrayal. This was encouraged by some observers and critics of the party from the left. I always found this ironic, since "cheaper insurance" is hard to compare with jobs equity, health care, and public education in a pantheon of values. But the hard political fact remains that when we moved on Sunday shopping in 1992 and on a social contract in 1993, the left carefully fashioned a myth that soon took on the status of an established truth.

These theories have an ancient pedigree: critics of social democracy have been quick to point to the "sell-outs," the "betrayals" of those who in power have made compromises and decisions that besmirched the purity of the cause and the movement. In the late 1950s, Hugh Gaitskell, then leader of the Labour Party in Britain, tried unsuccessfully to change the Labour Party Constitution. Its famous Clause 4 talks about the nationalization of the means of production as a fundamental objective of the party. When Gaitskell signalled that it was time to drop the clause (something Tony Blair just managed to do in 1995), Harold Wilson remarked that "you can't tell the Salvation Army there's no salvation."

← →

It was at Honey Harbour that I determined to get the party to come to terms with some of its most passionate symbols. My appetite for this grew the longer I was premier. I underestimated how hard this was to manage politically. I kept the caucus together, but never managed to rally the public and the party successfully behind another set of symbols.

The same week that we decided to drop public auto insurance, the government quietly agreed to take partial ownership of the de

Havilland Aircraft Company, a decision that was announced some time later. An activist government has a key role to play in society, something I passionately believed then and now. The forms of that activism and intervention will change. Too many on the left confuse form with substance. Policies and institutions become icons, missing the point that it is principles and values that matter. I have never been patient with orthodoxy.

But Harold Wilson's point was well taken: a successful politician has to manage change in order to retain and increase support. The change for many New Democrats was too abrupt, too jarring.

To put it another way, dropping car insurance, while a wise decision given all our challenges as a government, was seen by some to be a sign of loss of faith and loss of direction. A sense of populism had contributed to our victory in 1990. It was something we couldn't maintain. Moving from a party of protest to a government in power was more difficult than we thought.

That week in September of 1991, and the year that preceded it, had forced me to come to terms with things about myself as well. I was much more aware of the gap between populist rhetoric and what would actually work. Watching what was happening in other social democratic parties around the world—and indeed around the country—I was less enamoured of what had passed for salvation in party resolutions. I was determined to push ahead, but I was never completely sure that I had the full armoury of political skills personally, or the depth of support from my team, that would let us get there successfully. I was more determined to do "the right thing" than worry about how it would affect my own political success, and the success of the party. And, as time would tell, for that I would pay a price.

I also had the strong belief that doing the right thing and offering good government, as opposed to promises and ideology, was the better path. Whether it was to be politically successful I didn't know, and became less concerned about as time went on. The child is father to the man. My upbringing and my own roots have everything to do with the kind of premier I became and the government I ran.

Chapter One

GETTING THERE

Driving up Highway 15 north of Kingston, through towns and villages like Morton, Elgin, Crosby, and Portland, I have come to know that this part of Ontario is my home. We first came to Big Rideau Lake in 1954 and 1955, the summer my dad was in Hanoi, Vietnam. We stayed at a comfortable cottage called Bending Birches, on an island that belonged to Hamilton and Jacqueline Southam, great friends and colleagues of my parents.

The lake stands at the edge of the Canadian Shield—the water at the North Shore is hundreds of feet deep—and yet the landscape is greener and softer than Georgian Bay or Muskoka. Loyalists came across the St. Lawrence more than two hundred years ago, joined by settlers given land by Lord Simcoe and Irish labourers who survived the construction of the Rideau Canal.

Cottagers started coming to Rideau Lake late in the nineteenth century, and some great old buildings from that time still survive. In the fall of 1956 my parents bought a one-acre island, with boats, motors, cottage, and generating station. Since that time I have spent practically every summer "at the lake." It has been the centre in a growing-up that often meant travel and living away from Canada.

When we went to Portland in the fall of 1990, just after the election, I was stopped in the street by an old friend. "When you won on election night it was just like Portland won the Stanley Cup. Of course that doesn't mean we voted for you."

It was here that I learned to swim, to canoe, to fish, to sail; here that I had my first slow dance and my first kiss; here that I did so much of my growing up and my settling down. Here that my family spread my brother David's ashes and here that I know the same will be done one day for me. From my bedroom window I can see the sun rise in the morning, and from the back porch see it go down at night. In the times in between I try to share with my own children something of the joy of watching a beaver cross the front bay, the wonder of an osprey circling, circling, and then diving with incredible force to catch a sunfish in its talons. We watch the loons by day and listen to their primeval cries at night. I know that with any luck my three daughters will be doing the same with their children in a generation. This gives me more comfort than I can readily describe.

I was born in Ottawa on August 2, 1948. Not in a log embassy as I have often joked at my own expense, but in the Ottawa Civic Hospital. We lived at that time in a small house on Acacia Avenue, in the neighbourhood known as Lindenlea. My parents live there to this day.

My parents had moved to Ottawa in 1940 when my dad joined the Canadian foreign service. My earliest memories are of nursery school, where I was punished for trapping a girl behind a wall of blocks. I also remember I had a marvellous three-wheeled bicycle with a little trunk in the back. I used to chase after my older brother and sister and try to keep up.

My constant companion was Darcy Dunton, who lived just down the street, and whose parents Doff and Davey were among my mum and dad's closest friends. Davey Dunton was one of my two godfathers; the other was Charles Ritchie.

The year my dad went off to Vietnam—1955—Davey and Doff Dunton were like parents to me. The Duntons rented a cottage at Meech Lake (yes, that Meech Lake), and lying in a hammock Davey read *The Lion, the Witch and the Wardrobe* to us. To this day I have a recurrent dream about a door at the back of a closet leading to another world.

Davey Dunton gave me my first lesson in French-English relations in Canada. Driving down a dirt road, we picked up a monk. Davey started talking to him in French, which I didn't understand. When we dropped the monk off I asked him why he didn't talk to him in English. Davey said, quite simply, "Because this is Quebec and in Canada we speak both."

Darcy Dunton and I ran away from home twice, not as I recall in any state of deep rebellion, but more as an adventure. One escapade had two seven-year-olds taking an old row-boat out on Mackay Lake—and getting home very late. I can remember my dad being especially upset because he and my brother had to miss Milton Berle on television because they were out searching for us.

My sister was Jenny, and my brother was Johnny, and I was Bobby. We all still are to the friends who have known us since those days. It was a happy time—we fought among ourselves of course, but we had lots of friends, and we lived in a community that was remarkably close-knit. The war had brought together in Ottawa a group of bright, hard-working, and funny people (I choose each word carefully), who were enormously fond of each other, of each other's families, and who cared passionately about public policy and public service. These were my parents' friends, and this was the world in which I was raised. It was the Golden Era of Canada's public service.

← →

My parents met at a summer school run by Sir Norman Angell in Geneva, Switzerland, in the summer of 1937. They had arrived by very different routes.

My father's parents were from Glasgow. His father was the eldest son of Jewish immigrants from Lithuania, who had gone to Scotland in the 1880s. My grandfather would have been only two or three on his arrival in Glasgow, and grew up in the toughest part of the city, the Gorbals. He was, by all accounts, a character: charming, funny, handsome, and dapper, who fell in love with the girl known to the end of her remarkable life as Nell. Nell's family were proud members of the Church of Scotland, and my grandfather was already rebelling against the authority of his family and of his faith.

There was more than a little of the rebel in Nell as well. She was in love with the musical theatre, and would later tell us that her first two loves were with an Irish Catholic and a Japanese tenor at the music hall. This second romance she concealed from her parents by saying she was going to the baths (she swam until she was well into her nineties), and then wetting her hair on the way home in the horse trough. Seeds in her hair finally gave her away.

My grandfather's love of Nell and need for independence separated him from his family. So it was that in 1912 he did not head with the others to Cupar, Saskatchewan, where his parents, Herman and Polly Cohen, settled on a farm, but instead went to Hamilton, where he found rooms near the railway station in the north end of the city.

Nell joined him with their daughter, my Aunt Grace, a few months later. Writing years later about this voyage, Nell describes travelling steerage but sneaking upstairs to first class for tea after befriending one of the waiters. Her arrival in Hamilton by train from Halifax was marred by the fact that her husband was waiting for her at the wrong railway station, something that she recalled with enormous clarity eighty years later, as well as the fact that the rooms he had first rented weren't good enough. They found a small cottage to rent, near the Armouries, and then moved to Cannon Street. It was there, at home, late at night as the story would have it, that my father, Saul, was born on New Year's Eve, 1914.

My grandfather fought in the First World War with the Canadian army. Nell lost a brother in the trenches in 1916. I am named for him, Bobby Rae, as I am for my mother's grandfather Robert Oxenham. Nell and the two children were in Glasgow with her family during the war, but made haste for Canada again when the war ended.

Nell loved the music hall as a girl in Glasgow, and she passed on this love to her children, who numbered three with the arrival of my Uncle Jack in 1924. Nell's children were stage struck, with her encouragement, and under her strict supervision. Grace, the oldest, became a talented dancer, choreographer, and musician. Saul and Jack were naturals: comics, singers, dancers, piano-players, writers. Jack stayed in show business all his life, becoming the head of CBC variety programming in his early thirties. He is a producer, a song-writer, a singer, and leader of the Spitfire Band. He also had an extraordinary record as a young RCAF pilot in the Second World War. He was awarded the DFC for his part in the raid on Dieppe. Throughout my travels I have met great fans of Uncle Jack.

The "Three Little Raes of Sunshine" were launched in Winnipeg. On the wall of my office I have a poster from the Winnipeg Lyceum, where Saul is on the bill doing a Jolson imitation. He would have been all of nine years old. Their vaudeville act travelled, and came to the attention of Jack Arthur, who worked as an impresario for Famous Players Theatres.

With his encouragement, the family moved to Toronto in the mid-1920s. It was at this time that my grandfather broke all ties with his family and took Nell's last name as his own. He was known thereafter as William Rae.

My father attended Jarvis Collegiate, and when I spoke to students at Jarvis about sixty years after my father had been there, an enterprising teacher showed me pages from the yearbooks of 1930 and 1931: the President of the Dramatic Club in the first Jarvis Collegiate Radio Broadcast, "in his usual bright manner, told his listeners how to be happy by 'Painting the Clouds with Sunshine.'" That's my dad.

All his life he's had this brightness, this presence. I once appeared as the Duke of Plaza Toro in Gilbert and Sullivan's "The Gondoliers." I asked him how I did. He was proud of me, but said it looked as if I was holding back a bit. "No one's going to give you the stage. Just take it and when you're on don't let them ever forget you're there."

❖ ❖

During the Depression, the Rae family, like many others, had no money, but the kind intervention of the registrar of University

College, Professor W. J. McAndrew, made university possible. In 1932 the University of Toronto opened up a whole new world to Saul: the world of ideas, debates, politics, sociology, and study. He was a prodigious worker, and could still find time to organize the U.C. Follies, and summer shows at camps where he was a counsellor. He has continued to love music, comedy, and shows throughout his life. He only minds that some stuffy people don't understand that he could be fun-loving and dead serious at the same time.

He went to the London School of Economics as a Massey Fellow in 1936, and wrote his Ph.D. in sociology on "Public Opinion and Its Measurement." He attended summer school in Geneva with Sir Norman Angell, author of *The Great Illusion*, and my father became interested in understanding how the public made up its mind, how it changed its mind, and how this could be assessed and measured.

❮ ❯

He met and fell in love with my mother, Lois George, in the summer of 1937. His room-mate in Geneva was an American Rhodes Scholar named Walt Rostow, who also met his wife in Geneva. Saul went to Oxford in 1938, for a year at Balliol College, where he studied public opinion around the famous Oxford by-election, and made fast friends with what was a remarkable political generation in England, Canada, and the United States: his contemporaries at Balliol were Rostow, Madron Seligman, Phil Kaiser, Ted Heath, Roy Jenkins, and Dennis Healey.

Heath, Jenkins, and Healey all dominated British politics, in three different political parties. Madron Seligman became a member of the European Parliament; Phil Kaiser became an American diplomat; Walt Rostow was an adviser to President Kennedy and President Johnson, and a controversial figure for his support for the American presence in Vietnam.

It was at this time that Saul also met George Gallup.

❮ ❯

The election of 1936 in the United States saw, of course, the re-election of Franklin Delano Roosevelt. But as a footnote to political sociologists it was marked by another event as well: the Literary Digest had done a poll, based on those people who owned telephones, predicting that Alf Landon would beat F.D.R. This had so discredited the young "polling business" that George Gallup saw both his challenge and opportunity. The American Institute of Public Opinion was born, and my father joined it to write a book with Gallup about polling called *The Pulse of Democracy*.

↞ ↠

Saul and Lois were married in September of 1939, in Baltimore, Maryland, where they had travelled after my mother's arrival from England. There were two passenger liners travelling in early September, and my dad wasn't sure which one Lois was on. She came on the *Normandy*. The *Athenia* sank after a German U-boat attack.

↞ ↠

My mother was born in London, England, the oldest of three children. Her father, Stan George, was a doctor in suburban Hampstead. His own father, Willie George, was a successful businessman in Australia. There is a department store in Melbourne, Australia, that is called "George's," which was started by my great-grandfather. I'm not a part-owner, unfortunately.

Stan went to England for his medical studies, and while in London met and married Mildred Theobald, my grandmother, who died in 1991 at the age of ninety-nine. Her family were in the wallpaper business, and were quite successful. My mother was born in 1914, and was followed by her brother, Keith, and sister, Ruth.

Stan George died suddenly of kidney failure when my mother was fifteen years old. Mildred never remarried, and brought up the three children on her own. She was a lovely woman, enormously kind and generous, with a love of life and a gentle sense of humour. She stayed with us for extended visits when we were growing up—as did Nell—and I used to visit her all the time when I was a student at Oxford.

I did not meet or know either of my grandfathers, who died before I was born. But Nell and Mildred were a real presence in my life.

15

Nell left school when she was twelve, because that's what happened to girls in those days, and that injustice stayed with her. She loved to read, and could recite poetry and songs from memory. She believed fiercely in education and wouldn't hear of anyone leaving school or not doing well.

My first memory of Nell is visiting her in Toronto when Dad was away in Vietnam. I would have been seven. She let me cuddle with her in bed, and she told me stories about every dog she ever had, from the time she was a girl. She loved dogs, most of all Caesar, the boxer of Jack's who could sing and smoke cigars, do Churchill imitations and in all ways delight children.

She stayed with us in Washington, and again in Geneva, good, long visits. She loved to laugh, deep and full. She loved to sing "Rowan Tree," I remember, and show-business numbers. In her eighties she would entertain visitors with a club dance, a shuffle off to Buffalo, and a duet with my dad, whose words I can still recite from memory.

> *After I brought you the sunshine,*
> *You left me out in the rain.*
> *I played the part, gave you your start,*
> *Now I've been rewarded with a broken heart.*
> *You were the one I help to win,*
> *Now I'm the one to lose.*
> *You took the colours from the rainbow,*
> *And left me singing the blues.*
> *After I brought you the sunshine,*
> *You left me out in the rain.*

Once I came to Nell's flat and heard her shouting at the top of her voice, "Get him! Get him when he's down! Finish him off!" I thought it was a burglar. She was watching the wrestling.

Nell loved campaigning. She wasn't just a partisan supporter. She was a fiercely partisan supporter. No one could speak ill of her party or her candidate. Once in her early nineties she was visited by John Evans, who had retired as president of the University of

Toronto and was a Liberal candidate. She kept him talking and chatting for a couple of hours, showing him scrapbooks and pictures, and telling him all her stories. She told me later quite proudly that she'd kept him tied up all night.

She was a fighter, but she could also be gentle. She genuinely loved debating; she was a great reader. There was a restlessness about her spirituality—her eventual reliance on Christian Science was a perfect metaphor for the triumph of will over matter, but even that was tempered with her dictum, "always use common sense with C.S." This from a woman who stayed two days in bed with a broken leg because she thought she could get it to heal on its own. I've never known a stronger, more determined person. She loved with intensity, and she drew the same love and intensity in return. We buried Nell in 1994 at age 107.

❖ ❖

Mildred was a very different person, but equally strong and remarkable in her own way. My earliest memory of her is the summer she came to stay with us in Washington after my brother David was born. She had a white visor and a great laughing smile as she waved to us from the freighter in Norfolk, Virginia. No cruise liners for Gran. But I came to know her best when I was at Oxford and working in London. Tea and dinner perfectly served; we talked about so many things—people, family, ideas, music, and politics. She was reluctant to talk about herself, and literally couldn't stop thinking of ways to help others.

She lived almost as long as Nell, remaining vigorous until her death at ninety-nine in 1991. She wrote great letters in a bold flowing hand, and met all her great-grandchildren, whom she would remember at each holiday and birthday. She put up with my confusion when I was a graduate student in England and eventually urged me in the right direction.

In England I used to visit Nell and Granny George often at their flats, ten minutes' walk from each other. I think how lucky I am to have known them both so well and to have been able to share time and space with them.

After her father died, Lois went to Newnham College,

Cambridge, where she read History. She worked for the Royal Institute of International Affairs, for the National Film Board during the war, and then in audience research for the CBC. When we moved to Washington in 1956, she concentrated full-time on being my father's work partner and organizing the family. My brother David, a late arrival in 1957, became a full-time handful.

✦ ✦

My parents have been married for more than fifty years, and theirs is an extraordinary partnership. Saul's energetic spirit found its anchor in Lois's calm and steadiness; he provided an outlet for fun and irreverence, as well as a strong goad to do better and work harder ("98 per cent? What happened to the other 2?"). My mother has been at the heart and centre of our whole family life, a wise, calming presence for all of us.

My parents are far and away the greatest influence on my life. My dad's humour, his love for his work, his vitality surrounded me as a boy, as did his love for me and my brothers and sister. He dedicated his professional life to Canada's international public service, serving as minister in Washington, D.C., ambassador to the U.N. in Geneva and New York, and ambassador to Mexico and the Netherlands. The issues that are now widely discussed— globalization, Canadian unity, Canada's place in the world—were never abstractions for him, or for us. They were a natural part of his world, and therefore of mine. He has helped make Canada a better place, and I am proud to be his son. My mother's interest in everything around her, her prodigious reading, and knowing all that goes on around her continues to amaze me to this day. I was, and am, a lucky man to have chosen my parents so wisely. To grow up in such a warm place is not everyone's fate, but it was certainly mine.

Our lives were also marked by the strength of my parents' friendships, and the enormous pleasure they both found in their work. Much is now being written about the "mandarins" of that time and generation. None of it captures the spirit of something which at that time I thought was quite normal and everyday, but which I now see was quite unique.

When my dad joined the Department of External Affairs at the beginning of the war, it was a small group. There were only eight in his entry class. Others of his closest friends, George Ignatieff, Ed Ritchie, Arnold Smith, John Holmes, had joined just before or soon after. Four other men, Charles Ritchie, Norman Robertson, George Vanier, and Arnold Heeney, were to become great friends as well as mentors throughout his career.

They all shared certain core views about Canada and its place in the world. The British Tory view of Canada as a colony was rejected outright. The steady fight that had been waged since Confederation for Canada to be able to take its place as an independent and co-equal member of the world community was ongoing even after the Statute of Westminster in 1931. My parents had demonstrated against Munich as students in England, and had a deep and abiding dislike of appeasement and its protagonists. Any isolationist or pacifist sentiment they rejected out of hand as well.

Their politics were liberal and progressive, but not overtly partisan. Dad had been an early member of the C.C.F. club at the University of Toronto, and certainly his mother, Nell, was a strong Labour Party supporter from the old country. But he was also deeply pragmatic and practical, and an anti-communist even in the 1930s. His experiences in government were to deepen all these instincts.

He worked as Norman Robertson's assistant soon after joining "the Department" as it was called around our house. Norman Robertson was one of the wisest, nicest men I ever met as a boy. He was tall, wore dark three-piece suits, and had a round, oval head that was quite bald with a fringe of dark brown hair around the side. He was a remote figure when we lived in Washington and he was the ambassador. This all changed when he and his wife, Jetty, came to Geneva after he had been struck with lung cancer, and he was to preside over the GATT Kennedy Round negotiations of the day. Then he and his wife would come over to our house for Sunday lunch and he would quietly hold forth on Vietnam (a middle way had to be found); Britain and the E.E.C. (de Gaulle's incorrigible nationalism was impossible); and his memories of his own student days at Balliol—another common thread with my father—and the British General Strike of 1926.

Years later, after his death, Robertson was unfairly criticized for the decision during the Second World War to intern Canadians of Japanese origin living in British Columbia. This always struck me as too simple. He was an exceptionally open-spirited person. He was a career public servant who was an adviser to a government that made such a decision, just as a similar decision was made in the United States. He once looked at me wistfully as we were talking about how political climates change—we were actually talking about McCarthy and Alistair Cooke's book *A Generation on Trial,* which I had just read—and he simply said, "when you're there in government you always have a lot to answer for."

If he'd been asked to wear a cassock, he would have looked the perfect part of a very wise abbot. He was a complete sceptic in religious matters, and cared little for details of administration. He destroyed all his correspondence before he died, because he didn't think civil servants should talk publicly, and he also didn't want others picking on the remains. He never cared about making money and completely shunned publicity. He knew that his influence depended on trust from those in power, and that trust depended as well on their sense of his complete integrity.

These were traits common to this whole generation, in varying degrees and in different ways, of course. Arnold Heeney was ambassador to Washington when we moved there in 1956, and his style was in real contrast to Robertson's. He was a successful lawyer from Montreal, and an active Anglican. His view of life was robust, vigorous, and positive. He was politically more conservative than Robertson, more of a "people person," a strong administrator, and less of an intellectual interested in policy. He took an enormous interest in all the Raes and their progress, and welcomed me with open arms into his house even when I had long hair and views he must have thought odd.

✦ ✦

Charles Ritchie was my godfather. His visits to our house were always the occasion of great delight. Thin as a rake, he spoke in a high clear voice. He loved to gossip, he loved to joke about his school days. When he and my father started to mimic colleagues, cabinet ministers, journalists, it was more than a merry evening. It was hysterical. As I grew older, I came to cherish his wisdom and sense of perspective even more. And all this was long before I even guessed he was keeping a diary. He was very ill before he died, and when I last saw him a few weeks before he passed away, he said, "Whoever called these 'the golden years' didn't know what he was talking about. It's not dying I mind. It's the build-up."

This combined sense of fun and public service, of enormous interest in musical comedy, piano, radio and TV, ideas, issues and great friends from many countries was the air and water of my growing up. Very early on in life, I would sit at the top of the stairs at our house on Acacia and listen. If I close my eyes I can hear my father playing "Anything Goes," or "The Lady Is a Tramp," with his foot banging on the bass pedal, getting louder as the evening went on.

← →

Dad left home for more than a year in 1955, when I was just seven. He was Canada's representative in North Vietnam, and lived throughout that year in Hanoi. He came back much thinner, though still jaunty, and tougher in his views on the repressiveness of the Communists. One of my first real memories was going to the airport in Ottawa to see him leave. I was bawling my eyes out. Louis St. Laurent, then prime minister, was at the airport on his way to a Commonwealth Conference. He tried to console me.

"You should be very proud, your father is doing important work for Canada."

"I don't care! I want my daddy home for Christmas!"

No doubt there is a Freudian explanation for my relationship with the Liberal Party of Canada.

← →

The next year we moved to Washington, D.C., where we lived for six years. We lived in large, comfortable, rented houses in north-west Washington, and I went to Horace Mann Public School and Gordon Junior High School. I got into big trouble once because on the way to school my walking companion and I decided, for a lark, to take all the gas caps off the cars in the parking lot and bury them in a secret place. We were eventually caught by the police at the American University and were severely punished by my parents. Today I'd be a young offender.

I had two other brushes with authority at Horace Mann. Most kids took a bus to get to school, and those who had the responsibility of making sure those kids got across the street safely were members of the School Patrol. We were distinguished by the white belts we got to wear, as well as the fact that we got to drink hot chocolate before class. In Grade 6 three officers were chosen, and I was on the short list to be captain.

My career was cut short when I was seen, with my distinguishing white belt, throwing snowballs at passing cars after school on one of those rare afternoons when snow fell in Washington. My record was further sullied when I joined Frank, the artist in Grade 5 who had developed a skill at portraying the female anatomy. He decided to share this skill by instructing a group of us in the decoration of the doors on the boys' washroom. I was not made captain.

Together with Johnny and my best friend, Billy Paulson, I delivered one of the worst newspapers in the history of modern journalism, *The Washington Star*, a Scripps-Howard tabloid. We had some famous customers who lived in our neighbourhood in northwest Washington, notably then Vice-President Richard Nixon and Senator Estes Kefauver. Christmas time was the season when we would sell calendars, and try to extract as large a tip as possible. Mrs. Nixon gave Johnny ten pennies. Kefauver gave me a twenty-dollar bill, told me to keep the change, and wished me well. I have preferred Democrats to Republicans ever since.

It was in Washington that I developed a love of baseball that has never left me. I saw my first baseball game in the fall of 1956, the Senators at Calvin Griffith Stadium playing the Yankees. I saw the Senators transformed from a last-place team, which they were in the late 1950s, to a much better team, which happened when Harmon Killebrew and Earl Batty and Bob Allison came to play, and then finally to leave town to become the Minnesota Twins. I also used to watch the American University team play just around the corner from our house on Quebec Street, and I was bat-boy for a year.

I used to play baseball in a local little league, where I was platooned between second base and right field. When I want to punish myself on a particularly bad day, I can still conjure up the memory of being the last out—a fly ball to left field—in our quest for the championship. I was a singles hitter, on a good day, and reasonable with a glove.

Billy Paulson and I also invented a game, step baseball. A neighbour's house had steps going up a hill. Throwing the ball at the corner of the step, the ball would travel different distances depending on the angle and strength of the throw. On a fall or spring evening we would play for hours.

← →

Gordon Junior High was on Wisconsin Avenue, and I went there shortly after Brown vs. Board of Education, which integrated the public schools of Washington. I got a great education at Gordon. The teachers were terrific, but above all it was the sheer excitement of diversity, of different people from every background that made it fun. I threw myself into everything—plays, debates, the newspaper, and had a great time. I went to the finals of the regional spelling bee, which was held in Constitution Hall, and was eliminated because I couldn't spell "indictment." Not a mistake any post-Watergate kid would make.

Our school also fielded a team on the budding TV quiz show "It's Academic," and I was one of its members. We won, though I have gnawing memories of pressing the buzzer before the question was over and finishing the sentence instead of answering the question. Some traits stick.

Washington was my home from the time I was eight to the time I was fourteen. On my trips there now I find it still a place of great beauty in its public places, though more dangerous, and the gap between white and black, between rich and poor, is deeper than I remember it. At age twelve or thirteen we would think nothing of taking buses and public transit everywhere, two or three of us heading off to Calvin Griffith Stadium, buying a ticket, and sitting in the June heat watching the Senators get clobbered. We were all aware of race, and everybody listened to and told racial jokes. Washington was in many ways a Southern town, with Southern manners and morals. When my father sometimes drove up to our cottage with our housekeeper, Pearl White, who was Jamaican, there was always the issue of whether the motel on the way would let her have a room. My dad would never take no for an answer.

My little brother, David, was born in Washington, soon after we arrived. He was nearly nine years younger than me, and ran havoc with our lives. We learned to swear as teenagers, and so did he as a four-year-old. Once when my dad pulled and pulled on an old Mercury outboard to get it started, David said, at the top of his voice, "Ah, shit." Without missing a beat my dad said "Not ship, Dave, boatie, boatie." David was the fussiest of fussy eaters. He made life haywire, joking and laughing all the time, and, as we saw it, was spoiled rotten by indulgent parents who loved their "cadeau de Dieu."

← →

In 1962 we left Washington for Geneva, Switzerland, when I was fourteen. My dad was the ambassador to the United Nations, accredited to all the specialized agencies with their offices there, like the World Health Organization, the International Labour Office, and the High Commission for Refugees. Geneva was also the site for the ongoing, never-ending World Disarmament talks, and the so-called Kennedy Round of Tariff Negotiations. Because my parents had first met in Geneva it was a return to a city full of happy memories.

We lived in an old house in the middle of parklike grounds, on an escarpment which ran down to the Arve River. The house had a spectacular view of the Saleve Mountain, and to say I was a lucky kid was putting it mildly. I had a room to myself on the third floor, with my own sink, and when I describe all this to my own kids today, they just shake their heads.

Life was very different from Washington. The school was the International School, which was started with the birth of the old League of Nations. It ran from kindergarten to high school, and was divided into two sections, English and French, which in turn were divided after Grade 7 into English or American exams, and Swiss or French exams. During my time there the school was the birthplace of the International Baccalaureate, and I wrote the first exam in 1964. Weston Collegiate, in my old riding of York South, is one of several schools across Canada which now prepare kids for the "I.B."

When I got to Geneva I didn't speak a word of French, but I learned it by watching television and going to movies. I wrote for the student newspaper. I helped raise money in a school fair for refugees, and even have a picture of me handing a cheque to the brother of the Aga Khan. Talk about coals to Newcastle. I debated, ran for student council, made a movie (a remake of *High Noon*), played tennis, skied like mad every Christmas and Easter, and had a wonderful time.

I also read like crazy. My father told me to read Sinclair Lewis to understand the world around me, and I did. *Babbitt* is probably the best introduction anyone could have to the governments of Ralph Klein and Mike Harris.

I grew up believing that loving the life of books and argument, of imagination and the adventure of ideas, is loving part of life itself. I would walk through the back streets of the old town to the university bookstore near the Wall of the Reformation, and buy paperback novels and books on history and politics. Reading *A Portrait of the Artist as a Young Man* probably had as much effect on me as any that I read, exceeded only by my passion for George Orwell's writing before he wrote *Animal Farm* and *1984.* I'm a great believer in rereading as well, and every year I take down James Agee's *A Death in the Family* and read it again, knowing what comes next on every page. The first pages describing the summer nights in Nashville are still beautiful to me.

↞ ↠

Politics and public life was part of the air I breathed growing up. It was the conversation at breakfast and dinner. My father and I began to argue about politics in my teens, particularly when the war in Vietnam began to heat up. Having been in Hanoi for a year in the fifties, he had developed an intense dislike of the Communist regime there. He did not believe for an instant any assertion that what was happening in the South was some kind of spontaneous outburst of popular feeling. It was fomented from the North.

Being all of sixteen or seventeen, and armed with the latest book by Bernard Fall, I of course knew better. This was part of the continuing argument—and something of a rebellion—which continued through my time in university and lasted until well into my twenties. It is hard to write of this without smiling now, because it was all so much of the shift of the times, and with my own children coming into their teenage years I can see the patterns re-emerging. I only hope I am as patient, and remember to give as much space.

Chapter Two

STUDENT DAYS

In 1966 I came back to Canada to go to university. I got a job in the summer as a guide in the Parliament Buildings, and began my reimmersion into Canadian life. I would go down to the National Gallery to see Group of Seven paintings, and spent as much time as I could at our cottage on Big Rideau Lake. I gave tours in both English and French, which I could now speak much better than when I had left North America four years before. The Quebeckers were like Estes Kefauver, and always tried to stuff your pockets with a tip. The English Canadians seemed to me more like Mrs. Nixon, proper and reserved, and left no tips. Someone really did ask me how much the building weighed, and where they could find the Peach Tower. But the most interesting part of that summer for me was that we would spend evenings grilling politicians and journalists who were willing to spend the time with students.

In September I left for the University of Toronto, and one warm evening I walked up University Avenue toward Queen's Park. I knew in my bones that I had found my home. I lived in Sir Daniel Wilson Residence, and made friends that first year that are still my best.

Graham Fraser I knew as a little boy, but our paths had not crossed since we moved to Washington. He welcomed me like a long lost brother. His room was famous for being a mess, and the story was that someone had left a dog in his room over the weekend when he was away, just to see if he would notice. I am sure this is apocryphal. Graham awoke me to the movies, which he would go and see at any time of day or night.

When his father, Blair, was killed in a canoeing accident, it fell to me to tell Graham. I waited for him on the steps of his apartment and told him the terrible news. We spent the next several days and nights together talking, philosophizing, and crying. Ours is a bond that is stronger now than ever before.

← →

Jeff Rose lived in a room near Graham and I met him that year as well. Jeff was busy working on a teach-in on China that brought teachers, scholars, advocates, and everyone else to Varsity Arena in the fall of that year. Late one Saturday morning, after breakfast in Howard Ferguson Dining Hall (all these Tory premiers seem to get buildings named after them), I was holding forth to whoever was asking what I thought about the teach-ins. A tired, dyspeptic, undergraduate with dark glasses listened and fumed. Finally, he broke the silence, and he turned to me and asked who I thought I was. I answered with equal vehemence. Thus began a remarkable friendship.

My parents had told me to look up Michael Ignatieff. The Rae and Ignatieff clans had been connected for a long time. Michael's father, George, had been with my dad at Jarvis Collegiate and later at university and his mother, Alison, was the daughter of the dean of women at University College, a tremendous influence on the students of her time. George and Alison were lifelong friends of both my parents and had two sons, Michael and Andrew, but we had met only once as kids.

Look up Michael I did, and we have remained fast friends ever since. We debated against each other, argued late into the night, and finally roomed together in a flat at 618A Bloor Street above the Salamander Schmidt shoe store. Later I would invade

Michael's apartment in Cambridge, Massachusetts, as "the man who came for a weekend and stayed for six months." Many saw us as rivals, as our fathers had been both friends and competitors, but this is something we always resisted. Our friendship has been too important.

I threw myself into every conceivable activity. I didn't know many people; I hadn't gone to high school in Ontario, and was self-conscious about that. I knew that if I didn't jump in, life would simply pass me by. University College was a big place, and the university was even bigger; it was a matter of sink or swim. I swam, and I loved it. I worked as a volunteer on the teach-in, signed up for debates at Hart House, and got a part in the U.C. Follies. I loved musicals, had done patter parts in Gilbert and Sullivan, had heard my father reminisce about Wayne and Shuster. I also wanted to meet girls.

It turned out that I was the only guy in the Follies that year who wore old-fashioned pleated pants (before they became fashionable again). And I was the only guy who was a goy. The director—Allan Gordon—chose me because he wanted me to be the straight man who would mispronounce every Yiddish word, which I did, without knowing it. I didn't get the girl, that year, but I did make more friends and learn that while show business was a fun side-line, it couldn't be my career. This is a lesson I've had to relearn every few years.

← →

I first became aware of drugs in 1967. There was a sweet guy named Al Kamin, who in our first year was a hardworking kid from Windsor. The second year he and his buddy in residence would come into breakfast later and later with bigger and bigger smiles on their faces, sounding more confused and spaced out as the year progressed. Finally the penny dropped. Al became a strong disciple of Timothy Leary, and a soft-spoken proselytizer for LSD. He didn't make many converts, and only became more gentle.

Twenty years later I got on the Dupont Street bus, and at the back saw a familiar face. He was smiling gently at me, and asked me how I was and what I was doing with myself. At that time I was Leader of the Opposition and had been in politics for about ten years. Al was working for the Post Office, and seemed a happy soul. We parted on a friendly note.

The drug culture never did much for me. Maybe that explains why I can remember so much about those days. I had four main interests in my university days: my work as a student of history and politics, writing for *The Varsity* and other student papers and journals, student politics, and chasing girls. Some things worked out better than others.

I got into second year of the Modern History course, because I'd done Cambridge University "A" Levels at the International School. I took courses in Chinese, Japanese, and Russian history, as well as the old standards in English, European, and Canadian. In my final year I specialized in intellectual history. Again, as in every step along the way, I was blessed with outstanding teachers: Mel Watkins and Abe Rotstein opened up the world of economic history through the eyes of their mentor Harold Innis; John Beattie and Richard Helmstadter did the same for British social history; and Bill Saywell and Milton Israel helped build the foundation of my lifelong interest in Asia, where twenty-five years later I would lead three trade missions.

In my fourth year, three teachers in particular had an extraordinary impact. Carl Berger led a seminar on Canadian Intellectual History (yes, Virginia, Canada does have an intellectual history), and I thought from that class on that I would write my Ph.D. on Frank Underhill and teach that very subject. That was not to be. Jacques Kornberg led an exciting discussion of Marx, Freud, and Nietzsche. I sometimes stayed up all night reading the *Economic and Philosophic Manuscripts* and thought I really understood the young Marx. Kornberg gently persuaded me that there was more to understand, and with an unforgettable smile would point the way to more reading.

Finally, Gad Horowitz on a Friday morning would smoke incessantly (it was permitted in those days) and take a class of know-it-all political science students through the modern masters of critical, and cynical, political analysis: Michels, Mosca, and Pareto.

The greatest cynic, and critic, of all was, of course, Horowitz himself. He was aloof and somewhat abrasive but brilliant. His essay on Canadian political culture is still the best introduction.

My first foray into student government was not an entirely happy one. I was elected literary director of the U.C. Literary and Athletic Society, and was determined to out-do the previous director, who had run a show on the psychedelic culture which had been a tremendous success. I got it into my head that I would organize a show which would link the themes of propaganda, advertising, and the madness and mayhem of modern culture. Madness and mayhem became more than the theme of the show.

Two young artists, who went by the name of Sterbach and Wise, would build a total environment in the U.C. Refectory; there would be sound-and-light shows in Convocation Hall, run by their friend George, who had a black box that would control all the screens; there would be a film festival, speakers, and of course a major concert by the Mothers of Invention.

The show ballooned out of all proportion. I was frantically trying to get Sterbach and Wise to live within a budget. Hershell Ezrin, who was the president of the U.C. Lit, and a far better organizer than I, kept reminding me that we were not the Rockefeller Foundation. So, in due course, we both went down to Sterbach and Wise's loft on Queen Street, and lowered the boom on their budget. Now we had unhappy artists on our hands. They weren't sure, they told us, whether they could do it for less money, and in particular they weren't sure George could get his black box to work at that price. It felt like a shakedown.

The Mothers arrived three hours before their concert to tell us that they needed a new sound system in Convocation Hall, which we broke every rule to get. There was a total breach of the fire code, with the students lying in every conceivable position on every imaginable spot in the Hall. Frank Zappa was outrageous. Faculty were suitably outraged, and the Mothers ended their act by pouring shaving cream in every possible orifice of the huge organ at the front of the Hall. The university solemnly sent me a bill for the cleaning of the organ.

The black box didn't work. In fact, George didn't even show up. There were boos and whistles in every sound-and-light show, and the total environment from Sterbach and Wise was incomprehensible. Readers will not be surprised to read that the festival ran a deficit, which had to be paid off in subsequent years.

← →

No political event so galvanized opinion on campus as the Vietnam War. Canada, obviously, was not at war, but its halfhearted support of American foreign policy, and the presence on campus of many companies which supported the war effort, became a major preoccupation of student activists. We all knew people who had come to Canada either as draft resisters or directly seeking asylum. It was impossible to escape the issue, and it coloured the political attitudes of my generation like nothing else.

Dow Chemical was recruiting on campus, as all companies did, and this became the focus of a particularly dedicated campaign. After many demonstrations and much pressure the company did its recruitment off campus, which seemed a symbolic victory at the time.

I turned to writing in the student newspaper *The Varsity*, which published my long political tracts on Pierre Trudeau and George Orwell, and then I worked on the governing structure of the university as a whole. I got myself elected to the Students' Administrative Council during my last year, 1968-69, and together with Steven Langdon, who was president of SAC that year, spearheaded a drive that would lead to students taking an equal number of seats on a Commission on University Government.

Claude Bissell, the president of the University of Toronto, had determined that the time had come to change the governing structures of the university, and he wanted to fashion a more modern governing structure than the corporate-dominated Board and the Academic Senate. I developed a huge admiration for Dr. Bissell, a man of imagination and verve, whose life I no doubt made more painful and difficult.

He had not figured on the extent of student chutzpah, and we convinced the faculty association that the time had come to challenge all the existing structures: administration, Senate, and the Board. In the course of this debate we made a lot of people unhappy: there was incredible energy and nerve at the heart of the student movement, and we won a lot of arguments simply by our capacity to stay awake longer and louder.

The Commission on University Government lasted a year, and allowed us to see the whole university at work. It was a great lesson in building a consensus, and the report we produced, which I co-drafted with Larry Lynch, became the foundation of the changes to the University of Toronto Act of 1971.

My exposure to the full extent of university politics led me to a joke which I have often heard since. "The reason politics in the university is so vicious is because the stakes are so small." Years after this experience I returned to the campus as an articling lawyer, working on a tenure case for the faculty association. The former head of the History Department, Archie Thornton, shook his head in disbelief as he encountered me facing him across the table. "My God, Rae! I thought we got rid of you years ago."

In the winter of 1967-68 Lester Pearson announced that he was retiring as leader of the Liberal Party. By this time my brother John had joined the staff of a new young cabinet minister, Jean Chrétien, as his executive assistant. My sister, Jennifer, who had been away in England, came back to Canada to work on Pierre Trudeau's campaign media team.

I went up to Ottawa with my friend Tom Wood for the convention, and was roped into working on a little tabloid that we put out daily for delegates called *Trudeau Today*. My boss was Jeremy Brown. I admired Trudeau for his incisiveness, his wit, and his belief that ideas mattered in politics. As time went on I would come to worry more about the content of the ideas, but at that time, like a lot of people, I was won over by the style.

When Trudeau won, I sat with my godfather Davey Dunton high in the gods of the Ottawa Convention Centre, where he turned to me and said, "He's got it, but I worry he's too simplistic on Quebec." At that time, I had no idea what Davey meant. Now I do.

When I returned to Toronto after the convention, I got a call from a Toronto alderman by the name of Charles Caccia, who had heard of me from other Liberals. He was running for the nomination in the riding of Davenport. Would I help him?

I did, without hesitation. Charles won the nomination in a fight that had thousands of delegates crowding the Queen Elizabeth Centre at the C.N.E. When Trudeau called the election at the end of April, we were ready. I was a canvass organizer. My main co-worker was Bruce Barnett, who went on to become an invaluable Japan expert in External Affairs, and who years later shepherded me around Tokyo when I went there as premier. The sign chairman was Peter Stollery, now a senator. My star canvassers were Colin and Nettie Vaughan and Rod Robbie, later the architect of the SkyDome. The office manager for the campaign was Ursula Appolloni, who went on to beat David Lewis in York South in 1974.

Next to my own campaign in York South in 1990, I have never been in an easier contest. Charles was extraordinarily well known as a man of unusual integrity and singular determination. He had built Costi, an organization dedicated to improving education and training for immigrants, and was decidedly on the left of the Liberal Party.

Toward the end of the campaign, the leader's election tour called for Trudeau to come to Toronto for a ticker-tape parade down Bay Street in open cars. We made the usual plans for our candidate to be there, but we had made one small mistake. We failed to discuss the idea with Charles. After an evening's canvassing he came in to discuss the next day's activities. Charles listened quietly to the details of where he had to be and when. He looked up. "This all sounds very interesting, but I must tell you now that I will not be riding in a limousine."

"Charles," I explained carefully, "this is the big show of the campaign. All the other candidates will be there. There's a convertible with your name on it."

"Take my name off the limousine. I am running for working people. If I have to go in the parade I will ride my bicycle."

He wasn't smiling when he spoke this last sentence.

"You can't ride a bloody bicycle, Charles, you'll screw up the whole pattern of the parade. They'll never let you."

"Ask them."

I made the call, with the predictable response. I had learned something about Charles, but also about control and decision-making in the Liberal Party. Charles was "sick" the day of the parade. Throughout his political career Charles Caccia has always marched, or peddled, to a different drummer. Stubborn, determined, independent, completely honest, he is a remarkable politician.

↤ ↦

That summer of 1968 I worked in the Public Archives in Ottawa, researching Sir John A. Macdonald's correspondence, which seemed to be almost entirely about patronage. From all corners of the country came persistent entreaties on how much the correspondent had done for the party, how loyal he had been, how unqualified anyone else was, and how the failure to be suitably rewarded would result in disaster for the party and the leader, because the entire community was united behind the wisdom of the appointment and would be devastated if it went to Mr. X. instead of Mr. Y.

People no longer make requests in long-hand, but I have occasionally heard something similar on the phone, particularly between 1990 and 1995. History will record that I did less for my partisans than Macdonald did for his. But then he lasted considerably longer.

In the fall I decided to apply for a Rhodes Scholarship to Oxford University. I had to write an essay, get six references, and prepare myself for an oral interview. The chairman of the interview committee was General Guy Simonds, who had led Canadian soldiers through Italy. I had long hair and a scruffy tweed jacket, which would only confirm the stereotype of the Earnest Young Student. That night I got a call from the secretary of the committee telling me that, together with a student from Trinity College, Derek Allen, I had been successful.

Rhodes Scholars have often been described as "young men with a great future behind them." I can only say that when I left for Oxford in the fall of 1969 I felt the world was all ahead of me. I had come back to Canada after years away, made fast friends, thoroughly enjoyed student politics, and was about to attend one of the great universities of the world. I was a thoroughgoing democrat, whose socialism was never Marxist and always pragmatic. I believed then, as now, in community, and in finding ways to affirm it in the heart of a world in turmoil and fragments. I enjoyed the fray of the political battle, but even then insisted on the right of reflection, to be in the crowd but also apart from it.

Chapter Three

ENGLISH ADVENTURES

Going to England was in part a homecoming. My mother was born there, and my grandmother still lived in London, in a small flat on Brompton Square, around the corner from the Brompton Oratory. My Uncle Keith and his family lived in Maldon, Essex; my Aunt Ruth near Manchester, with her family. My Uncle Jack, Saul's brother, had left Canada in the fifties to work in British show business, and he occasionally appeared on television, wrote songs, and did production work for the impresario Lew Grade. Nell lived in London as well, in a ground-floor flat just off Gloucester Road.

The next five years I would go back and forth across the Atlantic several times, never quite sure where was really home, or what I wanted to do with my life. There were so many things about England that I loved: the humour, the history, the range of people, accents, and sounds. I even liked the food. There was a lack of curiosity about the outside world that drove me a little crazy, and a reticence that meant I had to be the person to start a conversation (not always one of my strengths). After several years I discovered how much of a Canadian I really was, and made my way back to Toronto. But not before having some adventures.

← →

My college at Oxford was Balliol, which in 1969 was a tremendously stimulating place to be. That first year I lived in a graduate residence, Holywell Manor, where I had a large, comfortable bed-sitting room. It was freezing cold, but so it was everywhere in Oxford, where central heating was to be a thing of the future only.

I decided to do a graduate degree in Politics. This would take me two years, and involved writing five exams and a thesis, plus what is a called a "viva," an oral exam. It meant that I had to work pretty steadily the whole time on course work, essays, and the thesis. Each term I would study with one tutor for one exam, and then spend most of the summer on the thesis.

Once again I studied with some extraordinary people. My tutors at Balliol were Bill Weinstein and Steven Lukes. Weinstein was an American from New York who had come to Oxford in the 1950s and decided to stay. The main consequence of this decision was that he spoke with the strangest mid-Atlantic accent I have ever heard, half Brooklyn, half London. There would be long contests among the students to see who could do the best imitation. Bill was a careful and thoughtful liberal theorist who put up with a ton of cheerful abuse from would-be Marxists who are now stockbrokers in the City of London.

Steven Lukes was a short, irrepressibly bright sociology scholar who had the dubious distinction of holding the Robert Maxwell Fellowship in Politics. Press baron Robert Maxwell was a substantial benefactor of Balliol College who late one afternoon, more than twenty years later, paid me a visit when I was premier. He used the Balliol connection to lobby for an end to the national rules preventing foreign ownership of newspapers. I demurred, saying I approved of the policy. He promised to support me editorially, which would admittedly have been a refreshing change. My purity remained intact after the stalemated conversation—he left me only with a copy of his authorized biography.

Lukes had just completed a massive intellectual biography of Emile Durkheim. His interests remained eclectic and diverse, and together with Tony Wright, now a Labour MP, we ran a seminar on British socialism and the Labour Party, which also became the theme of my thesis on Sidney and Beatrice Webb.

For my special paper on political institutions I worked with Philip Williams, who introduced me to the Oxford Labour Party. We canvassed voters and pulled identified supporters together when Harold Wilson lost in the summer of 1970. Philip was a deeply committed social democrat and Gaitskell supporter. He later joined Shirley Williams as a Social Democrat in the ensuing chaos on the British left in the early 1980s.

Isaiah Berlin was perhaps the most formidable "name" at Oxford, and when it was suggested that I might study with him for the exam on Hegel and Marx, I seized the chance. For two hours a week an American friend Joe Femia and I would sit in Berlin's room in Wolfson College and listen to the world's greatest intellectual conversationalist.

We would arrive soon after breakfast, and Berlin would start. It was a little like listening to someone starting a car on a cold day. The words rumbled up, rapid fire, comments, jokes, questions, gossip, prodding, passing our papers back, pausing only to look at us if we were bewildered. Femia would whisper to me, "What'd he say?" Berlin would point to the bowl in front of us, "Have a nut have a nut yes Hegel. To understand Hegel you must understand Fichte, and to understand Fichte you must understand Kant, they all see the world as a tapestry in which everything is in its place and everything fits, every piece of the carpet fits, you see, and nothing can be out of place. It's not an idea it's a system, you see? Yes? Have a nut. Have a nut. I'm going next week to New York and they've asked me to speak to the Policemen's Union I shall talk on Machiavelli eh? Yes, that will be quite something—yes that is one thinker they will understand… Now as I was saying about Hegel…"

Years later, in 1994, I nominated Berlin for an honorary degree at the University of Toronto and introduced him to the gathering:

> *He is one of the truly remarkable men of this century. He is remembered by his thousands of*

*students—of which I am one—as a lecturer of
unsurpassed eloquence, a teacher of great insight
and inspiration, and an adviser of enormous good
humour and kindness...*

*He distrusts revolutionaries with a simplistic
ideology, whether from the right or the left.
Pluralism is a fundamental aspect of what it means
to be human. "From this crooked stick nothing
straight was ever made"—Kant's aphorism is now
the title of the latest collection of Sir Isaiah's essays:
it reflects the healthy scepticism that is at the heart
of his vision and experience.*

← →

I had three good years at Oxford. It was not all work in the library. I helped to write musical shows, and put in a star performance as a dirty old man in our original panto production of *Cinderella*. I travelled in England and France, going back to Geneva to visit old friends, and fell in and out of love more than once.

Once again, I made great friends, from many countries and backgrounds. Balliol was very much an international place, with a strong representation from Americans, South Africans, and from all over the Commonwealth. Ira Magaziner, who only lasted a short while at Oxford, slept on my floor as he tried to figure out what to do with the rest of his life. He went on to do community organizing south of Boston, set up a consultancy, and eventually became a close adviser to President Bill Clinton.

Eddie Webster was a white South African completely dedicated to the end of apartheid, and later went back to teach at Witwatersand University in Johannesburg. He was arrested on his return, charged with "promoting egalitarianism." He got off with a reprimand from the judge for being "arrogant," to which Eddie's father shouted, "That's no crime." His wife, Loulie, is now writing the official biography of Oliver Tambo.

Oxford had traditional rules about more than one person in a room. They were especially vigilant about overnight guests of the opposite sex. In my case the line was drawn when a woman was observed occasionally leaving my room in the morning. I was summoned to the office of officialdom at Holywell Manor. When an assistant greeted me at the door she said, "Oh yes, Mr. Rae, it's about the fornication in your room." I'd never heard it put quite that way before.

My amorous pursuits almost led to self-incineration, if not worse. I smoked a pipe at the time, and, after one lunchtime, was sauntering back to the reading room at the Bodleian Library. For some time I had been trying, with absolutely no success, to catch the interest of a woman whose name was Rose. I tried to strike up a conversation with her as we entered the Library. No luck. Strike one. I absent-mindedly put my pipe in my jacket pocket as Rose and I climbed the steps to the library. Strike two. She declined very politely my offer of a sandwich and tea in the Balliol/Junior Common Room. I returned to my studies and was contemplating simultaneously the future of the world and my future with Rose when a librarian came to me and said, "Excuse me, sir, but I believe you are on fire." The smouldering in my left breast pocket was not my heart on fire. It was my aged Harris tweed jacket. I raced from the reading room to cheers from surrounding students. Rose was not amused. Strike three.

In my second year I lived in the country, in a village called Long Hanborough, just past the churchyard where Winston Churchill is buried at Blaydon. I shared a house with three philosophers and one physicist. While I enjoyed the great walks on the grounds at Blenheim and endless argument and conversation, I quickly realized that Oxford philosophy was really not for me. It seemed to analyse words and topics with ever greater precision, but did so quite absent from history and real politics.

My original plan had been to finish the two-year degree, and to come back to Canada, but I decided to take another year at Oxford instead. I taught and wrote a good deal in that third year, expanding my study of the Webbs into others of the Fabian tradition—Tawney, G.D.H. Cole, and Harold Laski, and for the second summer worked with Master Christopher Hill and other graduate students teaching sixteen-year-old boys from three different mining communities—Northumberland, Leicestershire, and South Wales.

The idea was to give bright kids, who had the potential to do more, a chance to live at Oxford for three weeks and do work that might inspire them to keep on studying instead of dropping out. We put on plays, organized field trips, supervised independent study, and I put up with being called "Yank" in three different accents.

It was the culmination of my Balliol experience. I left the College in 1972, not quite sure where I was headed. My encounter with the best and the brightest around the world had left me a little intimidated. I went home for a short visit and was increasingly unsure of myself.

Naturally my parents wanted to know what was next, and my response was to go silent. In fact I was becoming quite disconnected personally. It was only when I returned to England again in a kind of transatlantic quest for identity, that I realized I was in the throes of a depression. It had never happened to me before, and all told I would have to say it lasted for the better part of eighteen months.

I have rarely felt such utter loneliness and anxiety as I felt in that fall of 1972. Conversation was an effort; I couldn't read or write without feeling completely inadequate; my self-esteem was at zero; and several days would sometimes go by without my being able to do anything remotely constructive.

I was helped through all this by some remarkable friends who recognized the symptoms better than I did, and insisted that I do something about it. I tried travelling—staying for an extended visit with Michael Ignatieff in Cambridge, Massachusetts. But this only delayed solving the problem. I drifted back to England, where I began talking to a therapist in North London.

Two or three times a week I would ride my bicycle across from Islington to Finchley, and spend an hour getting the talking treatment—I would talk and he would listen. I felt embarrassed to be there, and yet I knew I needed help. I couldn't write, I couldn't sleep, I was stuck.

My grandmother Nell used to say, "When you don't know where to start, get all the facts, assess the situation, and just take the human footsteps," advice I still offer to bewildered visitors to my office who often can't figure out what I'm talking about. But I know what I mean, and so did Nell, and in the end understanding how to go forward is all that matters.

With more than a little help from my friends, I started taking the human footsteps. Initially more as work therapy than anything else, I started as a volunteer at a Legal Aid Centre on Hornsey Road in North Islington. Our clients were poor tenants from the area. I soon realized that the best and most practical therapy was for me to simply listen, learn, and then do my best to help. In helping others I helped myself. The way to break out of isolation is to break out of isolation, one step at a time. Take the human footsteps.

← →

Christmas of 1973, I was working at the centre, and heard a loud commotion in the front office. Mrs. Gloria Blair, a Jamaican woman who had come in to complain weeks ago of harassment from her landlord, was in the full throes of a completely hysterical breakdown.

When I had first met her, she had been completely confident, strong, demanding her rights, and unafraid to take on anyone who got in her way. Now she was right over the edge, crying, inconsolable, a rage as wild as any I have seen before or since. I convinced her and her two teenage daughters to get in my car and we would go together to the hospital. She was admitted right away (those were the days), and together with her two girls I kept a vigil through the night and into the next day.

The girls told the story of how the landlord was in fact her boyfriend, how he had beaten her and propositioned them both. He had thrown her out on the street. They had nowhere to live, nowhere to go. And Mrs. Blair had just broken down. The doctor said she would stay heavily sedated for a few days and he would see what to do next.

I got the girls into a council flat that I knew was vacant, and went back to see Mrs. Blair every day. Her recovery was as remarkable as her breakdown. By the beginning of January she was out of hospital, and had moved into the flat with her daughters. In a couple of weeks she was back to work, and came by the office to invite me over for Sunday dinner. "I couldn't have done it without you."

Those words meant more to me than any I had heard in a very long time. I had done something for Mrs. Blair, and in doing that I was starting to really reconnect with the world. I began working full time for a housing centre up the street, and then faced a choice. Almost all of the practical work we were doing brought me up against the law, not as I had studied the world of legal theory and jurisprudence at Oxford, but street law: stopping evictions, dealing with family violence, coping with rent control, and juvenile crime.

I knew I needed both a real intellectual and personal challenge, to do something that stretched my mind as well as the need to connect emotionally with people. I also realized that I had to decide whether I would pursue that career in England or in Canada.

I was twenty-five and had spent most of my life outside Canada. If I stayed in England to pursue a career in social law, which I was now determined to do, I would end up having made England my home. In the end, I was more Canadian than I realized: the class divisions, the sense that you were immediately classified as soon as you opened your mouth to speak, the simple fact that it wasn't really my home, all led me to come back to Canada. I was accepted at the University of Toronto Law School for the fall of 1974, and prepared to make my way home.

I almost didn't make it.

✦ ✦

In the summer of 1974 I went to Northern Ireland. One of the legal workers at the North Islington Law Centre, Sally Gilbert, was from just outside Belfast. Some lawyer friends there invited her to a meeting to discuss whether a community-based law centre could be set up in Belfast. I can't remember whether she invited me to Belfast, or if I invited myself. In any event, I went. My romantic interest in her was never reciprocated, but I kept trying.

I stayed at her parents' house, a large, drafty expression of Protestant respectability. Her father was a shy, charming owner and manager of a seed-merchant business which had been in the family for years. His name was Stephen Gilbert, and he wrote novels about rats, of which the most famous was *Ben*, later made into a major motion picture, as they say. I had always imagined the author of the book to be a twisted and unhappy sort, but such was not the case. He was very shy, fond of golf, a moderate in all matters pertaining to religion and politics, thoroughly decent and reasonable.

In any event, a trip to the Falls Road, Shankill Road, and Londonderry (or just "Derry" to the nationalists) and two days of meeting lawyers and social workers was all it took to convince us that a joint community law centre was an impossibility at that time. Police and soldiers everywhere, sectarian violence and hatred, no shared basis for common work in either the Protestant or Catholic working-class community, the real, immediate risks to everyone involved, all made it obvious that for the time being the community-based, liberal idea hadn't a hope of survival.

Two images, of sound and sight, have stayed with me. The eerie quiet in downtown Derry, broken by the tramp of shoppers' feet and the grinding, clackety-clack of the turnstile that everyone crossing town had to pass through with shopping bags open. Once, driving behind a jeepload of British soldiers, I realized that what war in Ireland really meant was looking at the barrel of a gun in the arms of a teenager. The skinheads and punks in the street, both Protestant and Catholic, were even younger. Kids fighting kids.

I stayed a while longer with the Gilbert family at their farm by the sea, quietly terrified that the real author of the rat books might emerge one night while I was sleeping. They kindly gave me a ride to the airport for the flight back to London. It was the middle of the day, and I was flying stand-by. At that time, the entrance to the Belfast airport was completely surrounded by a tall, wire fence.

The only gate was a makeshift wooden hut through which all passengers had to pass for the first security check.

I can remember being relieved that security was tight. I had one small bag, and opened it readily. The lady in charge went through everything—shirts, sweaters, underwear, papers, shaving kit, toothpaste, nothing left to chance. Through the ticket counter to another security check, equally painstaking, equally thorough again, overlooking nothing. I caught my plane, a mid-day direct British Airways flight to London Heathrow. It should have taken about an hour.

I sat in the middle seat of the second row, which on this plane was facing the passengers in the front row. Directly opposite me was a cheery woman in her forties, on her right her boyfriend, on her left a nun reading quietly. On my right was a businessman, balding, whose teeth were very yellow as he smiled a greeting. He wore a grey, dirty suit. The seat to my left was empty. As we prepared for take-off, I realized that no one was from England, because no one needed to be introduced before starting a conversation.

After the usual pleasantries, I started reading a book, *The Role of Sex in Human Loving*, by Eric Berne. Maybe as compensation for my frustrations in Belfast. Soon afterward, the flight attendant came around with lunch trays. The Irish Sea came up below a clear, blue sky.

In what seemed a split second, the same flight attendant came back and picked up our trays. We all objected that we hadn't even started eating.

"The captain will be making an announcement shortly." Terse, short, a trifle nervous. Something was up.

"Ladies and gentlemen. This is your captain speaking. We are going to be making an emergency landing in just a few minutes. Please listen carefully to the instructions from your cabin crew, and please remain calm as we make the landing. Thank you."

There was an appalling silence on the plane, broken finally by the cheery lady across the way.

"Did you know I was in the Navy?" I tried to venture gamely that I didn't.

"Well, I was, and let me tell you at least when you go down in a boat you've got a chance."

The nun put her book away, smiled, and began playing with her beads. Eric Berne fell to the seat beside me.

A rather officious steward asked for volunteers to operate the chutes. I thought I was in a movie. The plane came down very quickly, with more very nervous chatter from everyone as we listened to the cabin crew tell us to go down the chutes "like slides in a playground" and "run from the plane as far and as fast as you can." Everyone got off the plane without breaking a leg and without too much panic. We all ran along the tarmac and were picked up by an airport bus which took us to a hangar, where we were greeted by a man from British Airways. He distributed meal chits to us, but eating was not the first thing on my mind. We were then herded to a cafeteria reserved "just for our passengers." I stood in line behind someone I recognized from television, an Ulster Unionist MP named James Kilfedder. He told me he liked Ontario because he'd just been to an Orange Order Convention in Niagara Falls.

"There are lots of us in Ontario."

I muttered under my breath, "Us? Who's us?"

We were all hungrier for information than for cardboard sandwiches and cold meat pie. Another official came forward.

"I'm sure you're all wondering what has happened." The understatement of the year.

"The pilot received information that a device was on board the plane, and to err on the side of caution he decided to land. We're conducting a search of the plane right now. As soon as that's over, you'll be on your way."

A "device." What, a birth-control device? No, silly, a bomb. More waiting, polite conversation with Kilfedder, with the nun, but not with the smiling businessman with the yellow teeth. He'd disappeared. An hour passed as endless cups of tea were consumed.

"Ladies and gentlemen, may I have your attention please. Our search has been completed, and I regret to inform you that a device has indeed been discovered underneath the seats of the fifth row. I shall have to ask you to accompany me to identify all your luggage and belongings on the plane."

Another trip to the hangar. We were all lined up in a big circle around the pile of luggage, raincoats, briefcases, and books in the middle.

"Please identify your belongings as I hold them in the air."

Suitcases, raincoats, umbrellas were all carefully claimed, and then rifled through by yet another security check. My personal belongings had never been examined so thoroughly in one day. "Whose book is this please, *The Role of Sex in Human Loving*?" Sheepishly, to quiet applause, I went forward to claim it. The nun's eyes met mine. I was mortified, beet-red with embarrassment. I'd let the side down.

Another announcement. "Ladies and gentlemen, if I could please have your attention for a moment. The presence of the device on board the plane has rather changed our plans. Some officers of the C.I.D. Branch are being flown up from London to interview all of you. We would ask that you please join us for another meal while we await their arrival." The C.I.D. is the British equivalent of the RCMP Investigation Unit. Another trip back to the cafeteria. More cold meat pies and stale cheese.

In those days I had a beard. I was wearing my blue lumber jacket as a symbol of my Canadian identity. Kilfedder thought I was an anarchist. The nun thought I was a sex maniac. The man with the smiling yellow teeth had disappeared. The lady who had been in the Navy was drinking beer. She came over and said, "What's the matter, Yank? You're awfully quiet." I was vague, remote, exhausted. It was already seven o'clock.

The C.I.D. men finally arrived. We were taken upstairs to what looked like an old ballroom to be interviewed. There were chairs all around the room. We looked like so many wallflowers waiting to be asked to dance. I could hear the Navy lady answering questions.

"Did you notice anything odd or untoward in the behaviour of any of the other passengers?"

"Dunno really, but there was one thing strange about the American fellow across from me. He was calm, strangely calm— you know what I mean?—as we were going down. Sort of like he knew what was happening." That was me.

"Hey, wait a minute, that was me. I wasn't calm. I was scared."

"That's quite all right, sir, your turn will be next. You'll have a chance to explain yourself then." Explain myself?

"Sir, can you tell me please what you do for a living?"

"I'm a community worker."

"If you don't mind me saying so, sir, you look like a community worker." Like an anarchist you mean. "And where are you from, sir?"

"Well, originally I'm from Canada, but I'm working now as a community worker in London." Outside agitator.

"And what took you to Belfast?"

"Partly business, partly pleasure."

"Pleasure, sir, in Belfast?" He smiled. My whole story sounded so implausible.

"Visiting friends. But I was also looking into the possibility of setting up a community law centre in Belfast." I was obviously a prime suspect.

"Did you notice anything odd or untoward in the behaviour of the other passengers."

No, not that I could think of. I wasn't going to finger some innocent fellow passenger.

"Anything else you'd like to tell us, sir?"

"Well, yes, there is. The man sitting next to me on the plane. I haven't seen him anywhere since this all started."

"Oh, really sir? Are you sure?"

I looked around once, twice, three times. Those smiling, yellow teeth, the grey, dirty suit—they were missing.

"I'm quite sure."

"I want you to be doubly sure."

I asked the Navy lady. She had to admit she hadn't seen him. The nun, keeping her distance, couldn't see him anywhere either.

"I'll be back in five minutes with the Identikit." Sure enough, just like in the movies, another man came along with all the hairlines, foreheads, eyebrows and chins known to the artistic imagination of policemen.

Since it was black and white, I had to tell him about the yellowing teeth. I got an odd feeling of gratification from being able to help the authorities. Goody Two Shoes beats out the anarchist every time.

We were corralled into yet another airport bus, taken to the main terminal, and once more ushered through security. There was the same painstaking check of every possible item. It was approaching midnight, and we were at last lining up to fly back in a special plane to London. As I was handing my ticket over for one final inspection, I felt a gentle tap on my shoulder.

"Ish thish the flight to London?" The grey, dirty suit, the yellow teeth. I felt sick.

"Where have you been? I've just given your description to the police."

"As soon as I got here I knew it would be a long day, so I went to the pub. I've been in the pub the whole bloody day."

I collared him by his raincoat, and went looking desperately for the police. We found them, and explained everything. Luckily, they believed both of us.

We later discovered that the device, as it was innocently called, was a bomb which failed to explode. It has always been unclear to me whether or not this was intentional. Apparently also on board the flight was the head of the Royal Ulster Constabulary, a Catholic, Mr. Tom Flanagan, who was going to London to be honoured by the Queen. The decision had been made to take Tom away for all time, and all of his travelling companions with him. Whether someone thought better of this, or just wanted to show that no security system was safe, or whether the device (as I keep calling it) just didn't work, I'll never know.

It was only the next day when I saw the story in the newspapers that I started shaking. My anger about terrorism has ever since been more personal.

Chapter Four

THE LURE OF POLITICS

In September of 1974 I enrolled at the University of Toronto Law School, and moved into a small apartment at the top of a large house on Jones Avenue in the east end of Toronto. I got busy right away, and started working at the injured workers' clinic at the Dovercourt YMCA, as well as joining John Crispo as a teaching assistant in industrial relations. I shared duties with Jim McDonald, a fast friend with whom I later worked at the law firm of Sack, Charney, Goldblatt and Mitchell.

Walking from class one evening I ran into Peter Warrian, who had been president of the Canadian Union of Students in the late 1960s. He asked what I was doing, and I told him. He was working at the national office of the United Steelworkers, and thought they might have some extra work for me. I went up the next day to be interviewed by Lorne Ingle, who was general counsel to the Steelworkers in Canada. He said he needed help with some cases, starting with the proposed closure by Falconbridge of a mine site, and the lay-off of many workers. The Employment Standards Act protected workers affected by a "permanent shutdown," giving them greater rights to notice and severance. The company, wanting to save money, argued that while they were closing the mine, and had no plans to work it again, it wasn't being closed "permanently" since it was always possible that they might go back in. This seemed like a bit of a stretch to all of us, and it was my job to prepare the arguments that the legislative director, a marvellous Scotsman named Bert Munro, would make to an arbitrator.

I had found my feet: enough teaching and studying to know that my brain was active; enough legal aid to keep my hands in the fire of the politics of daily life under the Tories; and this new adventure with the Steelworkers.

An exposure to Tory politics in England made siding with them impossible. The innoculation has lasted my whole life. While part of me knows the Canadian political tradition is different, I have always seen the Tory party as an organized group to defend privilege. My problem with the Liberals was, and is, their smugness. People often express surprise at my choice of political family, but it followed a logical progression. I drifted from the Liberals as I realized how conservative Pierre Trudeau really was. I canvassed and worked for the Labour Party in England, and spent hours studying the history, theory, and politics of social democracy. My advocacy work in North London and in Toronto on behalf of tenants and injured workers convinced me that the existing power structures had to be opened up, and that a practical politics committed to doing just that could make a difference. In Ontario the Davis government was increasingly unpopular, and the NDP under Stephen Lewis was making great strides, following victories in Saskatchewan, Manitoba, and British Columbia. My work as an advocate led me to work for the Italian immigrants who made up the heart of the Union of Injured Workers. There was no blinding epiphany that led to a "conversion." The NDP came to feel more my political home than any of the alternatives.

My first journey on behalf of the Steelworkers was to Hamilton, where Local 1005 was facing a hearing because the executive had decided not to take a case to arbitration. In point of fact, they had thought about it, exercised their jurisdiction properly, and had decided not to take the case further because they concluded that the member had no chance of success.

My first meeting with the executive of 1005 was quite an experience. The union was rife with factions, each with their leader on the executive. Most of the members of the executive owed their positions (which were precious because they meant time off with pay from the plant) to a power base within the factory. The power base could be ethnic, or a section of the plant, or broadly political. But the effect was that there was no love lost among most of the members of the executive.

I had no idea of any of this when I turned up for lunch in a restaurant on Barton Street. Whenever someone would get up to go to the bathroom or to take a call, others would say, "Don't listen to Jimmy, he's a fucking liar." When Jimmy came back everyone smiled away, and then the same treatment would be meted out to the next sorry soul who left the room. Solidarity forever was not what it seemed. I got through the hearing, but it was quite an experience. All politics is more intense than it seems at first blush, and every organization has its politics.

I went with the Steelworkers to Las Vegas, where they had their convention in 1976. This was the year that a young staff representative from Chicago named Ed Sadlowski decided to challenge the union leadership in a general election. Sadlowski was outspoken, brash, and allegedly more radical than the stolid ticket led by I. W. Abel. In Canada the former research director at the national office, Don Taylor, was running to be the Canadian director against the slate's candidate, Gerard Docquier, who was the assistant to the director of District 5, Canada east of the Ottawa River.

I was in a difficult position. Don Taylor was someone I knew and liked, and it was natural that the National Office staff would support him. On the other hand, I was at the convention helping with the overall legal preparatory work for the convention, which meant I worked for Bernie Kleiman, the senior legal counsel to the slate led by Mr. Abel.

The first day I got to the convention, Don Taylor was chatting with Sadlowski, and I went over to shake hands. We joked about something, and I went on my merry way. When I got back to my hotel room, I got a phone call from Kleiman, saying Mr. Abel would like to meet me in his room.

I naïvely thought I was going up to shake hands with the boss, and be thanked for all my hard work. This is not exactly what I found. Like Orson Welles in *Citizen Kane*, Mr. Abel was at the far end of a vast penthouse, peering out the window, looking pensive. He turned to look at me, nodded me to a chair, and stayed standing.

"Your name Rae? You with the union in Canada?"

"Yes sir, and I can't thank you enough for the chance…"

He spoke slowly, in a deep, measured voice. "Let me tell you something, Rae. There are three kinds of people who are out to destroy our union. The first kind are lawyers (he made it sound like "liars") who think they're liberals but they're really just doing the companies' work. They take us to court. And they take us to the labour board. And they civil liberty us to death. Then there's the communists, and I've been fighting them in this union since I was sixteen years old. They don't give a shit about the union and they don't give a shit about people. They care about themselves and their god-damned philosophy. That's all they care about. And then there's young people who don't know any better. Now which one are you?"

He turned to me without a smile. He seemed to be implying that I might be all three.

"Well, sir, if you're talking about Don Taylor, he's got the support of a lot of people who've worked with him."

"Taylor? I don't give a shit about Taylor. You Canadians will do whatever you have to do. I'm talking about your supporting Sadlowski."

"I don't even know Sadlowski."

"Well, keep it that way."

As it turned out, Don Taylor lost by a very narrow margin to Gerard Docquier, who subsequently became a good friend as well. Ed Sadlowski lost by a wide margin in the United States, and so he remained on the staff of the Steelworkers.

I realized then that private practice might be a better place for me. I enjoyed law school and approached it with a different frame of mind than any other set of studies. I did well enough but didn't feel the same compulsion to ace every exam. Once again, I had great teachers: Bruce Dunlop, Horace Krever, Alan Mewett, David Beattie, and Michael Trebilcock. By third year I was teaching a full course at the Faculty of Management Studies as well as doing my work for the Steelworkers and handling my cases with the Union of Injured Workers. It never occurred to me at that point to article with anything but a labour firm, although I was asked to try out for the usual large downtown practices. Howard Goldblatt had the room next door to mine in Sir Daniel Wilson Residence back at the University of Toronto. He had joined forces with labour lawyer Jeffrey Sack after articling. Howard was enjoying it, and I went in to see Jeffrey for an interview. He offered me a job as an articling student and I accepted immediately.

There were four lawyers in the firm, when I articled there in 1977-78 with Ethan Poskanzer: Sack, Goldblatt, Michael Mitchell, who was a couple of years ahead of me in law school, and Gerry Charney, a great friend with an infectious laugh who had a considerable commercial practice as well as union clients.

Jeffrey Sack has one of the brightest, toughest legal minds I know, and he was a great taskmaster. But I was not long for the practice of labour law.

I had become active in the New Democratic Party, and since the east-end riding associations of Riverdale and Broadview, where I lived, were actually represented by New Democrats in the Legislature and the House of Commons, I had become friendly with both Jim Renwick and John Gilbert. John and Nora Gilbert and I travelled out to the convention in Winnipeg that elected Ed Broadbent federal leader, and I quickly got to know Ed as well.

Steven Langdon, who was president of SAC in the sixties, was running the Policy Review Committee for Ed at this time, and roped me in too. When the 1975 provincial election was called, I was approached to run but decided against it since I was in the middle of law school. But I stayed active and interested, writing occasional papers for the policy review process, canvassing for other candidates in '75 and '77, and continuing my work with the Steelworkers.

Soon after I started working for Jeffrey Sack in 1977 I got a call from John Gilbert. He was not going to run for re-election, he told me, and he hoped I would think about becoming a candidate in Broadview in the next federal election.

It didn't take me very long to decide. I had nothing to lose. If I didn't make it, I could stay with Sack and Charney. I was single, and didn't have to worry about having a family in Toronto and a job in Ottawa. Ed Broadbent wanted to help the party change by building on the ideas that were emerging in Australia, the U.K., and elsewhere in the Socialist International. We saw eye-to-eye on most policy issues and liked each other. All my legal colleagues and friends from law school and the Steelworkers were encouraging. I decided to do it.

I also had the support of Arlene Perly, who is now my wife. I first saw Arlene on the day Richard Nixon defeated Hubert Humphrey for the presidency in 1968. It was in the *Varsity* office, and she was standing on a chair to post a notice on the bulletin board. She got my attention. Without knowing her name I invited her to a party Mike Ignatieff and I were having at our apartment at 618A Bloor Street to watch the American election results.

She came, and laughingly suggested that she would come by the next day to make Michael and me a peach soufflé. She did, which was the first and last time I have ever seen her make this wonderful dish. As luck would have it, she was very committed to another person at the time, and while we would chat in the U.C. refectory or at a *Varsity* party, we never actually went out.

A mere five years later I phoned her up. She was studying toward her drama degree and was working for Air Canada to pay for graduate school. No, she wasn't married, but she was going out with someone else, and it was serious. Two strikes, but I persisted. We went for coffee, we went to movies, I pursued her with real determination, and it seemed we were getting somewhere.

She finally agreed to marry me in December 1979, and our wedding on February 23, 1980, was presided over by His Honour

Judge John Gilbert. Arlene's mother arranged the whole affair in a matter of days while we were busy fighting the federal election. No decision has brought me greater happiness.

← →

To win the nomination meant doing two things: signing up new members into the riding association, and convincing existing members to support me. My key support in all this, in addition to Arlene, was my sister, Jennifer. When I moved back to Toronto in 1974, I lived not far from where Jennifer was living with her two young daughters Johanna and Kate. We became closer than ever. Her extraordinary vitality and humour have been a mainstay of my life. I cannot, of course, be objective on the subject of my own sister. She combines whirlwind energy and intensity of purpose with a great love of people and sensitivity to their needs. She made my early political career possible, and at every transition since has been my friend. What brother could ask for more?

Jennifer was deeply involved in the St. David provincial campaign of Gordon Cressy in 1977, and knew all the key players who were active in the neighbourhood. Gordon had lost by just a few hundred votes. His campaign, however, had been a focus for a formidable group of community activists in Riverdale and Cabbagetown.

With Jennifer's help, and Gordon's encouragement, I signed many of these people into the party, and began my rounds through the winter of 1977 on the doorsteps of east-end Toronto. My opponents for the nomination were two well-known NDP stalwarts, John Harney, who had been an MP in the early 1970s, and Kay Macpherson, a lifelong feminist and political activist. John Harney later went on to lead the NDP in Quebec as Jean Paul Harney. Kay has remained active in the women's movement and the party all her life.

I won the nomination, by 50 per cent plus one vote, on the first ballot. It was a civilized contest, and no deep enmities were formed as a result. I had a better organization, and we identified our vote and got people to the meeting. Harney gave great speeches, as did Kay, but that's not what wins nominations—or as

I've since discovered, general elections.

By this time John Gilbert had resigned to become a judge. I opened a service office on Danforth Avenue, which we paid for with monthly subscriptions from activists in the riding. We weren't sure whether there would be a by-election, or if Trudeau would call a general election. I spent much of the summer canvassing door-to-door.

In the end, Trudeau called a slew of by-elections for October 16, 1978, and Broadview was among them. We were ready, but we knew it would be a struggle. The Liberals were hugely unpopular, and nowhere were they more unpopular than east-end Toronto. We were in a two-way fight with the Tories, and the local Tory candidate was Tom Clifford, a well-known local alderman, who had been born in the riding, grown up and worked there all his life, went to church, was a Kinsman, a Rotarian, a supporter of the Chamber of Commerce, God, Queen, and country.

The Tories' take on me was that I had never worked a day in my life, was a millionaire, an outsider, a dilettante, a godless socialist, and didn't know anything about Broadview or the people in it. Since this was my first campaign, I took great exception to anything approaching a personal attack. It would take several elections to grow a thicker skin. In Broadview it only made me work harder.

While Tom had the support of traditional Tory voters in the east end, the riding, like all of Toronto, was changing. Working-class Tories had turned NDP in the early sixties, when we won the riding both federally and provincially. There was a pocket of Italian voters, a substantial Greek community, and a growing number of Chinese Canadians in the south end. Younger professional families had begun moving in the late 1960s and early 1970s, and had changed the make-up of the riding substantially.

If we could hold on to our base, and broaden it to include many who in other times, places, and circumstances, might vote Liberal, we could win. By voting day, I had knocked on every door at least once, and many twice. Jennifer had stayed on as my key organizer, joined by party veteran Gordon Brigden as my campaign manager, and a crew of local activists. We ran a classic NDP by-election campaign, with four canvasses of each poll. By election day itself we had a good sense of what most voters were going to do.

Canvassing in the east end of Toronto had its moments. There was no better education, no better reality check. Sitting on a porch just off Broadview Avenue, I joined an older gentleman contemplating life with his dog at his feet. He looked well into his eighties, was friendly enough, and he asked me to sit down.

"You from around here, Bob?"

"Well, I am now, but I've lived all over."

"I was born right here in this house. My dad voted for Robert Borden. His dad voted for Sir John A."

"How about you?"

"I've voted for them all—Tommy Church, George Hees, I went for Dief. Hell of a guy, Dief. Then I went for John Gilbert. He came to my door every election. All wrong about hanging but how can you say no to him when he grabs your hand and gives you that basset hound look of his?"

"I guess you've seen a lot of changes over the years…"

"Changes? I went to bed, it was Toronto. I woke up, it's Hong Kong."

"I hope I can count on your support."

"Yes, I will. Froggy's had his day."

History, decency, and racism all wrapped up into one.

↢ ↣

Nationally the tide was against Trudeau, and in favour of the Tories. It was not a pretty feeling in Broadview either, but we were helped by the fact that Tom Clifford had real trouble expanding his base to include a lot of younger and immigrant voters. Nor did the voters' familiarity with Tom always translate into a vote. On the weekend before the election, canvassing with Gord Cressy and Jim Renwick, the local provincial member, I knocked on a door.

"I hope I can count on your support."

"Well, I've known Tommy a long, long time. We went to school together. Grew up together."

"That's fine. But this election is about who you think is really going to fight for you and your family."

"And let me tell you something. I don't mind paying Tommy's car fare to go down Queen Street to City Hall. But I'll be god-damned if I'm going to pay his air fare to Ottawa. You've got my vote."

← →

Election night was tense. I knocked on an apartment with the polls closing in fifteen minutes, pleaded with the woman inside to go and vote, and agreed to babysit and watch her dinner in the oven while she did. When I got to the committee room, it was an excruciating half-hour before the first phone call from a reporting station.

We won the first poll to report by 48 to 44 for the Tories to 15 for the Liberals. Gord Brigden looked at me soulfully and said, "It's going to be a long night. That was supposed to be a strong poll for us." The Liberal vote collapsed in the end to about 16 per cent. This was after they had always run a close second since 1965. We had been hoping they would hold on to about 20 or 25 per cent.

By the end of the evening, our own count had us ahead by just over 400 votes, but the Returning Office apparently had us ahead by only 80. As it turned out, we were right. We declared victory, and I was offered a glass of champagne. I declined, and joking about my "limousine liberal" reputation among the Tories, asked for a beer. It tasted great.

This was a wonderful moment for me. I enjoyed campaigning. I found that I liked canvassing, and I knew from all my casework that there was much I could do personally to help make a difference. All that I had done to get my life together had paid off. The people that mattered most to me completely supported what I was doing, and had helped make it happen. Arlene found she loved elections and campaigns, canvassed with great success, and won her poll with a huge majority—a clear case of people voting for the canvasser more than for the candidate.

I also met many wonderful people, and learned some simple lessons along the way. There is nothing more fun than working in a successful local political campaign. New Democrats lose a lot of elections, but in the east end we got used to winning, and it was a pleasure. Patti Park, who has worked in the party and labour movement all her life, went on to become chief organizer of caucus services when we were in government. Michael Lewis, Stephen's younger brother and probably the finest on-the-ground organizer I know, became NDP provincial secretary.

I learned the art of canvassing from many, but none so much as John Gilbert and Terry Meagher. They are genuinely interested in people's stories and also know how to close a sale. Always ask for support. Answer every phone call. Thank every supporter.

Canvassing brings out interesting contrasts between party activists. There's a deep loyalty among New Democrats that must drive other canvassers quite crazy. New Democrats are fierce partisans with a definite point of view. Similarly, the Tories that I have met on the doorstep are also clear on who they are. Many would refuse to shake my hand. To touch an NDPer might run the risk of infection. With lips tightly pursed, an elderly lady would say, "Not today, thank you" and firmly shut the door.

Liberals, on the other hand, are the classic swing voters. They smile, take the leaflet, and cheerily agree to take a sign, to go along with the two or three already up. "I'll keep you in mind" is the classic Liberal voter kiss-off.

Comparing stories, I'm told that dyed-in-the-wool New Democrats are in the "up close and personal" school of response. I think of the pride some of my fiercest partisans in the east end, like Bert Hunt and Vince Reilly, would take in having argued for hours with opposition canvassers, and I am proud and pleased they were on my team and not someone else's. It was Bert Hunt who told me the joke (repeated many times since) that the main difference between finding a Tory canvasser and a dog at his door was that the dog stopped whining when he let him in.

Chapter Five

UP THE HILL AND DOWN AGAIN

The morning after the by-election in Broadview I got a call from the icon of social democracy, Stanley Knowles. He urged me to make sure I had a scrutineer for the official count, good advice since I didn't even know what that was, and he invited me to come up to see him when we knew the exact date of the swearing-in. "We'll have lunch together."

The official count went off without any more hitches, and in the end the vote was Rae 8,388, Clifford 7,968, and Varelis, the Liberal candidate, trailing at 3,466. We knew this was the last election in the old riding of Broadview, and that the general election would be fought with different, and more difficult, boundaries. The riding would soon go well up into East York, and would lose strong NDP polls south of Queen Street. I had won the first round by a nose, but the second round was coming soon and would be much more difficult.

❧

I got to Ottawa the day before my swearing-in, and promptly went to Stanley Knowles's office. I fully expected that we would head off to lunch at the fabled parliamentary restaurant. I obviously didn't know Stanley very well. He was extremely friendly, and we chatted for a while. He then suggested that I go downstairs to the cafeteria, and get him an egg salad sandwich on brown and a cup of tea.

"Get yourself whatever you like, bring it back, and we'll go over some more stuff about your office." So began the high life in Ottawa.

← →

The NDP caucus in 1978 was a small group. Trudeau's victory in 1974 had come largely at our expense, and those who had survived were generally older, well-entrenched members, like David Orlikow from Winnipeg and Les Benjamin from Regina. Fonse Faour from Corner Brook, Newfoundland, had also won in the by-elections of 1978, and we became seat mates in the back row. The older members took a jaundiced view of both of us, to the point where Doug Fisher stopped me in the hall after a couple of days and said, "You'd better have a word with Arnold Peters. He thinks you're a horse's ass."

Arnold Peters was first elected in 1957, and had survived every election since then. He was a blunt, tough-talking populist, with little time for social theory, or anything approaching an intellectual approach to politics. We actually became good friends after a time, but it took some work on my part. His first reaction was typical of some of the older members, with the complete exception of Andy Brewin and Tommy Douglas.

Andy represented the neighbouring riding of the Beaches, and was an enormously decent man. A pioneer in civil liberties, he argued the case for compensation for Japanese Canadians who had property confiscated during World War Two before the Supreme Court of Canada, as well as the Privy Council in London. He managed to keep getting re-elected despite his preoccupation with international affairs. He took me under his wing at many key moments, and maintained his commitment and idealism right to the end of his remarkable life.

Tommy Douglas was, of course, a legend. He quickly dispelled any deference, insisting that I sit next to him at caucus meetings and regaling me with stories about his political life. The only book on his desk was Bennett Cerf's *Joke Book*, which he showed me with pride, and said, "This'll get you a lot further than Sidney and Beatrice Webb." He was right about that, and about most other things as well.

Tommy has become something of an icon to the left in our party, which is ironic in the extreme. He was extraordinarily proud of his success in Saskatchewan, which he kept reminding me came not because he was supported by the left but because he kept beating them back at conventions. In our caucus discussions he was a strong, loyal, steady supporter of Ed Broadbent's leadership, and a fierce critic of those who would push him further to extreme positions.

Tommy was a man of exceptional discipline and toughness. He kept to a vigorous regimen of walking and diet, and had even less for lunch than Stanley Knowles. His humour overcame everything—not just the set stories at the beginning of each speech, but the constant running repartee, often at his own expense. I asked him to speak at my fund-raising dinner in Broadview-Greenwood in early 1979, and Tommy said, "I'll walk naked down Yonge Street if it will help get you re-elected." I said a speech at my fundraiser would suffice.

It was an unforgettable evening. Tommy sat next to my grandmother Nell, and they discovered that they had grown up nearby one another just outside Glasgow. Nell sang, recited Burns, and then Tommy recited Burns. He gave one of his finest New Jerusalem performances, and it set us on the path to re-election in 1979.

I have always been amused by the number of left-wing New Democrats, and many even to the left of the party, who invoke Tommy's name and memory as justification of their particular hobby horse. In fact, Tommy ran a fiscally conservative government in Saskatchewan, and did not hesitate to part company with his left wing critics in Saskatchewan. He did not bring in medicare in 1944 when he was elected. That had to wait until the early 1960s. By temperament he was tough-minded and impatient with windy rhetoric, sentimental thinking, and attacks on the leadership of the party which he saw as divisive and disloyal. Tommy would have laughed out loud at the misappropriation of his name and memory.

I knew that if I was going to get re-elected I had to use my short time in the House to make an impact. Ed gave me his full support in this, and while some obviously resented this whippersnapper from Toronto pushing forward, others were more positive. I asked Minister of Finance Jean Chrétien a question on my first day in the House. It concerned the Bank of Canada and interest rates, and after Chrétien waffled a bit on his first answer, I shot back, "I may be a new kid on the block but I think I know when I haven't had an answer to my question." I gave my maiden speech the same day, and spoke in the so-called late show.

The next week I got a message on my desk announcing that John Diefenbaker would like to meet me. Would I please see him in the opposition lobby fifteen minutes before question period. I got there at the assigned time, and Dief motioned me to a chair.

The jowls were shaking, the eyes were popping, and he was giggling. "You're making quite a name for yourself. Let me give you some advice."

"I need all the help I can get, sir."

"Some people will tell you to take your time, to sit back, and wait your turn. My advice to you is…"

I was waiting respectfully.

"Don't take any shit from anybody."

I was taken aback at the candour, and the language.

"The only person around here who thinks question period is about asking questions and getting answers is Bob Stanfield."

The giggling by now was uncontrollable.

"And one more thing. When you ask a question…go for the throat…every time."

At this point he had thrown himself into a conniption of self-congratulations. As the other members filed in, he pointed a waving finger. "Remember, go for the throat every time."

Like most advice, it spoke mountains about the giver. He was an actor, and still, in what turned out to be the last year of his life, a phenomenon. But not a very nice man. When he died, Arlene and I walked with hundreds of others in the elaborate funeral cortège through Ottawa. She was shocked at the irreverent stories that Stanley and Tommy insisted on telling about Dief.

← →

I had one political task in the twilight of that Parliament, to do everything possible to make sure I had a chance at re-election. There was a Tory tide that was still rising, and few analysts at that point gave Trudeau much chance at winning another term. I somehow had to make a name for myself in Ottawa, and do my homework in the riding.

Being a new member of a small, officially recognized party was a huge advantage. Question period had only recently started to be televised, and I soon learned how to "give good clip." I didn't fully follow John Diefenbaker's advice, but you didn't need to be a rocket scientist to know that a televised question period was about presentation, punch, humour, and the ability to convey both information and emotion in as short a time-frame as possible. Superficial, aggravating for those looking for more depth, but politics nonetheless.

The Press Gallery was always looking for a new voice and a new presence, and, again, being part of a small caucus was a great advantage. In the age of blanket coverage, it didn't take very long to become well known. I quickly found that as I canvassed in the new riding of Broadview-Greenwood people recognized me and wanted to talk about the issues of the day.

I began to learn something about the media, an education that continues to this day. There seems to be a relentless cycle of curiosity that greets every new arrival on the scene (Who is this guy?). If you're lucky, this can turn into temporary infatuation (Wow! He's NEW and DIFFERENT from the other guy!). In Ottawa I was initially seen as bright, articulate, and never in danger of holding power, the perfect political fantasy figure.

I was later to learn that the cycle has other stages. When I moved to Toronto, I was greeted by suspicion (Dunno about THIS) and finally disenchantment (WHAT A JERK!). I have now discovered a fifth stage, nostalgia, which I share with people like

Robert Stanfield (MAYBE NOT SO BAD AFTER ALL).

The first two stages were great while they lasted. I milked the opportunities for media exposure mercilessly. I felt I needed to if I was going to withstand the Tory tide.

We canvassed the new parts of the riding in the depths of winter, and made a point of providing service to all the people in the new riding. I had an enormously capable constituency assistant in Valerie Lawson, who had worked for John Gilbert, and Jennifer kept a team of party activists going as we prepared for the inevitable spring or summer election.

The election call came on March 26, 1979, and the election was to be held on May 22, 1979. We had another tremendous local campaign effort, and in the end I increased my majority to over 3,000 in the new riding of Broadview-Greenwood. Joe Clark became prime minister, the leader of a minority Conservative government.

I was the only NDP MP elected in Metro. We did very well in western Canada, bringing in a whole new generation of MPs who quickly became close friends: Bill Blaikie, Jim Fulton, Pauline Jewett, Margaret Mitchell, Nelson Riis, Terry Sargent, Ian Waddell, to name just a few.

We all shared a great affection and respect for Ed Broadbent. We all rejected the neo-conservative edge of the Clark government. Morale and spirits were high as we prepared for the return of the House in the fall.

The Liberals at this stage were dispirited and ineffective in Opposition to Clark. Trudeau would occasionally show some sparks, but it was clear his heart wasn't in the battle. None of us was surprised when he announced that he was stepping down.

Trudeau and I have never exchanged more than a few words personally during our time in the House or since. He dominated the House as prime minister, but his humour was always cutting, and never self-deprecating. He never seemed to care very much what others said or thought, and certainly never went out of his way to chat or share a joke. Whenever Arlene or I saw him at an official function, he would ask one question, "How's Jennifer?"

I always felt a more persistent and personally persuasive Trudeau could have taken even more command of the House than he did. But that would have been to make of him a different person. As it was, his distance and aloofness proved to be both strength and weakness.

Joe Clark sealed his fate when he expressed the thought that he would govern as if he had a majority. This is like throwing yourself out of a plane as if you had a parachute. There were the mistakes of inexperience, of course, like the promise to move the Canadian embassy to Jerusalem, but these were inevitable and were hardly fatal. Above all, Clark made the simple, but fundamental, error of underestimating his opponents and misjudging the support of his friends. This can happen to anybody, and it did to him.

Ed made me the finance critic after the May 1979 election, and I loved the job. The Finance Minister was John Crosbie, who was a study in contrasts. Privately, John is a shy man with a quiet sense of humour. He closes his eyes as he speaks to you, and has difficulty looking you straight in the eye for long periods of time. I can remember once sharing a cab with him to a television studio in Ottawa. I had to do most of the talking, and he seemed extraordinarily deferential. He was like this all through make-up, and we were then ushered in to the interview.

The red light on the top of the live camera turned on, and suddenly so did Crosbie. The accent broadened, the voice was raised, and he went on the attack, never letting me get a word or an argument in edgewise. At the end, he smiled at me and said, "That, my son, is live television. They can't edit me; they can't cut me down; they can't do a god-damned thing about it, and neither can you."

I was later grateful for the lesson.

❧ ❧

Crosbie's first, and last, budget came down on December 11, 1979, a few weeks after Trudeau announced his retirement from politics. The Tories were obviously assuming the Liberals would not mount a root-and-branch opposition, since they wouldn't want an election without a leader. They also assumed that the small Creditiste faction would end up supporting them because they wouldn't want an election either. They knew that we would be opposed, but could always hope that some of our members might be conveniently away.

They assumed too much, and they assumed wrong. It is ironic, given today's circumstances, to note that Crosbie's budget assumed a deficit of $10.4 billion in 1980/81, which would be brought down to $9 billion in 1983/84. This was, admittedly, a time of much higher inflation (running at 10 per cent), but above all it was a time of very different public expectations.

The bone in the throat was the eighteen-cent-a-gallon increase in the gas tax. Crosbie clearly felt he needed a tax hike to deal with the deficit problem, and chose the most direct way to get it: a consumption tax that could also double as a tool for conservation. He also wanted to help pay for a down payment on mortgage interest deductibility, which if fully implemented would have become a fiscal disaster.

The reaction the night of the budget was sharp and swift. It was my first experience of the complete focus of the national media on a single event. The TV trucks set up a vigil outside the House of Commons that never left until the first budget vote a few days later. The very presence of the cameras, and the sense of crisis that they imposed, created their own momentum. Actors were being summoned to a stage, and like moths to the flame we all trooped out to the brightness of the klieg lights and performed our ritual denunciations.

Opposition parties in this context play a rhetorical game of their own. You tell a joke, I tell two. You call the budget terrible, I call it a calamity. You call it a catastrophe, I call it a tragedy. And on it went.

Subsequent Liberal mythology has it that on that very evening the craftiest among them began plotting the end of the government. I don't believe it. The Clark government died an accidental death from a self-inflicted wound. As we began telling each other how awful it was, in the constant presence of a few million witnesses, we became the captives of our own rhetoric. No one could back down, and in the end no one did.

When our caucus met to consider how we would craft the ritual non-confidence motion in the budget, it was still the conventional wisdom that the Liberals would have a few people away. We were not consciously pushing for the defeat of the government, since we felt that we needed more time to establish ourselves as the "real opposition" to the bumbling Tories. My personal view was also that a different Liberal leader would have his own problems, especially in Quebec, and that with more experience and time we could only improve our fortunes.

The macho dilemma was that if we crafted a budget amendment that the Liberals couldn't support (what we called in shorthand "a Regina Manifesto amendment"), we would lose face as being afraid to mass all our forces. The vote on the Liberal amendment would have come much later.

So we agreed to craft a motion that the Liberals would have to support. If the government was going to survive, it would be because Liberal and Creditiste members stayed away in judicious numbers.

I ran into Marc Lalonde in the elevator going up to a meeting. He looked worried.

"What's happening?"

"Marc, have you ever read Barbara Tuchman's book *The Guns of August*?"

"Yes, of course."

"Well, the Archduke Ferdinand's just been shot, and we're all stumbling to the finishing line."

Which is what happened on the evening of Thursday, December 12, 1979. Even that day, it seemed possible that something would intervene to stop the collapse of the government. But nothing did.

I spoke in the debate that evening. Since it was broadcast nationally, I played it to the hilt:

> ...*Some have called it a tough budget. Some have said that the budget was actually a courageous one. It was certainly tough on the average Canadian. While the Minister of Finance [Mr. Crosbie]*

*swaggers down Main Street in his mukluks, he is tip-
toeing softly through Bay Street and the corridors of
power in Calgary and Edmonton. Somehow Clark
Kent cannot find a telephone booth when he reaches
the Alberta border. This budget is courageous only in
the sense that the Charge of the Light Brigade was
courageous: "Into the valley of death rode the one
hundred and thirty-five."*

*The Christmas message from St. John's West is quite
simple. It is an old message; to them that hath it
shall be given.*

*Perhaps we could put the lesson another way. If
you drink, don't smoke; if you smoke, don't drive; if
you drive, don't drink; if you drive, smoke and drink,
don't think, because if you think you will wonder
why you ever voted Conservative in the last election!*

Clark didn't have the numbers, and Crosbie was left to shout and sputter into the television lights. The same day our wedding invitations went out in the mail, I embarked on my third election in fourteen months.

↰ →

As it turned out, Trudeau came back from the twilight, and was kept quietly hidden from the public for the election. Locally I ran against a Trudeau acolyte who claimed to have known me as a kid. He had been a journalist who published under the name of Philip Deane. His father was a Greek general, and Philip Deane ran against me as Philip Gigantes.

He was a strong candidate, and given the change in the wind this time it was the Liberals I was running against. It was remarkable how things had changed. A short fourteen months before, Trudeau was a swear-word on the Danforth. As the election approached in February, we were praying that we could keep him short of a majority. No such luck. On February 18 I was back in as part of a slightly larger NDP caucus in a House of Commons with a Liberal majority.

Arlene and I were married on February 23, 1980, five days later. She finally succumbed on the fourteenth canvass.

At the wedding, Ed mentioned to me that Trudeau had talked to him about the NDP joining the government. He said he had reflected on it for a while, and told Trudeau that this was not something he could recommend to the caucus. I told him it would have been worth discussing, but that once Ed had nixed it, we couldn't very well have raised it ourselves.

It was a curiously lopsided House. The Liberals had virtually no representation from the West, and almost all the seats from Quebec. The Tories were bitter, angry at having lost the government: I was naturally at the top of their "least favourite" category, having made the final speech and proposed the motion that defeated their government. If Ed had brought Trudeau's request to caucus, I would have insisted on our looking at it carefully. We would not have had much leverage because of the Liberal majority, but our regional strength would have given us presence and credibility.

These were arguments I would participate in again in Ontario in 1985. As it turned out, as far as the constitutional arguments of 1980-81 were concerned, we became partners with the Liberals in any event. My own view was that with positions at the cabinet table we would have been able to exercise considerably more influence.

← →

It soon became clear that the issue that would predominate the early years of the last Trudeau government was the constitution. Trudeau had agreed to stay on, and to serve another term, on condition that he be freer to determine the political agenda. In particular he wanted to fulfil his constitutional dream: patriation of the constitution with a Charter of Rights.

Having won his majority, he then proceeded to mount a successful defence of the country in the Quebec referendum, but did so with a price: the commitment at the Paul Sauvé Arena on a May evening in 1980 that a firm "Non" would be interpreted by the Quebec Liberal MPs as a mandate for constitutional change.

→ ←

General de Gaulle had gone to Algeria to meet with the French leadership there in 1957 and 1958, and made a famous remark when he left: "*Je vous ai compris.*" This bit of demagoguery was followed by an inevitable French retreat, and a sense of betrayal from the colonists who saw Algeria taken away from them. So with Trudeau. His bold appeal at the Forum was taken every which way by those who wanted to strengthen Quebec's hand with a "Yes" but who remained nonetheless loyal to the idea of Canada and so voted "No" on the strength of Trudeau's promise.

The ambiguity of Trudeau's promise won him the referendum, and won him time in negotiating. But in the end, the difference between what he delivered and what many perceived him to be promising left a legacy of rancour and misunderstanding that still lingers.

Brian Mulroney would make this point at his nomination meeting in Sept-Îles in 1984 when he said:

> *Not one Quebecker authorized the federal Liberals*
> *to take advantage of the confusion that prevailed in*
> *Quebec following the referendum in organizing to*
> *ostracize the province constitutionally.*

❖ ❖

Arlene and I went on a honeymoon in Greece and Cyprus that August and September. I managed to miss being in Canada for the inevitable meeting of the first ministers in September of 1980. Trudeau's broad federal package was rejected by the premiers. When I came back to a caucus meeting late that month, Ed reported on meetings he had with Allan Blakeney, and how it did not appear likely that any agreement could be reached between the federal government and any of the provinces.

I made the observation at that meeting that the simple message of Canada having its own constitution, with a Charter of Rights, was a popular message in my constituency, and that there was more sympathy for that than for the complicated power-manoeuvring of the premiers. But I was in a decided minority at that time.

That was the only full discussion we had as a caucus prior to

Trudeau's historic television address to the country announcing his constitutional package. I was actually in Vancouver, and was as surprised as anyone when Ed came on after Joe Clark and basically endorsed the package of patriation, a Charter of Rights, and an amending formula, all to be carried forward unilaterally in the Canadian Parliament. I defended that position that night, and on many other occasions, yet it was obviously a decision that was to divide our caucus and party very badly for months and even years to come.

The attack on Ed came from three camps, not just one. First, there was the group in the party who had been consistently sympathetic with Quebec nationalism. The Quebec NDP itself was a truly pathetic little group, with a new leader popping up every six months, representing no identifiable group within the Quebec spectrum. Federalists in Quebec were Liberals or Conservatives. Nationalists in Quebec were either activists for the Parti Québécois, or a source of pressure within the Union Nationale/Conservative Party family. There was no room for us, but within the party there was still a group determined to find room for Quebec nationalism within Canada, and they didn't like the Trudeau formula.

The second group consisted of those New Democrats, led by Allan Blakeney, who didn't like the unilateral move by Ottawa because of what it did to the provinces. They were also opposed to an entrenched Charter because of the power this would give to conservative judges. Allan and Roy Romanow, his attorney general, were exceptionally eloquent in their presentation of this view, which had considerable support in the party.

The third group was led in the caucus by Svend Robinson and Pauline Jewett. They wanted the Charter to go further, to be stronger, clearer, more inclusive, and to cover more subjects. They didn't care about provincial power, and rejected the Blakeney argument as well. They also included people who wanted to do more about aboriginal issues, and who thought the Charter of Rights should be broadened to included group and social rights.

We would therefore discover what all Canadians have since discovered about the constitution. There is nothing more difficult, and more divisive, than discussing the fundamentals of the country. The NDP on this issue was simply a reflection of the country: friendships and loyalties were strained to the breaking point as we struggled with the toughest issues of principle and identity.

The entire political leadership of the country was focused on this issue for a full two years. By this time we were beginning to enter a serious recession, yet no one seemed to be paying attention. We would pay a huge price as a country for our constitutional obsession.

When the votes in caucus were counted, I was very much in the Broadbent camp. I thought it would be politically fatal for us to oppose the patriation of the Constitution with a Charter. In my own province, Premier Bill Davis had made the same calculation. There was a practical Canadian pride that said it was time to bring the constitution home, and that the entrenched protection of civil liberties was an important expression of who we are as Canadians.

The divisions in the caucus and the party were almost unmanageable. We kept hoping that by wrenching some concessions from Trudeau on natural resources it would be possible to bring Saskatchewan into the fold, but after a series of conversations between Trudeau in Ottawa and Blakeney in Hawaii in January of 1981, Allan decided to stay with the other dissenting premiers and continue the assault on the Trudeau package.

The mood in the House of Commons was awful, as divisive and bitter as any time I can remember in politics. The day we agreed publicly to support the Trudeau package fully, after he had agreed to some amendments, the Liberals moved closure. That night Harvie André from the Tories and Ron Irwin from the Liberals almost came to blows.

We were badly wounded internally, and unable to mount an effective opposition to the government on other issues. Luckily, my mind was elsewhere. Our first daughter, Judith, was born on August 1, 1981. National crises began to fall into some perspective. I forgot about the constitution for a month and began learning how to change diapers. Finally in September of 1981 the Supreme Court ruled that political convention required more support from the premiers for constitutional reform than the government had been able to get. The stage was set for yet another round of talks as the premiers descended on Ottawa for one last try at consensus in early November 1981.

At this point we felt like powerless spectators. One day, it appeared that Trudeau and Lévesque would agree on a referendum formula. All that was changed when Roy Romanow, Roy McMurtry, and Jean Chrétien worked out a deal to allow the use of a "notwithstanding" clause as a safety valve for legislatures upset with a court decision on the Charter of Rights. When the final package, which included a confused amending formula which required unanimity for some things but not for others, was agreed to by everybody except Quebec, we accepted that it was time to go forward.

We were able to insist on better and stronger language on equality and aboriginal rights, and call it a day. In early December 1981, the House of Commons passed the resolution supporting the whole package by a vote of 246 to 24. It had been a messy process that had divided the country, to say nothing of our party, very badly. Like a great many people, I was unhappy about Quebec's not being a formal signatory, but felt that to a considerable degree the P.Q. was responsible for its own misfortune.

Lévesque had done a deal with seven premiers in which he had made a cynical concession about the veto; cynical because he did not really believe for a minute that the deal of the "gang of eight" would ever become constitutional law. The spectacle of the Quebec delegate general to London wining and dining underemployed British Tories in an effort to stop patriation was nauseating. Finally, the support of the Liberal MPs from Quebec made me feel that there was a substantial feeling in Quebec about patriation, and that there was nothing in the Charter itself which should be offensive to Quebeckers who wanted to stay as part of Canada. If we waited for a separatist government to approve a change, we would never get there.

As it turned out, Lévesque and the P.Q. were able to turn the very process of patriation and their own rejection of that process into another powerful myth about the "betrayal of Quebec." The kitchen meeting became the "Night of the Long Knives." You can only get there by completely rewriting history, and ignoring the blunders of the Lévesque government along the way. Yet this is precisely what revisionist history has done.

By the time the vote on the patriation package came, in December of 1981, my mind was elsewhere. After much to-ing and fro-ing I was a candidate for the leadership of the provincial party in Ontario.

Earlier that year the minority government of Bill Davis had gone to the people and had received a significant mandate, largely at the expense of the NDP. Stephen Lewis had been the dominant force in the Ontario party as leader through the elections of 1971, 1975, and 1977. A man of enormous eloquence, he had deep roots in the party, and an unparalleled capacity to move activists to take on the complacency of the Tory government.

His decision to leave electoral politics in 1978, after we lost the status of Official Opposition, had been a hard blow for the party. His successor, Michael Cassidy, was never able to garner the same emotional support, either in the broader public or the caucus. The defeat of 1981 was laid at his door, however unfairly, and in the spring of that year Cassidy announced that he would not be seeking the leadership at the next convention, which was then set for February 1982.

I immediately began receiving calls from people in the party and the labour movement asking me to think about running. I couldn't pretend it was something that hadn't occurred to me. It was partly a case of the grass being greener. The tensions over the constitution had taken some of the original joy of politics away from me, and I had a hard time seeing how we could mount an effective opposition to a Liberal administration that in some respects was progressive and interventionist.

I was genuinely divided in the choice. I enjoyed federal politics, and was close to my caucus colleagues. My work, as well as my one-liners, were appreciated. When I said that Crosbie's economics were not just pre-Keynesian, but pre-Cambrian, some people got the joke, just as they did when I said that Allan MacEachern reminded me of nothing so much as the piano player in a brothel who pretended that he didn't know what was going on upstairs. I got to see the country, travel widely, and could speak on behalf of the party wherever I wanted.

But there were equally powerful arguments on the other side. My personal life had changed. The prospect of commuting between Toronto and Ottawa, spending three or four nights a week away from home, seemed less attractive.

I went back and forth, mentally weighing both sides, and a group was formed to help me make up my mind in favour of running. Stephen Lewis was a strong supporter, as was his brother Michael, a long-time party organizer with a good ear to the ground. My old campaign manager Gordie Brigden weighed in, as did about half the Ontario caucus at Queen's Park. I had my detractors as well.

Jim Renwick was the provincial member for Riverdale, the over-lapping riding with Broadview-Greenwood, and he had never really been a fan. The feeling was mutual. Jim was bored with constituency work, and with riding politics, and so had left the day-to-day task of building the base and keeping the constituency happy up to me. He disapproved of my position on the constitution, and let me know it. He had his own preferred candidate for the leadership, Richard Johnston. Renwick made it clear that if I ran he would oppose me, and that if I was successful he would never give up his seat for me.

We never argued personally about this, and at a certain level our relations were quite cordial. But newspaper columns kept being written, with disparaging personal comments that could only have come from Jim. He was not alone, of course, and so I came to realize that nothing is more difficult than a leadership contest within your own party.

Partisan contests don't have to be personal, and the appeal to the general public is usually based on issues and programme. It is possible to explain rejection by the electorate in purely partisan terms. "They liked me but they didn't like the party's programme." This always makes it easier to carry on and live to fight another day.

Contests within a party are quite a different story. They turn on personalities, on who people think is better qualified to do a job, on who they like. It is a test of loyalty and affection, and always hard to manage. Because differences of philosophy are rarely that great within a party, they are always exaggerated in order to create a sense of difference.

I decided not to run. I told a couple of key people of my decision. Marilyn Roycroft, who had been a researcher in Stephen Lewis's caucus and was well known as an organizer in the party, had been co-ordinating the "draft Rae" campaign. I let her know that the answer was no, and word spread.

The lobbying started again with a vengeance even as well-wishers came to see us at the hospital just after Arlene had given birth to Judith. Ironically, Arlene's room looked right out over Queen's Park. Brigden was particularly shameless. "Do you think fate would have given you this room if it wasn't meant to be?" The answer was still no.

The lobbying didn't stop however, and even followed us to my parents' cottage a week or two later at Big Rideau Lake. Marilyn, Peter Mosher, and Hugh Mackenzie came up and took me out on a boat together to keep up the pressure while Arlene and Judith slept one afternoon. The *coup de grâce* was a lunch conversation later in August with Donald C. Macdonald, the leader of the C.C.F. in Ontario in the fifties, and leader of the NDP until 1971. Donald was the leader of the group in the caucus that wanted me to run, and he was persistence itself.

He played on every emotion: guilt, ambition, flattery, loyalty. I had a duty to run. I was the only person who could bring the party to power. If the NDP could crack Ontario, anything was possible. Finally, Donald said, he would give up his seat in the legislature and let me succeed him in York South.

I eventually succumbed. I was sad to leave Ottawa, and the company of good friends in the caucus, but I felt that on balance the challenge of leading the party in Ontario would be even greater. Arlene, who had favoured the move, was happy, since it would mean we could focus our activities in Toronto. I announced my decision on Labour Day 1981. I was leaving the bright lights of Parliament Hill for a very different world.

The hardest part of the decision, in the end, was not leaving Ottawa. It was saying goodbye to my constituents in Broadview-Greenwood who had elected me three times in as many years. I had found a political home and built it up. I had knocked on every door and knew thousands of people. It was like giving up a first love.

Chapter Six

NO SOFT LANDINGS

Losing a beloved federal riding was bad enough. Battling for the leadership was harder. It was a long contest, over six months, since the convention wouldn't be held until February of 1982. My opponents were Richard Johnston, who was Stephen Lewis's successor in Scarborough West, and Jim Foulds, the MPP from Port Arthur. We had more than fifty all-candidates meetings all over the province, and it got to the point where we could almost recite each other's speeches by heart.

I was immediately cast as the "establishment candidate," fair game for attacks from the party's activist left. Richard Johnston carefully crafted his coalition to include this group; as well as strong supporters of his ability and record. Jim Foulds was running as an effective member of the legislature and as someone who had thought long and hard about issues he cared about. He clearly felt he deserved to win, and deserved support, and that neither Richard nor I had the experience to do what had to be done.

My campaign manager was Marilyn Roycroft, who did an exceptional job in marshalling the votes we needed. André Foucault from the Paperworkers worked on building support among trade union delegates. Dave Cooke was the chair of my campaign within the caucus, and Thérèse Bain from Temiskaming co-chaired for the wider party. Dave Cooke is one of the great politicians in our party, with an almost infinite capacity for hard work and good judgment. He would prove to be one of the truly outstanding ministers in the 1990 government.

My message to the party was simple enough: we had to present a credible, contemporary message to the electorate in our opposition to the Conservatives. There was no point in going back to the details of the Regina Manifesto; there was no particular salvation there, and the public wasn't interested in being saved. My underlying strength was the feeling among delegates that with me as leader the party would get more attention, and would be able to mount a more effective opposition to the Davis government than could the Liberals.

There was the inevitable personal acrimony. I was labelled arrogant, aloof, and a right-winger more at home in the boardroom than in the union hall. At the time, this bugged me. Then I became known as "thin-skinned." This bugged me even more. Then I realized that this was more of a ritualistic hazing than anything else. The front-runner always has to bear the brunt. That's the way it works.

In the end I won the convention with a substantial majority on the first ballot. Richard and Jim were gracious in defeat, and there was remarkably little bitterness when it was all over. In fact, Richard's main caucus supporters, Floyd Laughren and Ross McClellan, became key advisers and friends throughout my career as leader of the party. Frances Lankin, who nominated Richard, became an outstanding minister in my government ten years later and a trusted friend. And of course, my own nominator, Mel Swart, went on to become one of my great critics.

I had left one or two hostages to fortune. At one point in the convention I had improvised a speech to the delegates in which I talked of the Tories' Ontario as "Toryland" which was essentially a country club in which women and people of colour were not welcome. Hugh Segal was a commentator on the convention, and immediately seized on this as a sign of my own inexperience.

Other commentators—in addition to the inevitable Clare Hoy—
took off as well. Looking back, the comment seems particularly
apt. It certainly aroused an angry response which often means a
target has been hit.

My landing at Queen's Park was not a soft one. Television had
been a great equalizer for me in Ottawa. As soon as I resigned my
seat in March of 1982, I lost my favoured position with the
media. "Who does this guy think he is?" became the collective
media question, and life was very different. Frost to Robarts to
Davis was even more unbeatable than the famed baseball combination of Tinkers to Evers to Chance.

The Tories at that point seemed impregnable. I was thirty-three
years of age, and had known no other party in power. Forty years
in power—it would become forty-two—put them outside anyone's
league in the world's real democracies. One would have to turn to
the Party of the Institutionalized Revolution in Mexico for a North
American comparison. There was no revolution in Ontario—
then—but institutionalized and entrenched they certainly were.

I had no seat in the House, and would have to find one. The
Liberals had their own convention, and had just elected their new
leader, David Peterson. Replacing them as the "real opposition"
was going to be harder than it looked.

Donald Macdonald made good on his commitment to leave
York South, but only after a painful episode with both Jim
Renwick and Marion Bryden declining to retire. I had hoped to
be able to stay in the east end, but that was not to be.

The west end of Toronto is different from the east. York South's
boundaries stretched from Bloor Street to Highway 401, from the
Humber River in the west to a shifting boundary through the
middle of the City of York. Broadview's ethnic base was Greek and
Chinese. In York South it was Eastern European in the south;
Italian, Portuguese, and now Caribbean in the centre and north. In
each case an older, Anglo-Saxon working class provided a rock-solid
core for the New Democratic Party. Younger professionals could

be persuaded to come our way, but they could also shift with the political winds.

Arlene and I took a deep breath and started canvassing again. The very first day, we started downwind from the packing plants on St. Clair Avenue (now mainly closed). The deep breath was not a good idea, particularly since Arlene was by this time pregnant with our second daughter, Lisa, who would be born on February 6, 1983. We kept going. We had the support of the entire New Democratic Party, but we also had a strong and particularly unpleasant opponent, John Nunziata, now the federal member for York South.

Arlene, canvassing for the first time in the west end of Toronto, came to the door of an elderly Polish gentleman, and asked if she could put up a sign.

"Madam, I do not like a party that is red or pink or…even orange."

Later, walking along Bloor West Village, behind two Eastern European ladies who are also doing their shopping, we overhear this conversation.

"You know about the Jews?"

We flinch.

"They've stolen…"

We stay frozen.

"…all our recipes."

Our intermarriage has brought its own mixed identities. Our youngest, Eleanor, watched "Sesame Street" in both versions, Canadian and American.

"Some people say zed and some people say zee."

"That's right. Which do we say?"

"We say zed."

"Why?"

"Because we're Jewish."

Speaking at a dinner just before the election, I launched into my emotional, ungrammatical, but politically comprehensible Italian. As I was leaving the hall, an enthusiastic, elderly woman grabbed me to kiss me on both cheeks. As she embraced me she shouted in Italian, "All my life I've only heard two men who can talk like that."

"Yes?"

"Pierre Trudeau and Benito Mussolini."

Luckily the reporters covering the event had already left.

→ ←

Nunziata had been an NDPer earlier on, but had left after an internal row over a municipal campaign. In 1982 he was an alderman, running against the millionaire socialist outsider who'd never worked a day in his life, me. I had been through all this before, but not quite so unpleasantly in Broadview. There was a nasty edge to the Nunziata campaign. No point complaining, but victory on November 6, 1982, was very sweet.

The old village of Weston, the neighbourhoods of Silverthorn, Mt. Dennis and Harwood, the apartment towers on Jane Street, and the mixed income neighbourhood south of Dundas Street— we had strong support throughout the riding, which would last for the elections of 1985, 1987, 1990, and 1995. My eyes and ears were Tony Romano, whom I hired as my constituency assistant and who kept me elected. I was very conscious of the fact that as leader I simply couldn't focus on the riding as I had done in Broadview-Greenwood. At one all-candidates' meeting during the by-election, I was beginning to feel particularly vulnerable to the "outsider" charge, and announced that the Raes would move into the riding, something which came as a surprise to Arlene.

After Lisa was born in 1983, this is exactly what we did. We bought a house in the south end of the riding, in a valley below Baby Point, on a quiet, tree-lined street. Many of our neighbours were younger couples with young children. Bloor West Village became our new "High Street," replacing the Danforth. This is our home to this day.

← →

William Grenville Davis, eighteenth premier of Ontario, had finally won his majority back in 1981. First chosen premier in 1971, he had spent six years between 1975 and 1981 as the leader of a minority government. Advisers and cabinet ministers came and went. Davis stayed, and by the time I became NDP leader he was doing a pretty good imitation of Old Man Ontario.

Shrewd, with progressive instincts, Davis governed cautiously, and spoke in continuous circumlocution. He was incapable of expressing a thought in a straightforward way. As the saying goes, it worked for him. He had also survived the fire of his first administration, which had been marked by ministerial fiascos and even charges of corruption. He had learned to govern with more confidence and humour. By the time I entered the scene, he was very much in charge, and I was the new kid on the block who had to be brought down several pegs.

↔ →

David Peterson was someone I had known for many years, though never well. He had been at law school in the sixties with Colin Coolican, and the Coolicans are close friends of our family. I had actually first met him at the Coolicans' cottage at Big Rideau Lake. I was never able to overcome my initial impression of him: witty, caustic, superficial, and someone who felt charm would get him further than hard work. He was known to his friends as "Boot" and "Squire."

At a personal level, I quickly developed a good relationship with Bill Davis, which has carried through to this day. Friendship and partisanship are two different things. There are people in my own party I dislike personally (and many who may well dislike me), and people in other parties I like a great deal. My relationship with David Peterson was marred by the simple fact that we were rivals in the period between 1982 and 1985 and opponents in the House and three elections. There was no love lost between the NDP and the Liberals going well back into the 1970s. Bob Nixon, on the other hand, I admired enormously, and still do, though Bill Davis and Nixon never really got along at all.

Bill Davis dominated the political horizon completely by 1982. The hope in the party that my arrival would eclipse the Liberals was quite misplaced. Peterson remade his image, shedding his glasses and a few pounds. He successfully took hold of the issue of the takeover of a trust company by Leonard Rosenberg, and the flip of some apartment buildings. Benefiting from good sources in the trust industry, he dominated question period effectively.

There was no direct television broadcast from the legislature. The cameras, perched in the press gallery, got a great view of the top and back of my head. The Queen's Park media gang was only too happy to take me down a few notches: I was the outsider, supposedly the hotshot from Ottawa parachuted in to build the party, and every gaffe was given its due prominence.

I have no doubt that if Bill Davis had run for another term in 1984 or 1985, he would have won a resounding majority. Everyone's polling showed the same thing: with Davis, the Tories had well over 50 per cent support. The Liberals were a distant second, and we were just behind them.

The chemistry suddenly changed with Davis's decision to retire, which he announced in the fall of 1984. The day of his press conference we were half convinced he was going to call a election. He did not, and quit instead. I noticed that he understayed his welcome, which was wise. He was also responding to a strong desire to move on to different challenges. I was particularly grateful for the decision, because it gave us time to welcome our third daughter, Eleanor, who was born on November 19, 1984.

Bill Davis's departure left no heir apparent. A number of strong candidates emerged: Frank Miller, Dennis Timbrell, Roy McMurtry, and Larry Grossman. Miller was actually older than Davis, and cut from a very different cloth. He was affable enough, but determined to take his party to the right. His plaid jackets spoke of another era. His references to Reagan and Thatcher spoke of an ideological agenda that, to that point, had been foreign to the Ontario Progressive Conservative Party.

Frank Miller's message seemed to be the one the party faithful wanted to hear in early 1985. When the Tory convention was held, the delegates rejected younger, more progressive voices. The great beneficiary of this choice was not me but David Peterson. I did not fully realize this at the time, nor did I understand that the more effective I was in demolishing Miller, the more I was simply opening up room for Peterson.

Three-party politics in Ontario create a unique dynamic. For the better part of my lifetime, the success of the Ontario Tories had been their ability to occupy the middle, forcing the Liberals often to the right, and us to the left. When Stephen Lewis won thirty-eight seats in the minority parliament of 1975, second to the Tories, and ahead of the Liberals, it amazed me that there was no consideration given to his becoming premier with the support of the Liberals. It was apparently never discussed. Davis carried on, failing to get a majority again in 1977, and only becoming a majority premier in March of 1981.

The choice of Miller put the Tories well to the right, and created a generational divide as well. The Liberals' campaign in 1985 was well organized and well presented. Mine was less confident at first, and by the time we gained our voice it was too late. We didn't have enough money, so I had to share a bus with the press. Someone gave me an electric piano, and I drove them crazy with what I thought were clever songs about Frank Miller and the Tories. At the same time, David Peterson was cruising with confidence, promising beer and wine in the corner store, and looking and sounding more like a winner.

Just before leaving Ontario politics, Bill Davis decided that it was time to provide equal funding to Catholic high schools. The issue of full funding for separate-school education has been a difficult and emotional issue in Ontario politics for its entire history. Our own party went through some painful internal debate in the time leading up to the election of 1971. One powerful body of opinion favoured greater integration between the two systems, public and separate, with no additional funding for Grades 11, 12, and 13 in the Catholic system. (Catholic schools were only funded up to Grade 10.) The other, which I personally favoured, said that there were two publicly funded systems guaranteed by the Constitution of 1867 (and long before), and that discriminatory funding of the last three years of high school couldn't be justified.

Bill Davis had run hard against this second view in 1971, and beaten up on both the Liberals and the NDP. It was obviously an issue that troubled him as the province's population continued to change. The changes in his own home town of Brampton must have helped change his mind as well: a huge influx of Italian and

The Toronto Sun

Portuguese constituents had not lost their commitment to "their" schools. Whatever the reason, Davis changed his mind, and thereby divided his party.

In the last two weeks of the election campaign, the outspoken Anglican Archbishop of Toronto, Lewis Garnsworthy, decided in his wisdom to weigh in on this issue by denouncing separate-school funding as a sign from the Tory government that they had decided Catholics were better than the rest of us. The effect of pouring this particular brand of holy oil on the flame was predictable. Frank Miller could only do his best to blow it out.

He was not helped by his advisers. They told him to avoid a debate, which he did, but at a great price. This also hurt me because I enjoy a good verbal fight, and probably helped Peterson. Miller also decided that he didn't need the help of the Big Blue Machine, since they were allegedly too progressive and not personally loyal to him. The result was a disastrous lack of focus and organization. There is everything to be said for using the best people you have, regardless of who they may have supported in a leadership campaign. This simple truth was lost on Miller.

⟵ ⟶

Election night, May 2, 1985, was a surprise for Ontario. The Liberals and the Tories tied in the popular vote, at about 37 per cent. We came in at just under 25 per cent. The Conservatives were ahead in seats, with 52; the Liberals had 48; and we had 25. That night, Ontario went to bed believing it had elected another Conservative minority government.

I personally felt very differently. I had no animosity for Frank Miller, yet I didn't see how our political base would long tolerate our support for a Tory government led by him. The day-to-day roulette of minority government didn't have much appeal for me. The leverage it was said to represent was overblown. I had spent many hours discussing these issues with members of the federal party when I was in Ottawa. I was to spend the next several weeks arguing about it with my caucus colleagues, with leaders of other NDP parties across the country, and of course with party activists.

The first thing I did, on my own, was to place a call to Hershell Ezrin, who was David Peterson's principal secretary and chief of staff. I knew Hershell well. He had been president of the U.C. Lit at the University of Toronto, and had invited me to his home for a Friday night supper when we were students together. He joined the Department of External Affairs, and had kept in touch throughout his career. During the constitutional round of 1980-81, he had been put in charge of federal propaganda on national unity, and naturally our paths crossed then. I had been disappointed when he accepted the role as David Peterson's chief of staff in 1982, since this made our friendship more difficult, and I knew he would do a good job.

I phoned Hershell at home, congratulated him on his success, and said that I wanted to speak directly to David Peterson. We arranged for a time on the weekend when we could talk, and talk we did.

I told Peterson that we should think about a different kind of government. I said it would be a difficult issue for both our caucuses, but I wasn't ruling anything out, and we needed to find a way to negotiate a programme for a new government. I told him that I would be going to my caucus that week, and would be appointing a team of negotiators, who would have a mandate to begin discussions with both the Liberals and the Conservatives. He joked that there were some people in my caucus he would have trouble working with. I said the feeling was mutual, but that wasn't the point. We had the chance to break the mould of Ontario politics. It took him a while to realize that I was offering to make him premier.

❦ ❧

Our own caucus meeting of May 17, 1985, was a long and emotional one. It started with the inevitable recriminations on how we could have run a different and better campaign. With the exception of 1990, when everyone took credit for their foresight and brilliance, these post mortems are rarely pleasant, and always feature fingers pointed clearly at the leader. Once the air cleared a bit, we focused on the choices ahead.

There were essentially three camps: those who wanted a formal coalition with the Liberals, with NDP members joining the cabinet; those who categorically rejected this idea, and wanted to manage the minority government experience much as had happened in Ottawa between 1972 and 1974, and at Queen's Park between 1975 and 1981; and those who felt the Tories had to be replaced but couldn't stomach joining the Liberals in government.

I decided to listen carefully before acting. The first caucus meeting was attended by many from outside the caucus— members of the party executive, for example, who were much more strongly opposed to the idea of a coalition than the caucus itself. My personal preference was for a full coalition, but I wasn't sure enough of my support within the party, or of myself, to push ahead in the face of strong opposition.

Stephen Lewis, Michael Cassidy, and Donald Macdonald were all against the idea of a coalition, and all expressed their feelings in vehement terms. My own self-assurance had been dealt a blow by the campaign itself, and I was reluctant to enrage the gods. I have no hesitation in saying that if I had to do it all over again I would have insisted on the NDP taking cabinet seats in a joint Liberal-NDP government in 1985.

Ed Broadbent shared this view, and expressed it to me equally strongly when I had a private meeting with him the weekend after the election. To say "there wasn't enough support in caucus or the party" would be a cop-out, because these intangibles can change in the face of persuasive leadership.

I chose to steer a more cautious route. Summing up after that first caucus meeting, I said that it was clear there was strong opposition to a coalition with the Liberals, and at the same time enormous ill-will toward the Tories. We therefore had to find a path which would allow us to maintain our continuing identity, and at the same time avoid what I eloquently called the "day-to-day blackmail bullshit" of previous minority experiences.

I appointed a committee of three—Ross McClellan, Mike Breaugh, and Hugh Mackenzie—to meet with the other parties. The Tories appointed Bob Elgie, one of their most progressive members, Larry Grossman, and John Tory, Jr.; for the Liberals the team was Sean Conway, Bob Nixon, and Hershell Ezrin.

There was an air of total disbelief among the Tories. They could not believe that they might come to lose the election, and couldn't accept that the chemistry of 1985 was very different from 1975. Coming back from the first meeting with the Tories, I asked the team whether there was any philosophical objection to any of our programmatic suggestions. Mike Breaugh laughed and simply said, "Are you kidding? It's a candy store."

Our approach in discussions with the other two parties was to insist on a set of policies that the new government had to pursue, as well as on a new way of doing business at Queen's Park. We wanted an agreement on parliamentary reform, including the idea that the government could be defeated on a bill and wouldn't see this as a matter of confidence.

One important aim was to ensure stability, to show people that minority government didn't have to constantly teeter on the edge of collapse. Another was to be able to point to an agenda that was clearly identified with us, so that in the endless quest for credit and responsibility, we could point with some credibility to a document that had been authored by us.

After a while, the negotiating team was uncomfortable with continuing in-depth discussions with both parties. Guile and deception did not come as easily to our group as might have been helpful in our self-interest. Once we had the outline of a deal with the Liberals, we announced that we were going to stop dancing with the Tories.

There was the inevitable "principled denunciation" by Frank Miller. He said that no self-respecting government would agree to limit itself with a written agreement. We knew better. The Tories would have mortgaged their grandmothers if it had meant they could have stayed in power.

The discussions with the Liberals carried on for several more sessions. Peterson and I had one final meeting in which he said he was having trouble with the idea of accepting defeat of individual tax measures without turning these into a matter of confidence. I laughed and said there was no budging. The haggling ended and we shook hands. The signing was scheduled for the next day.

The morning of May 29, 1985, I got a call from Hershell saying Peterson wouldn't be attending any joint signing ceremony. We should go ahead with separate press conferences. At that point I had lost my bargaining room, and realized that the premier-in-waiting didn't want to be seen within a hundred miles of the guy who'd made him premier.

We signed the accord with the Liberals on May 29, 1985. It represented a breakthrough in Canadian politics. It made possible the end of the forty-two-year Tory reign of power in Ontario. It presented a clear programme to the legislature for two years. The political programme included: jobs and training for young people; an end to extra billing and support for medically necessary travel for northerners; nursing-home reform; a new tenant-protection law and support for non-profit housing; equal pay; equity legislation; first-contract legislation for trade unionists and better severance arrangements; pension and child-care reform. It set out a practical, progressive agenda. It also changed a number of parliamentary conventions about confidence, when a government had to resign, and how much scope there would be for private members, backbench members, and opposition parties, that were a real advance.

But for all this, I signed with mixed feelings. I didn't believe all the commentators, from the right and from the left, who said that I was signing my own death warrant. But I felt at the pit of my stomach that I'd missed an opportunity by not insisting, both to my own party and to the Liberals, that the NDP join the cabinet. I also knew that while many good things would be done by the new government, as prescribed by the accord, the Liberals would invariably get the lion's share of credit.

As a minor footnote to history, I moved the motion of non-confidence in the Miller government after a bizarre throne speech in which the Tories promised to do everything for everybody. This meant that I had been responsible for the defeat of two Tory governments at both the federal and provincial level. So there are some things I can still tell my grandchildren with enormous pride.

← →

That summer I kept busy explaining to all who would listen what we had done and why it was important. Arlene and I went with our three young daughters to the Commonwealth Parliamentary Association meetings in Quebec City and Malbaie, where I was savaged by Bob Williams, a tough partisan NDPer from B.C. The common feeling in much of the party was that we were in danger of losing our identity because we had "gotten in bed" with the Liberals. This of course spoke to a deep syndrome in the party: in the minds of some, the party's role was as a voice of protest, a movement of values that was only comfortable in opposition to the prevailing capitalist culture. A compromise with this culture in the form of an accord or coalition was a sell-out of the basic values of the party.

This is a vision of the party I have never shared. Commenting on Claude Ryan's angry dissent from the War Measures Act, Pierre Trudeau once turned Lord Acton's famous dictum on its head: "powerlessness corrupts, and absolute powerlessness corrupts absolutely."

Throughout my political life I have disagreed with the perspective that it is more moral to be out of power than in; that being on the margins waving a placard or shaking a fist is ethically superior to making decisions which often require us to choose, not

THE TORONTO STAR

between black and white, but between shades of grey. Edmund Burke, in *Reflections on the Revolution in France*, wrote that

> *the rights of men are in a sort of middle, incapable*
> *of definition, but not impossible to be discerned.*
> *The rights of men in governments are their advan-*
> *tages; and these are often in balances between differ-*
> *ences of good—in compromises sometimes between*
> *good and evil, and sometimes between evil and evil.*
> *Political reason is a computing principle: adding,*
> *subtracting, multiplying and dividing, morally, and*
> *not metaphysically or mathematically, true moral*
> *denominations.*

In this sense, I have always seen the pursuit of power as a responsibility. Power is not immoral. It is a fact of political and public life. Within the Canadian left, as elsewhere, there has always been a tendency to see political power itself as something to be spurned, as a force that would demand only compromise.

Compromise is an essential and necessary part of the discourse of politics. Just as it abhors a vacuum, a healthy politics rejects absolutes. The revolutionary left and the radical right both start from a very different premise: that they are armed with truth, and that this truth is incompatible with the blurring tendencies of parliamentary life and coalition politics.

Even beyond the revolutionary left, many in the party are fundamentally more comfortable with opposition than with the difficulties of power. Those who were unhappiest with the accord were those who kept saying, "We're losing our identity because we're getting in bed with the Liberals." The maintenance of a separate identity, loyalty to what Burke called "the little platoon," was more important than anything else. People like Mel Swart and Bob Mackenzie, both long-time party members and deep loyalists to me, were extremely uncomfortable with the accord.

Then there were those even more extreme: if we ever actually won an election they would demand a recount.

BOBBY AT THREE YEARS.

THREE GENERATIONS.
WITH MY MOTHER, LOIS, AND MY
GRANDMOTHER MILDRED, 1951.

My mother, Lois, leaving Newnham College, Cambridge, 1935.

Johnny and me at Canada House Christmas party, 1952.

A PICTURE I TOOK OF GRANDMOTHER NELL AT LAKE SIMCOE,
AUGUST 1955.

SUMMER DAYS AT THE COTTAGE.
WITH MY SISTER, JENNIFER, MY MOTHER, LOIS,
AND MY BROTHER JOHNNY.
THE GIRL DOING STUNTS AT THE BACK IS DARCY DUNTON.

A SERIOUS YOUNG MAN IN A VERY OLD
JACKET, UNIVERSITY OF TORONTO, 1968.

MY FATHER, SAUL, GIVING A SPEECH AT A ROMAN CATHOLIC
MISSION IN GUATEMALA AROUND 1970.

THREE AMIGOS. MIKE IGNATIEFF, ME AND JEFF ROSE,
SOUTH OF FRANCE, AUGUST 1970.

MY BROTHER DAVID AT RIDEAU LAKE IN
THE LATE 1970S.

MY SISTER-IN-LAW GINNY RAE AND HER SONS
JONATHAN AND CHRISTOPHER, 1995.

THE RAE CLAN SUMMER OF 1977.
BACK ROW: DAVID, SAUL, LOIS, BOB;
FRONT: KATE, JENNIFER, PHYLLIS, NELL, JOHANNA AND JOHN.

THE NEXT GENERATION!
FROM LEFT: JONATHAN, ELEANOR, BEN, CHRISTOPHER,
LISA, AMY AND JUDITH, 1991.

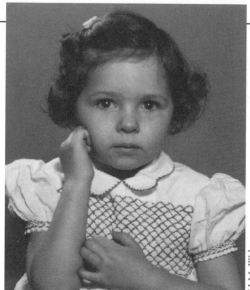

H.M. Walters

ARLENE, 1953.

ON OUR HONEYMOON IN GREECE, 1980.

THE HAPPY COUPLE, 1981.

WEDDING GUESTS SAUL, NELL AND JACK, FEBRUARY 23, 1980.

CALL TO THE BAR, 1980.

Susanne Jeffrey

THE FIRST OFFICIAL PHOTO WITH ELEANOR AT TWO WEEKS. THAT'S
JUDITH NEXT TO ARLENE AND LISA ON MY LAP, CHRISTMAS 1984.

AL AND HANNAH PERLY WITH THEIR THREE GRANDCHILDREN.
NOVEMBER 1984.

Jennifer, Saul and Lois at the cottage in 1994.

The Toronto Star

"Don't blow it Daddy!" Celebrating two birthdays
(mine and Judith's) in August 1987.

Chapter Seven

IN THE VALLEY

The weekend of August 17 and 18, 1985, took me to a party meeting in Halifax, where once again I was defending this new course for the party. I got home on the afternoon of Sunday, August 18. Arlene had spent the morning with the girls and her parents, Al and Hannah Perly, and we were planning to have dinner together at home while her parents joined friends.

At about 6:30 that night we got a call from Al and Hannah's dinner companions. They had expected the Perlys for dinner, but they had not turned up. We could not find them at home, or anywhere else, and thought that they might have forgotten and gone out to a movie. On the off chance that something had happened, I phoned the Toronto police, and they said nothing had been reported. I then phoned the police in York region, and there was a studied silence on the line. They asked me to identify myself, and then phoned me back with the unbelievable news that Al and Hannah had been killed, together with their friends the Goulds, in a car accident.

Their car was hit head on by a speeding car that had spun completely out of control on Major Mackenzie Drive, in the middle of a sunny afternoon. Two officers came to the door to confirm the news.

Nothing could possibly have prepared us for this moment. Arlene was wild with grief. I made several desperate phone calls, and the family gathered around in a state of uncontrollable anger and tears. The days following are a blur.

← →

Al Perly was born near Radom, Poland, and came with his parents and brothers to Hamilton in the early 1920s. He worked first in his father's paint and wallpaper store, and then came to Toronto where he started work in a shoe store. He then went into the theatre business and was a movie theatre manager for Nat Taylor. After that he set up an upscale steam bath, first with a partner, and then on his own. Finally, he and Hannah went into the travel business, and together they ran a successful travel agency for years before selling it to one of their employees and retiring.

Hannah Florence was born in Zidikai, Lithuania, the second oldest of five children, and was raised in Peterborough, Ontario. She met Al in Toronto during the war, and was his partner in every sense. They were wonderful people, who accepted me completely and without reservation, from the time of our very first meeting in 1977. Al had a gentle, joking quality about him, and loved to tell stories. Hannah was the organizer, the centre of the family, a great cook, and a lively presence. She was an enthusiast about almost everything. They both adored and doted on our daughters.

Al used to take me to the steam bath at the Primrose Club, where he was a regular, and it was there that I heard the best summary of the choice being offered in 1979 between Joe Clark, Pierre Trudeau, and Ed Broadbent.

"Isn't democracy wonderful. We get to choose between ignorance, arrogance, and socialism. This is a choice?"

Hannah used to give me a key insight into politics in the age of television. We would regularly have a conversation which went something like this:

"Saw you on the news last night."

"What was I talking about?"

"I have no idea. I was busy doing something else. But you

looked terrific (or tired, or grumpy, or whatever)."

Politics is in part a game of impressions, of feelings, of momentum and shifting perspectives. New Democrats are notoriously people of the book, obsessed with policy more than with the punch and feint. Hannah always reminded me that most people come at life differently.

Our lives were changed drastically by losing Hannah and Al. Arlene became an orphan, and the kids lost their "Toronto grandparents." We also had to survive the absurdities of the justice system. The case of the young man eventually found responsible for the accident went up and down appeals, delays, and reversals for nearly eight years. We couldn't say or do anything, complain or comment, as would any ordinary citizen.

I threw myself back into politics, but for Arlene it was more difficult and painful. At the time of this tragic upheaval, our daughters were very young—Judith was just 4, Lisa 2 1/2, and Eleanor only 7 months. Arlene was trying to put on a brave face for them while barely keeping body and soul together herself. After a few years, she started writing about children's books, which she had come to know and love through reading to our own children, and watching them fall in love with stories themselves. We came to learn that life goes on, but never in quite the same way.

The second blow came at Christmas 1987. My brother David, the baby of the family, was diagnosed with a lymphatic cancer which had entered his central nervous system. He had been feeling poorly in early December, and after a brief delay the doctors determined the cause. It was a bitter, bitter blow.

David was nine years younger than I, born in Washington after my father returned from his stint with the International Control Commission in Vietnam. I can remember so clearly sitting on the sun porch at Quebec Street in Washington when my parents told us the great news: our family, in which I had been the youngest for nearly nine years, was going to have a baby. David was born on May 15, 1957, a long and loud arrival. We soon realized— Mum and Dad more than any of us—how much this boy would change our lives.

David was precocious, funny, and always stretched life to the limit. He did an M.B.A. and went to work for the Bank of Montreal, who sent him to New York. He then moved on to G.E. Capital and became an investment banker. He met his wife, Ginny, in Mexico City, and with their two boys lived in Connecticut. They all moved to Toronto in the summer of 1987 where he was to set up G.E. Capital Canada. It was only a couple of months after his arrival that he was diagnosed with cancer.

When the doctor told him he had a one in three chance of living five years, David instantly replied with a brave joke, "Too bad about those other two guys." That summed it up: an extraordinary, determined defiance. Before his illness, like most older brothers, I would have said he had a low pain threshold. How wrong I was. The treatment was gruelling throughout. He took it all with incredible courage.

But courage was not enough, and David's ordeal lasted for a full year and a half. There was enormous hope, but numerous setbacks. He spent the entire time in three excellent hospitals— Mount Sinai, Princess Margaret, and Toronto General—under the care of an extremely dedicated team of doctors and nurses headed by Hans Messner. Many are good friends still. His condition was further complicated by an attack of Guillain-Barré Syndrome, which left him unable to walk.

After several months of treatment, the doctors suggested we try a bone marrow transplant. My parents, John, Jennifer, and I were all tested and I was found to be the most compatible donor. When we talked of the transplant, he and I joked about the irony of the banker getting the donation from the social democrat.

"What if it makes me a socialist?"

In June of 1988 we did the transplant, which for the donor is a few days of discomfort. For David the ordeal never ended: the whole family became expert in the lingo of rejection, drug reaction, low blood counts, which became a way of dealing with the illness and the growing understanding that none of this heroic medicine was going to work for David.

The assault from the early drugs and radiation had done too

much damage. He beat the cancer but died from the effects of the treatment. The deterioration was slow at first, then relentless.

During the last months he drove us all to distraction with the insistence that the smoked salmon, the sushi, the smoked meat, the cappuccino, be just so. In a reverie, scarcely able to move, David beckoned to his dear friend Leon Pressman and whispered quietly, "I know this terrific doughnut shop..."

Literally days before he died, David had us all watch a video presentation about mahogany boats: they were the best boats made (of course they cost a fortune), and he wanted to make a point.

David finally succumbed to his illness on June 6, 1989. At his funeral I said:

> One evening a few days ago David in a kind of
> dream told Uncle Jack and me, "I am returning to
> the city of my birth." It will be a city of good music
> and good food and good times, of dancing and song,
> of belly laughs and warm embraces, of friendships
> bravely treasured, family from age 2 to 102 all
> around, boisterous conversation about basketball
> and politics, horse racing and the market, of life
> and love. It will be a great and good city because
> David is there.

My parents had moved down from Ottawa to be with David and all of us throughout this long night. We learned the hard way that modern medicine can't save everybody, but it can certainly prolong the ordeal. None of us had ever imagined that something like this would happen to us—and then we were taken aback at the resources we found within.

We took turns sleeping at the hospital as he slipped into a coma. We cried a lot, and also learned the value of humour. David and I spent hours watching tapes of "Yes, Minister" and "Fawlty Towers," and the night before the transplant held hands as we laughed uncontrollably at *Throw Momma from the Train*. My mother was less amused.

Politics through all this became less important. I had always been something of a driven soul, my mood fluctuations depending on the success of a question period or the latest press review. After the loss of Arlene's parents and then my brother David, nothing the media or opposition could do or say would ever have the same impact. It's just not on the same scale.

Since leaving politics in 1996, I have become the National Spokesman for the Leukemia Research Fund. I do this gladly in David's memory, in the knowledge that we will eventually beat this cruel disease.

↤ ↦

In 1986 I had brought Robin Sears back from a stint at the Socialist International in London and, together with David Agnew and Chuck Rachlis our research director, had turned our shop into an effective fighting unit. Robin is a tough professional, a good friend, and a controversial character, who had his detractors. These always partly flowed from the petty jealousies and internal bickerings that are inevitable in a political family. Most important for me, he freed me up to do what I most wanted and be where I felt most comfortable.

The nervous nellies in the party had convinced themselves that the accord with Peterson would finish us off. I was convinced of the opposite, that by changing governments, and forging an agenda without political uncertainty and the game of political blackmail we would emerge stronger. I was eventually proved right. Handling minority governments the "traditional way" had not worked for us federally in 1974 or provincially in 1977.

Yet our approach had its own challenges. We met regularly with members of the Liberal government and reviewed the progress of the accord. We passed an extraordinary amount of progressive legislation in less than two years. For a time it was the Tories, and not us, who became irrelevant.

Above all, on difficult issues, like the end to extra billing and changes in Ontario's Human Rights Code, we held the Liberals' feet to the fire. Our convention in June of 1986, instead of being the blood bath some had feared (I'm speaking of my own blood here), was a triumphant love-in. The caucus walked in together after an all-night debate to cheers all around.

The extra-billing issue had been hard fought. I first encountered the problem in Broadview. Several constituents came in with bills for hundreds of dollars from their doctors. I raised the issue in the House of Commons, as did others. Monique Bégin, the Liberal Minister of Health and Welfare, eventually brought forward the Canada Health Act, which withheld money from provinces permitting extra billing by doctors.

The provincial Liberals did a pre-election flip in 1985, and agreed to the ban in the accord. The Ontario Medical Association, not realizing how much the political ground had shifted around them, launched a root-and-branch campaign against any change, eventually launching demonstrations and a strike of sorts.

They only succeeded in making the accord look good. The doctors were seen as selfish and shortsighted. Their loyalty to the fundamentals of medicare was challenged by the public. They lost more ground with each angry confrontation.

← →

"What does an opposition leader actually do?" The key is to remember the political goal: to do your job in such a way as to make victory possible in the next election. That seemed remote in the aftermath of the 1985 shift in power. The polls showed a constant 45 to 55 per cent of the electorate supporting David Peterson, with us trailing well behind.

There is invariably a tension in opposition between wanting to attack the government for its inevitable mistakes and feeling a need to present an alternative. Traditionally Liberals have felt less compelled to worry about this. But New Democrats are nothing if not driven by policy.

Stephen Lewis was a great opposition leader, and might well have become premier if he had stayed on as leader. Ed Broadbent, very different from Stephen in other ways, spent as much time thinking and developing policy ideas as he did building the party. He did both with great skill.

My own approach drew from both, whom I like and admire.

Question period, particularly after the introduction of television, was the key media event when the House was sitting. The game was to invent a clip, which would catch the 6:00 p.m. news, to be followed by a scrum outside the House for both questioner and victim. Keep the questions short and sharp enough to make your point. Make it colourful enough to get quoted. Get your facts straight. Try to avoid shooting yourself in the foot.

But even in opposition that's only the tip of the iceberg. Not all questions jump out from the news. On rent control, nursing-home reform, car insurance, and extra billing, for example, we built province-wide campaigns. Questions flowed from what was happening door-to-door and on the ground. You always hoped people's stories were accurate. On car insurance, we constantly had to battle over which complainer had the right story.

There was never a weekend when I wouldn't be speaking some-where around the province. By car and plane, the pace was relent-less—from the Empire Club in Toronto to the auto workers' hall in Windsor or Oshawa; from the church basement in Powassan to the Legion Hall in Ridgemont; every university, community college, teaching hospital, institution for the developmentally disabled, paper factory, day-care centre—there wasn't a corner in the province that went unvisited.

It was a wonderful experience, and if my political career had ended without my becoming premier, I would not have been unhappy. I got to meet people and do things that made it all worthwhile.

For example, just outside Windsor, in the flat farm country that stretches for miles east along Lake Erie and north-east to London, lies the village of North Buxton. I had never heard of it before becoming leader. It was, for years, a black community. Every Labour Day people come from all over northern United States and south-western Ontario for a picnic and reunion. The church rocks with voices singing, shouting, chanting. There's a ball game. Howard McCurdy, at the time a city councillor in Windsor, took me for a walk through the village and to the graveyard near the church.

"Some of these names are runaway slaves. And you know something? When I was a kid we still had segregation in parts of southwestern Ontario."

Ten years later I would get an invitation to a museum run by the Walls family. Dr. Bryan Walls is a Windsor dentist who has made it his life's work to tell his family's story. Almost singlehandedly he's built a museum dedicated to the Underground Railroad and the courage of those who built the Freedom Trail. On a sunny day in August 1994, I got to share a platform with Rosa Parks, who refused to go to the back of the bus in Birmingham, Alabama, forty years before. She now lives in Detroit. She spent the day with young black children telling them how the world had changed and how she had helped to change it. Let freedom ring.

← →

Or, again: Soon after being elected leader, I realized I needed to learn more about the north of the province. And so learn I did. I visited, listened, and made speeches in union halls and church basements, hearing stories of the Cobalt Symphony, Sir Harry Ochs and Kirkland Lake, pitched battles between miners and police, communists and social democrats, French and English. I went ice fishing on clear blue days at 20 below and handed out flyers at plant gates at 5:30 in the morning when it was even colder. Down every sizable mine (and some not so), through every paper and pulp mill in the province. I went to wakes for miners killed in Sudbury, Timmins, and Kirkland Lake, and made one small boy a little happier when I got him tickets to a Leafs playoff game after he'd lost his father.

One summer I spent weeks driving across the north, and stopping to head into the bush. My best guide ever was George Marek, just retired from the Ministry of Natural Resources. He wanted to show me the "second forest," what was growing back from the first cut. He made himself unpopular with the paper companies because he was a tough conservationist. He taught me the difference between red pine and white; jack pine, spruce and balsam; poplar and aspen. A Czech immigrant with a powerful sense of his responsibilities as a scientist, George railed with profanities against governments of all stripes and companies of all sizes. None were paying enough attention to the long term.

Invited to dinner at his house in Beardmore, I couldn't help noticing paintings on every wall, bold colours, great light: the north in all its splendid variety.

"Whose work is this?"

"Mine."

I bought four paintings from him on the spot. They've hung in my office ever since.

← →

The 1987 election was, in good measure, a Peterson love-in that confirmed the direction of the accord government. The economy had improved dramatically from the recession of 1981-84. Unemployment was low. The deficit was declining steadily. David Peterson's personal standing was high. He promised to fight free trade.

The result of the election confirmed the shift of opinion that took place as soon as the Liberals assumed power in 1985—with more than 45 per cent popular support the Liberals captured 95 seats, with the NDP getting 19 and the Conservatives 16. The lopsidedness of the House exaggerated, as it always does, the popular vote.

The election gave us the status of Official Opposition, a psychological and tactical advantage. Larry Grossman, the Conservative leader, resigned and his party decided to delay the leadership convention until 1990. Peterson's huge majority after 1987 became an easier target as an impression of aimless disdain and complacency replaced the defined purpose of the accord.

I thought briefly but very seriously about running to succeed Ed Broadbent as federal leader when Ed decided to retire in the spring of 1989, but my new mood led to a very different decision. I decided to stay in Ontario and fight one more election, not believing for a minute that this would change my status as an opposition leader. I also wanted to be able to spend more time thinking and writing about politics, to find a way to put it all in a broader perspective. My plan was to campaign as leader in one more election, and then to leave electoral politics.

That September in 1989 I celebrated this new-found feeling of freedom by accepting an invitation to sit in on a road in the middle of the Temagami Forest. This was a rather unusual step for an Opposition Leader. I met earlier with Chief Gary Potts, and he had stressed to me that it was crucial for the band to have some say in the future of the resource around them. The magnificent stand of old pine near the Old Squirrel Road was an important part of the native claim. No one seemed to be listening, or paying attention. I decided to do what I wanted to do.

Two O.P.P. officers are now the proud owners of a photograph which later became a postcard. It is a picture of me, with officers on either side, holding up the number "4." I was arrested together with dozens of others and politely escorted to a police wagon in the late afternoon of September 18, 1989, and driven in the company of other conscientious objectors to the nearest town, Elk Lake. There we were not actually charged, but simply warned that if we were found trespassing again we would be charged. A few days later the Crown got an injunction, and those that defied this court order were all arrested, charged, and in many cases convicted.

Arlene waited for me at a Blue Jays game that evening, for which I never showed up. After a few innings she heard about my arrest and called the family lawyer. As it turned out, his services were not required.

I had not gone on the Old Squirrel Road with the express purpose of getting taken away in a police van. I also knew that some others on the road were against all logging at all times and in all ways. I was there because Gary Potts had said he needed the support and attention that my presence would provide. I also believed then, and I do now, that those ancient trees should not be logged. The publicity in southern Ontario from this event was predictably mixed, but the Liberal government did not want to press the point since they themselves were badly divided on what to do.

I earned the enmity of those completely opposed to the native land claim, which didn't upset me, and also the strong anger of members of the International Woodworkers of America, whose leader at that time was the irrepressible Jack Munro. Never the shy or retiring type, he phoned me at the first opportunity.

"Are you sitting at your wooden desk, you stupid shithead?"

I had taken a risk by doing what I did, but in hard political terms it was worth it. I upset Jack Munro, but when I refused to cave in and urged him to come and talk with Potts he did just that. We met informally in Temagami. He still kept ranting about wooden desks and wooden doors and where the hell did I think these things came from, but Munro came away understanding that this was not about hugging trees but about managing a resource and protecting that which was priceless. No group of workers were stronger supporters in 1990 than the IWA. I had taken a stand, and gone beyond traditional politics.

Some in the caucus were happy, and others most decidedly were not. But this was always the price I paid for doing something. I felt freer to express myself and say and do what I wanted than ever before. I wanted more opportunities to broaden my perspective than the usual rants at question period.

During our time in government some years later, we almost got an agreement on a comprehensive land claim, but it failed to pass in a band referendum by a handful of votes. Development in Temagami is now controlled by a Tory government which has expressed its strong opposition to the land claim. They are also planning to allow more logging and development in this unique area than even recommended by the local community council.

We also developed an Old Growth policy which protected more land and trees than ever before, but of course earned the inevitable opposition of those who saw any logging or forestry as evil in themselves. They now have Mike Harris and the Tories to contend with.

❖ ❖

In late 1989 I was approached by the Lithuanian community, along with a number of other politicians, to be official observers of their first democratic election in the winter of 1990. Ontario's Baltic communities had always been resolutely conservative, and never particularly friendly towards New Democrats, but Richard

Johnston brought me into contact with a new generation that was ready to include us in their political spectrum.

So it was that Arlene and I went to Poland and Lithuania in the middle of the winter of 1990. We went partly to see what life was like as communism was collapsing, partly to see the first election in Lithuania since before the Second World War, and also to see the world we all lost in the Holocaust. Our first stop was Poland, where we visited Warsaw, Lodz, and Treblinka. We came away with a jumble of impressions.

An acquaintance in Poland told me about buying a car. He made instalment payments every month for eight years, finally getting his car in 1988. A year later, he had a small accident, and had to get his back fender repaired. It cost him more to repair the car than to buy it. He paid 750,000 zlotys for the car. Today the same car would sell for 21 million zlotys. "It wouldn't be so bad if it was a real car."

In Lithuania, some workers in a factory were approached about taking shares in the enterprise and becoming its owners. One worker asked, "But who will do the work if we are the owners?"

There was country-and-western music in the elevators, and the three international hotels in Warsaw had casinos. Unemployment figures were being published monthly. Legislators argued about which building should contain the proposed new stock exchange. Hotels were full of visiting business and investment delegations from around the world. One could overhear conversations in English, Russian, Japanese, and German.

We passed through Moscow for a day on our way between Warsaw and Vilnius. In Moscow at 10:00 in the morning the line-up for MacDonald's stretched out and around Pushkin Square, three and four deep. At lunch it was twice as long: it would take more than two hours to get served. The food was expensive, but in addition to the novelty, the only explanation for the line had to be that the food was better than anything else around. Some estimated that more than a million people came into Moscow every day just to shop for food.

These economies were crumbling: from bread basket to basket

case in a generation. Pollution was everywhere: cars, trucks, buses, factories fouled the air, the water, and the land. The extent of ecological damage was probably more catastrophic in Eastern Europe than anywhere on the globe.

A status-ridden economy, rigidly planned, oppressive, inefficient but one where minimal food and rent are cheap, was being dismantled. The institutions and, more important, the attitudes to take its place were not yet there. Free fall without a net.

The joke about the communist bargain was "You pretend to work and we will pretend to pay you." How to replace that with something approaching a market economy has proven to be an enormous challenge, and one that could not be met without cost, which is why the old Communist parties are now making a comeback.

Stalinism produced a lasting deformity in public life. When everything was controlled by the state and the party, every failure could be blamed on them. There was a complete break between what people said and thought in their homes and on the streets, and what was said officially. It was assumed (for the most part, correctly) that all the "politicians," i.e. the Communists in power, lied as a matter of course and a matter of survival. Public discourse was a caricature of the Orwellian world: to be a "public person" was to be someone who twisted the meaning of words, to the point where simple words like "brother," "democracy," "peace" became code words for the party.

I do not know how anyone can come into contact with these societies without becoming resolutely anti-communist. Conflict about the language of politics symbolizes deeper problems. In the Stalinist world "blame the party, blame the regime" were understandable and necessary reactions. Today, cynicism of this kind is literally unaffordable. The transition from a society where no one has any responsibility, to a very different world where blame for failure and success must be shared, is truly revolutionary.

And we found there are no guidelines as to how this could be done successfully. A revival of pre-World War II political parties no doubt brings nostalgia, but the plague of consultants, con artists, speculators, get-rich-quick schemesters that has now descended on every Eastern European capital is not the answer either.

We left Poland with a sense of profound depression. In Warsaw you can see swastikas daubed on the walls of apartment buildings in the new and tiny "Jewish quarter." The monument to the Warsaw Ghetto Uprising is in a square surrounded by blocks of flats. It has red paint on it and other anti-Semitic graffiti. At Treblinka the cobblestone road built by the prisoners still stretches for two kilometres: some of the cobblestones have bits of Hebrew writing, since the Nazis forced the prisoners to use broken grave-stones to build the road. We were there on a Sunday, quite alone. Almost anyone who could mourn or remember is dead or gone. And the willingness of Polish society to acknowledge the depth of the tragedy is limited.

We then went on to Lithuania. There are precious few examples of a country in the twentieth century gaining independence only to lose it again. The Molotov-Ribbentrop Pact of 1939 did just that to the three Baltic States—Estonia, Latvia, and Lithuania. A half-century after their annexation by Stalin, independence for these countries was once again on the political agenda.

With the first step off the plane from Moscow to Vilnius, I felt as though I was in a different country. The entire architecture of Moscow conspires to deliver one message: you don't count. Massive buildings, whether apartments, offices, or monuments, stretch for city blocks. There are line-ups and shortages every-where. Stalinism was a complete catastrophe. The difference between now and even ten years ago is that everyone knows it, and everyone is saying it.

Vilnius is a small, warm city. Its university, its squares, its archi-tecture, design, ambiance—the whole feel—were all at polar opposites to the crumbling impersonality of Moscow. Nor could there be any sharper contrast than that between the sleek, orga-nized, ruthless dogmatism of the Communist Party and the cheer-ful, if resolutely amateur, openness of Sajudis, the democratic and nationalist opposition to the Communists that was successful in that 1990 election.

Sajudis headquarters stood right across from the Cathedral at the main square. Outside was a wall of brutal photographs, graphic reminders of the bloody repression in Baku. Inside was friendly chaos: the third-floor office jammed with visitors, volunteers, phones ringing, voices shouting. In the eye of the storm, seemingly unruffled by the constant buffeting of phone calls, media interviews, and foreign visitors, was Vytautas Landsbergis, a professor of musicology, chairman of Sajudis. Modest, smiling, shrewd, he seemed almost bemused by what was happening. Three days before the election he left his meeting with us to give a musicology lecture at the Conservatory.

He was typical of most of the leadership of Sajudis. They were professors, lawyers, writers. Gorbachev initially dismissed what was happening as a revolt of the intellectuals. He couldn't believe it had the support of the people. He had to go to Lithuania to see how wrong he was.

We came away with the deep feeling that the independence train had left the station. In a polling house in the small town of Zidikai (where my mother-in-law was born), I was embraced by a woman who'd lived there all her life. She'd survived the dictatorship of the pre-war, Soviet takeover, German occupation, Soviet invasion again, and the hardships of the past thirty years.

"In our soul," she smiled, "we have always been free." She had voted Sajudis, she told me. I jokingly reminded her it was a secret ballot. She laughed.

"Let the world know. Tell them in Canada we're voting now just like them. We don't have to be afraid any more."

The election was remarkably relaxed, understated, low-key. Families turned up together to vote, and parents showed their kids the ballot before dropping it in the box. We travelled the length and breadth of Lithuania, and saw no sign of the Red Army or even policemen. There were no street demonstrations, before or after.

But the quiet was deceiving. The command economy didn't work, nor did the Sajudis government last. First, there was a bloody and terrifying encounter between Soviet troops and the

Lithuanian parliament, just a year after our visit. The hard fact of the complete integration of Lithuania into the Russian economy made change too difficult, as did the presence in Lithuania of a substantial Russian minority.

As I write now, the Communists have come back. Sajudis lost subsequent elections because they simply couldn't manage the economy. The apparatchiks, suitably cleansed and laundered, have returned.

But politics was far from the only purpose of our visit. I had asked our Lithuanian hosts in Toronto if it would be possible for us to stay with a Jewish family in Vilnius. The billets also assisted the Canadian delegation to gain entry. A more "official" U.S. delegation of observers was not permitted entry to Lithuania by the Soviets. We were billeted with a truly remarkable man, Gregory Kanovich, a writer in his early sixties, whose family had moved to Russia after the Soviet invasion and so had survived the Nazi sweep of 1941. Gregory's wife, Olga, was Russian, not Jewish, and she quickly adopted Arlene and me for the next ten days. Gregory and Olga spoke Russian, Lithuanian, German, and Yiddish, but little English. We communicated mostly by waving and gesturing. As chance would have it, his oldest son, Dmitri, lived in Toronto, and so we have maintained a connection to this day. In the early 1990s Gregory and Olga moved to Israel, because he had, as he put it, "nothing left." Their younger son Sergei had already made "aliyah."

Before the war, Vilnius ("Vilna") was a world centre of Jewish life and learning. There is now just one synagogue (as there is in Warsaw); the community is leaving in droves for Israel. Some stay behind because it is the only world they know. Ninety-four per cent of Lithuania's Jews were killed in the war. Those that survived often went deeper into the Soviet Union upon annexation in 1940.

"Those who remember are gone." Yes, but why? The outrage of the Holocaust has been followed by a profound denial, by neglect, by silence. Outside Vilnius, at Panaraius, the site of one of the great massacres of the ghetto, there is no separate recognition to the stark, tragic fact that people were killed because, and only because, they were Jews. The Soviets would not even allow that simple acknowledgment. On the stone monuments they are hollowly called "Soviet citizens."

Gregory had been elected to the Supreme Soviet a year before. He summed up the Soviet Union with a simple phrase, "nation, stagnation." He was profoundly pessimistic about what would unfold as the uglier side of Russian nationalism was given full expression.

We asked our hosts if we could witness the election in the tiny village near the Latvian border where Hannah Florence was born. They readily agreed, finding it a bit odd that we would not choose to see the transformation from the perspective of a larger community.

Sitting in a tiny room at the back of a wooden house, Arlene and I began a conversation with Maria Petruliachene, an eighty-four-year-old widow living in the village of Zidikai. Election day was sunny, bright, and unseasonably warm. I visited the polling station, and the local museum, and we took pictures of houses and the old stone church.

Arlene started to cry as soon as we got out of the car. I tried to explain to our hosts the emotion of the visit. Hannah had been born here, and come to Canada at age five with her mother and brother and sister in 1928. Her father, Meyer Florence, had preceded them by a year to get settled and find a job. They had left behind a Zidikai where there was a synagogue, schools, shops, and a community of more than three hundred families. A few left between the wars—to South Africa, to North America, to Palestine. But most stayed.

Those who stayed were killed, all of them, in the summer and fall of 1941. When we visited there was no sign that they were ever there at all. Maria remembered Hannah's family, remembered the widow, Hannah's grandmother, who ran the small store with her daughter, remembered the names. Another old man we talked to could recall the name of Arlene's grandfather. There was a memorial in the town to Lithuanian independence. There was a Christian graveyard on the main street out of town.

But if you didn't ask, and didn't talk to the older people who remembered what this town, and hundreds of others, were like, you would never know Jews had also breathed that air, and walked those streets, and worked that land, for centuries before the Nazi invasion. To see it now, and to receive the official version, you would never know the Jewish community had been there at all.

The Nazis overran Lithuania quickly and brutally in the summer of 1941. They eliminated entire Jewish communities as soon as they arrived. Maria described how the Jews in Zidikai were gathered up (one wondered how they were so speedily identified), and locked together in the synagogue. "They were kept without food and water for five days. Then the men were separated from the women and children. Some of our children ran messages between the two groups, took letters, and the priest took up a collection from the village to get them some food. After a week or so, they were all put on a train to Mazeikai (the neighbouring town), taken to the Jewish cemetery, and shot. That was the end."

We asked if we could see the cemetery in Zidikai, and discovered that there was no road to get there. Two or three kilometres across a snowy, muddy, impassable field, there were some stones amid bushes and trees. Nobody had been there for fifty years.

We made the journey to the cemetery in the neighbouring market town of Mazeikai, and found there were a number of marked monuments to leaders of the political resistance to the Nazis, as well as one unmarked stone that we were told had been recently set aside to recognize the Jews who died. Right next to this little fenced-in enclave was a clump of trees and broken, knocked-over headstones. Looking more carefully, we could, with difficulty, make out the Hebrew inscriptions, moss-covered, overgrown. This was the cemetery where Jewish families had buried their dead for hundreds of years, and was the mass grave of thousands of Nazi victims. If neglected for much longer, it would be completely unrecognizable.

More than a century ago, my grandfather's family left the coastal town of Palanga for Scotland. The Palanga we saw was a beautiful seaside resort, with a fine bakery and an amber museum.

Brezhnev had a dacha there, right on the Baltic. In late June of 1941, Jewish children were at summer camp in Palanga. They were murdered in the first Nazi sweep through the town.

Arlene and I spent our tenth wedding anniversary in a sailors' resort hotel in Palanga, reflecting on how dramatically different was our world from that of our grandparents.

We came away from that visit glad at last to have seen the village of Zidikai, and to have walked the beach at Palanga. But we left feeling that the absence of a simple acknowledgment of the past was too much to bear.

← →

Several months later, I got a phone call from a woman in Hamilton. Had I made a visit to Zidikai? Yes, I replied. I was told to expect a package, which arrived in a couple of days. The covering letter explained that after our visit, the people in the village had talked about what they could do. They asked the oldest people in the village to sit down and draw a map of the village which would show where all the different stores and houses had been, together with the synagogue. They enclosed the map, which showed stores marked "Florence" and "Lantin," and a description of what they sold.

The package also contained a package of photographs. Our guides had walked out in the spring to the small grove of trees which had overgrown the Jewish cemetery, and taken a picture of each gravestone. In front of each they had placed a single flower.

Chapter Eight

HOW SWEET THE TASTE

When we came back from our trip to Eastern Europe, I wrote a number of articles about the experience, which evoked a strong response. My strong dislike of the remnants of Stalinism and what I saw as Gorbachev's inability to grow sufficiently out of his imperial roots led to new contacts and discussions with the Eastern European communities in Toronto.

It also contributed to my feeling that I was now able to draw on all my experiences and background as the political atmosphere warmed up in preparation for another election. I was an international Canadian who had decided to root myself in provincial politics, at least for one more try, and if that meant speaking out on the constitution or on international matters, so be it.

I told my caucus in 1987 to be ready for an election in 1990. They all thought I was crazy to be thinking that way, but I felt that Peterson's huge majority would lead him to call it at a time when he felt he could come back with another majority. Both the constitution and the economy encouraged him to go early.

I'm sure that Peterson felt the collapse of Meech would cause enormous problems, and he didn't want to be facing those at the tail-end of a mandate. Similarly, the steam was clearly out of the economy, and after several years of inflationary growth he would not want to face the people in the middle of the recession.

Peterson seemed unbeatable. The initial reaction to what happened at Meech was a big boost in his popularity. Many say now that they advised him against calling an election in 1990, but this was certainly not the conventional wisdom then. When he made the walk to see the Lieutenant-Governor in late July, he seemed impregnable. While people treated me with a kind of cheery respect, the thought that I would become the premier of a majority government was fanciful in the extreme.

It was my third campaign. I told Arlene that summer at the cottage it would be my last. Robin Sears had left as principal secretary the year before, and David Agnew took over. We had worked together for more than a decade, and were completely at one on the kind of campaign we wanted to run. It would be hard-hitting, aggressive, and populist. We asked Gerry Caplan to write a paper outlining a broad strategy, which Gerry did, and that too confirmed our own feelings on what might work.

We also found an advertising agency, Ryan MacDonald and Edwards, that was prepared to take some risks, since we felt that we had little to lose. The ads had some bite but were also creative and funny. They used TV news as the backdrop and focused directly on the public's distrust of politicians. They struck a chord. We wanted the voters to hear something that was irreverent as well as more hard-edged against the Liberals. We were convinced that while Peterson had governed during a time of growth since 1985, there was increasing feeling that the good times had not necessarily been fairly shared.

This impression was fuelled by a couple of startling examples of corruption and mismanagement. Patti Starr, whom David Peterson named to be head of Ontario Place, proved an enormous liability when she roped a slew of ministers into a scheme which blurred the line between charitable and political fund-raising. She would eventually spend a brief time in jail, but did not go quietly into the night. To this day she has a law suit against Peterson. She was certainly never friendly to me or my party, but proved to be an unwitting ally.

Peterson's beheading of his loyal staff member Gordon Ashworth, and a cabinet shuffle, in which a huge array of ministers—from Chaviva Hosek to Lily Munro to Ben Grandmaître—were made to walk the plank in the summer of 1989, had failed to expunge the bad odour.

The Peterson government had formed the kind of links to developers and big business which were no doubt fun while they lasted but left a bad aftertaste with the public. The clearest flaunting of this was the SkyDome project, which Bill Davis had promised would come in at less than $200 million. When the Liberal cabinet agreed to add a hotel and a fitness club, the costs began to climb through the retractable roof. The taxpayers were left holding a very large bag.

Hannah Perly's edict about politics being about impressions led to David Peterson's victory in 1985 and his defeat in 1990, just as surely as it did with me in 1995. People liked David because he seemed young and bright and modern in 1985. They disliked him because he seemed too smooth and too arrogant and too far removed from their pain in 1990. He unwittingly gave the impression of taking the public for granted.

Not once, but several times he would pat me on the shoulder and say, "You may be a good fellow, Bob, but you'll never be premier. Get used to it." What had been a flawless Liberal effort in 1985 and 1987 completely missed the mark in the summer of 1990. The Liberals thought they could flip hamburgers on the picnic circuit in 1990, not promising too much but simply presenting an affable leader. Their ads had no edge or bite, just the assurance that at a difficult time all you had to do was put your faith in David.

The Liberal campaign started with an unfortunate blip. Gordon Perks, an environmental activist, sat in the front row of the opening press conference, and interrupted Peterson in mid-flight. He wouldn't leave, and he wouldn't stop, as the ritual denunciation of the environmental record of the Liberal government was carried on every evening-news report. Everyone wants a smooth, clear takeoff. David Peterson's was hardly that.

I took the media mainstreeting in Kensington Market, and was struck by the friendliness of the response. Going out to meet the public with the media in tow is always a huge risk. You can have ten good encounters and one grumpy one, and depending on the breaks it's the negative that usually gets the headlines. I didn't want to be accused of running an uptight campaign afraid of meeting the public, and indeed wanted to create the opposite impression to what I knew would be an imperial tour by Peterson. Most elections you don't always succeed in public impressions matching private aspirations. This time we got lucky.

We were lucky as well with the Tories. When Mike Harris was chosen to succeed interim leader Andy Brandt, I had shared my feeling with him that an early election was coming. He clearly didn't want to believe me, and for good reason. He was relatively unknown, and was labouring under the long shadow of Brian Mulroney. Harris had a single, simple message, that he was a tax-fighter, and would not raise taxes any more. It would take one more campaign, five years later, for the message to get the resonance the Tories thought it deserved. That the Tories had died a spectacular death in Ottawa and were no longer an albatross ended up making Mike Harris's job easier.

Peterson was so confident of victory that when he went to the premiers' conference in Winnipeg in the middle of the campaign, he shared the fear that he would come back again with an unmanageable majority.

Our own polling showed that he might well be right. The overnights from the first days of the campaign were so bad that David Agnew refused to share them with me. They improved slightly at the halfway point of the campaign. But certainly no one was planning the first cabinet meeting. Our pollster David Gotthilf had his ceiling, and my retirement plans seemed cast in stone.

↤ ↦

Leadership debates are, again, a ritual of impressions. Miller had lost in 1985 partly because he had refused to participate. Some thought I had won the debate in 1987, and that my performance helped me become Leader of the Opposition. My disadvantage in debates is that people expect me to do well. I can therefore never benefit from the gamesmanship which says, "The way you got up off the stage after you slipped on your mike cord really showed dignity." Besides, the Oxford style of sharp confrontation and verbal dexterity doesn't always work, or leave the right impression. You can win the argument and lose the game of impressions.

I came away from the debate in 1990 convinced that I had lost. There was a great cheer from the Peterson camp when it was over, and mild relief from Harris's people that he had made his points to his own audience. As luck would have it, my first feelings were misplaced. There were no "defining moments," but the impression of Peterson as nervous and on the defensive stuck. Whatever the reason, the poll numbers started jumping around in an extraordinary way after the debate was over.

The NDP "universe" suddenly exploded, which shows how "exact" a science polling really is. Peterson showed the true size of his desperation in a move which we knew had to be hastily improvised: the promise in Cornwall, two weeks before the election, to lower sales taxes by one point.

People knew in their gut that the recession was bigger and more real than the experts were ready to acknowledge. They didn't like the early and unnecessary election, and didn't believe any of his explanations as to why he had called it. With the failure of Meech, they also had the impression that Peterson had "gone too far" in responding to Quebec. The splits in his own party, with the opposition to Meech being led by Pierre Trudeau, hurt him more seriously with his political base than any of us knew at the time.

It's ironic that just as Peterson benefited from the split in the Tories over separate school funding, while supporting Davis's position, so too was I helped by the split in the Liberal base over Meech, even though I was just as strong a supporter of the Meech Lake Accord as David Peterson.

Ten days before the election David Agnew sat me down on the bus and said, "Unless there's a big change in direction and momentum, you might just win." Neither of us really believed it, and neither did the media, although public polling from Angus

Reid was beginning to show the same thing. Certainly the mood of our crowds was good, and in unlikely places. Rolling through Huron County on the way to a small farm for an evening picnic, we got an exuberant phone call saying we were now in the lead (which we refused to believe), and there were more than 150 people ready to share corn with us, an unheard of number for that part of Ontario.

✦ ✦

Arlene had focused for the early part of campaign on York South to which I returned about once a week. When that seemed secure she set out on a mini-tour of the province with Julie Davis, president of the party and secretary-treasurer of the OFL. Everywhere they went, they met New Democrats who didn't know why but were certain they were winning. They checked out London Centre, and no one believed either of them when they insisted the canvasser marks were in Marion Boyd's favour over David Peterson.

The nastiness of the last week of the Peterson campaign convinced me that our numbers had to be on the right track. "Children would starve under the socialists" ran one headline. Many around me were upset by these attacks, and wanted me to get angry in response. I knew they were the giveaway signs of an unhappy and frustrated campaign. I sensed that David Peterson knew the bottom had fallen out, and he had to lash out at somebody. You only get a lot of stuff thrown at you when you're ahead.

As it turned out, the last-minute Liberal scare attack had some effect, bringing some people back to the Liberals from the brink of a vote for the NDP. When you throw mud, some hits the mark, but some sticks to the thrower. Our overnights had us into the 40s before the attacks started, and then falling back slightly at the end. I went to bed on September 5 convinced that we had a shot at forming a minority government, and that we would probably win the most seats. Given Peterson's final outburst, I didn't rule out the possibility that the Liberals and Tories would combine to keep us from forming a government.

The Sunday before election day, Arlene went on the press bus for a last interview. As is always the case, the media ran a pool on the election result. She wasn't allowed to see who chose what result, but they did show her the numbers. No one predicted a majority for the NDP. Most predicted a majority government for the Liberals, some a Liberal minority. Only two showed the NDP with the most seats.

On election day I had a meeting with Stephen Lewis, Gerry Caplan, David Agnew, and some other key supporters. We would need to be ready for any eventuality. We began to prepare for the possibility of a transition to government, although some almost superstitiously refused to admit that this was the most likely possibility. At that point I asked Stephen to head up the transition, which he readily agreed to do.

That night we went to the Triumph Hotel on Highway 401, which is the closest hotel to York South. I was joined by family and a few close friends, and we watched the results with a sense of giddy disbelief. Nothing had really prepared us for the number of seats which fell into our hands. Rural ridings where we had struggled past the election announcement to even find a candidate were coming in with healthy majorities. When news came that Premier David Peterson had lost his seat by thousands of votes to the director of a women's shelter, Marion Boyd, I realized the source of the anger and bitterness of the last few days. This was not something any of us believed was even remotely possible only two weeks before.

Peterson phoned, and was gracious. "Listen, let me tell you something. The tide comes in and the tide goes out. This is an unforgiving business." We agreed to meet soon, the following Monday, to discuss transition.

I phoned my parents, and we cried about brother David not being there to savour the moment. I also called the girls at home. Lisa—then seven—has always had an uncanny ability to be both funny and hit the mark.

"Daddy! You're now the boss of everybody!"

I pulled myself together and drove with Arlene down to the La Rotonda Ballroom, at the corner of Dufferin and Eglinton. It was always the site of our workers' rallies at the end of a campaign. We shared the local victory party with the neighbouring riding of Oakwood, where the NDP had also run a successful campaign, and Tony Rizzo was elected.

The place was bedlam. Arlene and I struggled to get in, helped by a phalanx of smiling but big steelworkers who kept shouting supporters and media at bay. Slowly we made our way to the platform, where Jennifer, David's widow, Ginny, and Arlene's sister, Jeannie Conn, and brother-in-law, Gary, were standing in the same dazed bewilderment that I quietly shared.

This was an unforgettable moment. People who had worked and sweated and campaigned, some all their lives, never really believing that victory was possible, were shouting and cheering till they were hoarse. Someone started chanting, "Bob, Bob," and then someone else added "Premier Bob." The name stuck.

I struggled to find the words, and started with the Italian greeting "cari amici." (I got a call the next day from someone asking, "Why did you start by talking about Gary Ameche?")

I continued, "Maybe a summer election wasn't such a bad idea after all."

Chapter Nine

"No, Premier"

My first phone call on the morning of Friday, September 7, 1990, was from Secretary to the Cabinet Peter Barnes. It says something about our parliamentary system and the silly isolations of it that I had scarcely met Barnes apart from one brief encounter in Ottawa during the Meech Lake Accord. He had on that occasion spoken briefly at a staff meeting to convey the message from a senior bureaucrat in Ottawa that "Premier Peterson is a very great man for what he has done for Canada."

Peter Barnes is the son of a British civil servant who spent much of his career as a magistrate in East Africa. Peter was educated at Cambridge, he came to Canada first as a management consultant, and then joined the Ontario Public Service. He served as the deputy minister of community and social services under John Sweeney, and was chosen by David Peterson as cabinet secretary to succeed Bob Carman.

I used to jokingly call Peter "Sir Humphrey," after the British television series, "Yes, Minister," and "Yes, Prime Minister." Since I had grown up in a civil-service family myself, I knew something of the inside jokes and the views that public servants inevitably have of their political "masters." Our government was to be no different. We had our jokes about them as well.

I agreed to meet Peter Barnes and David Peterson the following Monday morning, and arranged to be joined by David Agnew. I rested over the weekend, went to a ball game with the family, where our picture was shown on the big screen and we got a warm round of cheers and applause. I continued to go to ball games throughout my time as premier, and insisted on sitting in the stands—the boxes were too far removed from the game. My picture on the big screen was never subsequently greeted with the same positive enthusiasm, and in fact on one occasion I turned to my companion, Charles Pascal, a deputy minister, and berated him for his evident unpopularity. It was Charles's stroke of genius after the Jays' World Series win in 1993 to tell me to simply hold up a card saying "No Speech Today. Hooray for the Blue Jays." Like any politician who exploits the captive audience of sports fans celebrating their heroes, I risked getting booed off the stage. This was one of the best pieces of speech advice I ever got from a deputy minister, since as soon as I held up the sign, the boos turned to cheers.

The Monday morning meeting with David Peterson was not pleasant. We were able to agree on a transition date, October 1, which was a little long but we all knew the last two weeks had been a great surprise to everyone. I told them that Stephen Lewis would be chairing our transition team, and Peterson promised "full co-operation." The meeting could have ended there, but the discussion turned to Toronto's bid for the Olympic Games. The decision was to be made in Tokyo in a few days' time, and I asked Peterson to go, since he was still premier and it was obviously impossible for me to leave the province in the middle of the transition. He had been working on the bid for months.

He point blank refused, and said that he would only go if I went as well. It wasn't quite a shouting match, but it went back and forth in a way that was less than productive. We eventually agreed to ask Lieutenant-Governor Lincoln Alexander to represent the province, and I sent Floyd Laughren with him. I suspect that Peterson knew full well that Atlanta was likely to be chosen, and that he didn't want to be associated with an unsuccessful bid.

That was to be the only discussion I had with Peterson before taking office in October. He had been more wounded by the loss than his brave face and speech had revealed. He and his staff slipped away without sharing very many tips of office organization, management, or pending provincial issues. When we moved into our offices on October 1, 1990, the room was completely bare. Inside the empty desk were the words "Good luck, David Peterson."

↞ ↠

Months before our election in 1995, I asked David Agnew to approach both the other parties about a possible transition. I told him to give them briefing books, and to prepare the way for whatever might happen. This was done. There were the inevitable statements about "how we never knew." There is still an adversarial immaturity to our system that needs to be broken down.

I asked Ross McClellan to join Stephen at the heart of the transition team, and they eagerly began the preparations for forming the government. Ross would become the head of the policy team in my office, joined by Chuck Rachlis, the former research director to the caucus when we were in opposition. David Agnew became my principal secretary, and I hired Lynn Spink as executive assistant. She had worked for John Sewell as mayor, and for Jeff Rose when he was president of Local 79 at CUPE, and brought to the job a good-humoured, no-nonsense approach which I liked. I was sorry when she decided to leave two years later. She was succeeded by Ana Lopes who did a superb, unflappable job right to the end. Richard McLellan, with whom I've worked since he served as Tommy Douglas's assistant in the 1970s, agreed to manage the office, which he did with extraordinary grace and efficiency.

I strongly resisted the advice to move Peter Barnes out of the cabinet secretary position. I came to the office with the view that the public service's neutrality and professionalism were to be respected, and had no reason to doubt Peter's loyalty to the elected government. I did want, however, to strengthen the role of cabinet office in the government, particularly its capability to generate and co-ordinate policy. Michael Mendelson had experience in the

Schreyer and Pawley governments in Manitoba, and had been hired by Peter Barnes to come to Ontario, together with Jay Kaufman and Marc Eliesen. I scarcely knew Michael, but he was highly recommended, and I asked him to join Peter Barnes as the deputy cabinet secretary with the rank of deputy minister.

Together with David Agnew and Ross McClellan, Michael stayed at the heart of everything our government did for its entire five years. He paid the price for his loyalty, and was fired by Mike Harris, as were Jeff Rose, Jay Kaufman, Charles Pascal, and a host of other very talented and dedicated people.

My views about the government and civil service changed dramatically as a result of my experience. There were, in fact, layers upon layers of internal politics and cronyism within the public service. It was impossible for much of the bureaucracy to escape the inevitable consequences of having been an integral part of forty-two years of Tory governments. Peterson's natural response was to quietly move in his own people wherever and however he could, but the system kept beating him back.

The cabinet secretary's power rests in his or her ability to recommend appointments to the premier for deputy ministerships. It was impossible for an incoming premier to be able to judge the talents and capabilities of the forty-four deputies, and difficult to assert control and authority. The Conservatives solved this problem under Bill Davis by combining the roles of principal secretary to the premier and cabinet secretary in one person, Ed Stewart, who had been Davis's deputy minister in education. It would be two full years before I reached the same conclusion, and for this I would inevitably be accused of "politicizing" the public service. From everything I saw over the years, it was already very political, though this was expressed in the inevitable code of options, warnings, and the sideways murmurings that were eventually fed full bore to the outside world.

There is probably no worse training in the world for becoming premier than spending a career in opposition. It is hard, if not impossible, for an opposition leader to meet and be briefed seriously by the bureaucracy on an ongoing basis. This is even truer for NDP leaders than for others. The suspicions are simply too great. The reluctance to share information is based on the natural apprehension that anything important will be immediately used to partisan advantage in question period.

The theatrics of question period is the central forum for opposition leaders. For premiers and governments it is at best a sideshow, which can occasionally be used to partisan advantage, but which has relatively little to do with the nuts and bolts of governing. Opposition creates the illusion that there is good policy and bad policy, and that political life is simply a matter of choosing the good over the bad, in a relatively painless way. Rhetorical dragons are slain with rhetorical swords, and evil is drowned in a flood of eloquent words.

← →

As the briefing books piled high in my living room, it was hard not to be overwhelmed by the sense that I was singularly ill-prepared for the task ahead. Sleep was an elusive companion for the next year. It wasn't hard to see the gap between the level of expectation in the party as well as the broader public and the difficult reality of an economy in free fall. We kept getting wonderful poll results, showing a huge increase in our public support even in the first weeks after the election. I found it hard to square that with what I knew was going to be difficult news.

It was equally clear that the bureaucracy had not absorbed the changed nature of the economy and the province's finances. Robert Nixon's budget in the spring and the update in August had shown a balance. Out first briefings from the Treasury officials showed this wasn't the case in September: revenues were off, and expenses were up. We shared this news as quickly as we could, but the extent of the discrepancy between the Peterson budget of 1990 and what we were to face for the next several years took some months to discover. The Liberals had built up a structure of spending that meant the province had a structural deficit of over $8 billion when the full impact of collapsed revenues was felt by the spring of 1991. This meant our own approach had to change, and change dramatically. Having chosen my immediate team, I moved on to the task of picking the cabinet. There were many jokes about our caucus. Two downtown lawyers meet after the election. One of them boasts that one of his juniors went to law school with the premier. The other laughs, "That's nothing! My cleaning lady's in the cabinet." Or, "Bob Rae had an easy time choosing his cabinet. All he had to do was pick the guys with suits." Both these jokes tell us a ton about the essential snobbery of the business élite. Even caucus members who had been elected for well over a decade were unknown to most of the movers and shakers in the business and media worlds.

We had managed to elect seventy-four members in all, a truly remarkable achievement given that we had received just under 38 per cent of the vote. More than fifty of our number were entirely new to the legislature; most had never been elected to any public office. It was a group full of life and determination but short on experience.

The other reality was that a great many of the caucus were people I hardly knew. We had managed to elect members in seats where we had never before received more than 15 per cent of the vote, and while I might have met them at a fund-raiser or shaken

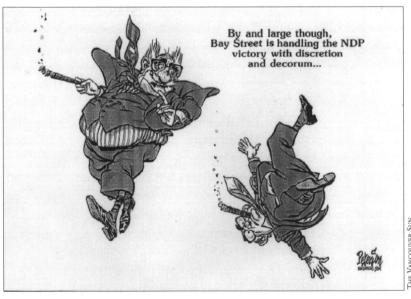

By and large though, Bay Street is handling the NDP victory with discretion and decorum...

hands during the campaign, a great many were as new to me as they were to the Ontario public.

I was never one to have an inner circle within the caucus. I didn't want to be accused of playing favourites (an inevitable charge), and kept my private friendships and family to another part of my life. This was a style I maintained right through the government, which once gave rise to one of my favourite exchanges with a reporter.

"Why don't we know more about your private life?"

"Because if you did, it wouldn't be private any more."

My choice for deputy premier and treasurer was Floyd Laughren, and this proved to be wise. Floyd was elected in 1971, having worked as an economics lecturer at Cambrian College in Sudbury. He was well liked in the caucus, and well regarded by the other members of the legislature while in opposition. He had a steady hand and always displayed a marvellous sense of humour. We had not always seen eye to eye on all issues—in the seventies Floyd had been a voice on the left of the party—but since my becoming leader he had been a tremendous source of quiet support. He had an enormously difficult job in the government, and he never wavered or flinched.

My other senior colleagues were all people I'd worked with for years, with the significant addition of Frances Lankin, whom I first made responsible for Management Board. Together with Frances, I had a capable team with people like Dave Cooke, Evelyn Gigantes, Ruth Grier, Bud Wildman, Shelley Martel, and Howard Hampton. These were all people whose friendship and hard work I had valued in opposition, and their appointment to cabinet was natural. Bob Mackenzie got the job he'd always wanted, Minister of Labour, and carried it out with a sense of mission for four years until heart trouble forced him to step down near the end of our term. Newcomers to provincial politics like Tony Silipo and Elaine Ziemba were effective, thoughtful ministers.

One of my best appointments was Elmer Buchanan in Agriculture. The son of a farmer, Elmer held the portfolio for five years. He was a constant source of sound advice, political savvy and practical intelligence. He was a great Minister of Agriculture, who was liked and respected in rural Ontario.

Allan Blakeney gave me some advice in the early days, which I should have followed. He urged me to keep the cabinet very small, and enlarge it only if necessary. I listened instead to others who encouraged me to make the cabinet as inclusive as possible, and give people a chance to learn on the job. I appointed more women to the cabinet than anyone in the history of Canada. I also threw a great many rookies in at the deep end. Many excelled. Others did not, and there is no quiet failure in this business. Learning to play the violin in front of ten million people is not the easiest thing in the world. I gave Blakeney's firm advice to both Kim Campbell and Mike Harris, and they both took it. Too soon old, too late smart.

I also decided to give a cabinet job to Peter Kormos, a particularly flamboyant character from the Niagara peninsula. Agnew's view, which I fully shared, was that it was, to borrow Lyndon Johnson's proverbial phrase, better to have him inside the tent pissing out than outside the tent pissing in. The problem was that he ended up inside the tent pissing in. And that made his cabinet membership necessarily short.

Every day brought worse economic news, and the kind of headlines that I dreaded—"NDP hopeful promises this." The press were all over us, and I had at least two or three scrums a day. I wasn't used to people hanging on every word, and then running with whatever interpretation came to mind. But the first weeks, as busy and crowded as they were, were still full of an extraordinary optimism. Bay Street was worried but Main Street felt good about itself.

← →

We were sworn in on October 1, 1990. My parents and brother John, with his wife, Phyllis, flew in the day before. We had a quiet family dinner, remembering David, and reflecting on how quickly change can come. Some things in our life were transformed dramatically, and others were not. We lived in the same house, and paid the same mortgage. The girls all went to the same school. My life became more regimented, and I was joined for almost every waking hour by the premier's detail of the Ontario Provincial Police. Strange at first, we eventually got used to their constant presence, mainly because they're such fine people. May our jokes remain forever sealed.

The biggest change was the realization, which did not take long to sink in, that my time was not my own. My schedule was planned weeks, even months in advance. My every waking hour was accounted for: from reading newspapers and files in the car on the way to work, to briefing sessions with staff and deputy ministers, cabinet committees, question period briefings, trips around the province and around the world, meetings to deal with crises and to avoid them in the future. I was swept up at a pace I couldn't easily control. This never changed for the next five years.

We all turned up at Convocation Hall on a beautiful morning, to be joined by a crowd of nearly two thousand, with more enthusiastic supporters outside. Lincoln Alexander and I joked about our relationship over the years—I'd cost him his job as a cabinet minister in the Clark government—and I gave a short speech, which I'd written the weekend before in which I said, in part:

> They say that the greatest joys in life are those that are unexpected. This day and this ceremony certainly fall into this category. The new government that is taking office today is made up of women and men from across the province, from all walks of life. Few of us ran in the last election feeling our party would win the election on September 6th: we ran because we had a message to bring to the Ontario public, because the cause of social democracy made sense to us and, in some cases, because no one else was willing to run....
>
> We must also remember that while recessions have their inevitable impact—as we have learned—on governments at all levels, by reducing revenues, and by requiring more money to maintain people's incomes, above all they affect people, their jobs, their

income, their security, their hopes. There is already too much poverty in Ontario. A recession will bring more, and that alone makes it worth fighting.

No one government can, on its own, spend its way out of a recession. Where that has been recently tried, it has failed. But we must respond—by investing wisely in the future of the province, and by encouraging others to invest as well. Ontario needs a partnership for recovery. That task begins today....

Kipling reminds us that triumph and disaster are both impostors. We know our election will be followed quickly by tough questions. We need the help and advice of all members of the legislature, and indeed all the citizens of the province. We understand that the responsibility we have been given can be taken away, and that public trust is a fragile thing.

Lincoln Alexander responded with a warm and crowd-pleasing speech based on the refrain, "Do I know the premier?" A seniors' choir sang "Oh We Ain't Got a Barrel of Money." That soon became clearer than we ever wanted to know. At the end of the formal part of the ceremony, my irrepressible daughter Lisa flew up the stairs to the stage and into my arms. All three girls were young enough not be embarrassed by their dad as "celebrity" and were bursting with the excitement of the day.

Later that day we opened up the legislature to the whole public. For the first time in living memory, people from all walks of life flooded the building in a major celebration, and took tours of the premier's office. Irma Douglas, Tommy's widow, came for the swearing-in, and gave me her favourite picture of Tommy, which stayed on my desk throughout my premiership. Nothing can take away from those celebrations or the sense of pride and inclusion and triumph of those early days. Better a celebration and an open building than demonstrations and a barricade.

Chapter Ten

JOBS, JOBS, JOBS

It wasn't just that we didn't have a barrel of money. It was worse than that. The bottom had fallen out of the Ontario economy. We had seen the problems of unemployment coming, but saying that provided little comfort to the thousands who were joining the ranks of the unemployed. Our election allowed businessmen who knew better to turn and blame us. This line of attack had little influence over opinion in the first few months of our government. But after about a year, the mantra began to sink in.

The truth is that the "adjustment" to free trade, high interest rates, and a dollar that was over-valued was every bit as painful as we said it would be when we urged a very different set of policies in the 1980s. David Peterson had won an election on opposing free trade in 1987, but had folded his tent once Mulroney won his own mandate in 1988.

There were hundreds of small factories, and some large ones, that began closing in late 1989 and 1990. I'm convinced that this, as well as Quebec, is what persuaded Peterson to call the election in 1990. By that time the people were ahead of Bay Street, and ahead of the pundits, in understanding that a storm was coming. The Ministry of Industry and Trade, as well as the Premier's

THE TORONTO STAR

Council, had in the late 1980s produced studies showing how vulnerable we would be to the sea-change. But we found that precious little had really been done to prepare for its impact.

Many in the labour movement in that first winter of 1990-91 sported buttons with the brave refrain, "We refuse to participate in the recession." This captures the spirit of defiance and denial of the early days of the government. In the end, of course, we had no choice but to participate in the recession. No one government could stop it, and we could hardly ignore its effects. Workers paid heavily: 300,000 manufacturing jobs lost between 1989 and 1992, with hardly any let-up.

Our first response was to move quickly to expand the capital budget of the government, and to get projects up and running that had been too long in the planning stage. We announced this expanded budget in the Throne Speech, and put ministries to work on longer term plans for major projects: highway construction, like Highway 407; subway and rapid-transit expansion, which finally got through the planning process in 1992 and 1993 (only to be scuttled in 1995 by the Tories); and whatever other capital works could be brought off the shelf quickly. The decision to proceed with the Princess Margaret Cancer Hospital on University Avenue was made in this context.

The only exception was our decision not to proceed with the Ballet Opera House in downtown Toronto. This was the subject of a long and painful cabinet discussion. Opposition to the project was widespread, inside the government and out. I was torn, but eventually accepted the majority view. The problem was its cost, and my certainty that the government would have been asked to bail out the project at several points along the way. When I asked at one cabinet briefing who was really behind this $300 million theatre, some wag shouted out "the wives of the people who built the SkyDome."

This decision earned us the anger of some leading business people who had been pushing this project for years, as well as many members of the arts community. They portrayed us as left-wing philistine rubes from the sticks who didn't care for High Culture. The real story was that the committee responsible never even tried to come in with a smaller, more affordable plan, and that in subsequent years we kept trying to get a focus on what I called a "nineties idea rather than an eighties idea."

Ed and David Mirvish managed to build the Princess of Wales Theatre for less than $30 million. I found it hard to understand why the Ballet Opera House had to cost almost exactly ten times that much.

We agreed instead to expand arts funding in the community through increasing the budget of the Arts Council by some 25 per cent, which, given the recession, was a wise thing to do. The vast majority of this funding directly funded employment in the arts, which again, and to serious consequence, has been slashed by the Tories.

My favourite right-wing columnist Barbara Amiel wrote a wonderfully misplaced column soon after the 1995 election of the

Harris government, where she expressed the fond thought that with the defeat of the proletarian rabble high culture would at last get a government that cared. Fat chance.

The second thing we had to do was begin a substantial change within the government itself. I quickly concluded that Peterson had handled his frustration with the bureaucracy by trying to go around it. He'd had enough money pouring in that it really didn't matter. The dramatic fall in revenues meant we had to do things differently.

I asked Tim Armstrong to take over the Ministry of Industry and Trade. He'd been deputy minister of labour in the Davis government. I got to know him better in his next job, as agent-general for Asia in Tokyo. Peterson had invited me to join him on his trip to China in 1986, and Tim was a leading presence on that trip. I enjoyed his sardonic humour and broad perspective. He liked to read, and he liked to joke, and had little time for bureaucratic gamesmanship, which endeared him to me.

Tim had the tough task of doing two things: responding to the big jobs crises—which meant leading all our restructuring negotiations—and changing the culture of the ministry. I realize now that it was unfair to ask him to take on both tasks, although they both got done. In the first job Tim had the able assistance of Peter Tanaka, who really was a delight to behold in tough discussions, and in my view one of the unsung heroes of our effort to get Ontario companies back on their feet.

↔

I became personally involved in several major restructurings. Each came to take up an extraordinary amount of time and effort. I shall tell the story of just three of them: Spruce Falls Pulp and Paper in Kapuskasing; Algoma Steel in the Sault; and de Havilland in Toronto.

Spruce Falls
In the fall of 1990, not too long after I was sworn in, I got a visit from a man named Darwin Smith, the president of Kimberly-Clark, one of the largest paper companies in the world. Pulp

prices were low, demand was way down, and the industry was in deep trouble. Kimberly-Clark was the 51 per cent owner of Spruce Falls Pulp and Paper, which was the only employer of any significance in Kapuskasing; *The New York Times* owned the other 49 per cent.

Kap had been built as a model town by the owners of *The New York Times*, who originally took a paternalistic interest in the community. I had visited there many times as opposition leader, and knew the mill well. I'd also taken two tours of the wood-lot operation over the years, and gotten to know the managers of the mill as well as the leaders of the local union. Our MPP Len Wood had been on the executive of the Paperworkers Union in the mill, and had been elected after a tough battle with both the Liberals and the Tories in 1990.

My first impression of Mr. Smith was that he was Darwin by name and Darwinian by nature. He came with a gruff message. The mill was not losing money, but it was not making as good a use of his capital as he wanted. He planned to shut down the current operation, and replace it with a single, new machine. Employment would drop from about 1,400 to about 250.

This was terrible news. The company was the reason for Kapuskasing's existence. A lay-off of that size would be a disaster, not just for Kap, but for all the communities in the area: Hearst, Moonbeam, Smooth Rock, Cochrane. But I knew that Mr. Smith had not just come to give me bad news; that he could have done over the telephone. No. He, like almost everyone else who ever came to see me as premier, was there because he wanted something.

The company had dammed the Kapuskasing River, and sold power to themselves and the local community. It guaranteed cheap power to the company and made the mill profitable. If Ontario Hydro would buy the dam, and give him his money, he might consider selling the mill to the employees.

At our first meeting I told him it was unthinkable for there to be a lay-off of a thousand people, with all the multiplier effects, when the mill was making money. He was holding some cards, and so were we, and I encouraged him to engage in some serious discussions with the local community as well as with Ontario Hydro.

Darwin Smith played a high-stakes game. He distributed a video in which the community got the message that a shutdown was a possibility. Hydro felt it couldn't spend money without an assurance of a reasonable return, and that meant knowing they would get approval to upgrade the dam, and do other work on the river to generate power.

The entire upper river valley was the subject of a long-time claim by the Cree of Northern Ontario, which added to the complexity of the issue and Darwin Smith's conviction that this whole problem was too complicated for a solution.

Finally, the community began to get involved, as did the employees. But it was clear that the workers on their own would have enormous difficulty managing the mill. We needed to find an interested third party to take a strong interest in the project as well.

First efforts proved unsuccessful. Darwin Smith's "deadline" of June 1991 came and went without anything approaching a solution. An army of folks from Kap came down by car and camper and pitched their tents on the grass in front of Queen's Park. No doubt these days they'd be billy-clubbed and dragged off to jail. I met with them, and asked for their suggestions.

I also asked for a meeting with the local union, and told them in the Cabinet Room that if there was going to be a successful restructuring it would mean fewer work rules, less fights over jurisdiction between different unions, and a willingness to trade some wages for share capital. This did not make anybody happy. Their NDP premier was telling them they'd have to take less.

I then spoke to Darwin Smith on the phone, and asked if he could come in for a meeting. He agreed. Marc Eliesen, who by that time was chairman of Ontario Hydro, Brock Smith, the deputy minister of northern affairs, Tim Armstrong, and Gerry Charney, who had been acting as a negotiating adviser to the minister, all met in my office to prepare for this meeting, which was to be a purely private chat between me and Mr. Smith.

As if we did not have enough problems and complexities, Darwin Smith was upset that we had found another investor, Frank Dottori of Tembec, who might join in the management of the new company. His own efforts to sell the company in 1989 had been unsuccessful. It appeared that he didn't want someone else horning in on what he thought was a singular act of corporate statesmanship. My objective in the meeting was to get him to come back to the table, and to participate fully in the sale and restructuring to save as many jobs as possible. I wanted him to take away the hammer of plant shutdown, and to accept our good faith in finding a solution to the problem with Hydro and the native claims.

We met for dinner in his hotel room. My voice was raspy. So was his. He asked me what my trouble was. I told him I'd just had a bout of pneumonia, and had been left with some asthma. I waved my puffer for sympathy. He smiled and said his problem was permanent. He'd been diagnosed with sinus cancer years before, and had been given massive radiation, which had stopped the cancer but left him with this gruff voice.

"So how are us old guys going to deal with this problem?"

"Take the threat of closure away, and I think we can get a deal."

"Will I get paid for my dam?"

"Yes, if we can agree on a fair price."

"What about the natives? These claims and these environmentalists are causing us headaches all over North America."

"That shouldn't be your worry. We'll have to deal with that over time."

"Anything else you want from me?"

"Accept the fact that Tembec and Frank Dottori are in, and part of the deal. And that's got nothing to do with you. Give the employees the plant for a dollar, and let them deal with Dottori on how they're going to raise money in the future. Get us a deal on where we can sell paper, if you can, and give us access to financing."

I was following my instructions from Charney. Smith didn't blink.

"I understand you're some kind of socialist."

"I want to save jobs and I want to give the company a chance to survive in the real world. Let's just forget the labels."

"I can do a deal on this basis."

Darwin Smith and I shook hands, and I asked Gerry Charney, who was waiting in the next room, to start discussions right away.

There were many twists and turns along the way. For the workers to accept concessions, and still see some lay-offs, was very difficult. The trade union rhetoric of the previous fifty years had been to treat the employer as the enemy, to use the adversary system for every possible partisan advantage, and to expect improvements in wages, working conditions, and contract language at every round of negotiations.

We were asking people to take less in pay, to give up the protection of job rules, and, most dramatically, to become the employer. This was not a quick or easy sell. The leadership of the Canadian Paperworkers Union, Don Holder and John McInnis, were initially sceptical, and worried that what happened in Kapuskasing might set an industry pattern for wage concessions.

The persuading they needed came more from the local workforce than from me. The people in Kap wanted their jobs. A spirit which broke down some of the old language and arguments about the company and the workers had emerged in the town. If there was no company, there wouldn't be an employer to get mad at. If the company had a strong base in the community, it wouldn't be possible to demonize an absentee landlord.

I developed a grudging respect for Darwin Smith, who was a tough but fair negotiator. He got fair market value for his dam, and Hydro got our assurances that we would negotiate over environmental assessments and native claims, which we did. He didn't get any money for his mill, and he was good to his word on assistance with financing.

The New York Times still buys some of its paper from Spruce Falls, but it pays more for it. Frank Dottori from Tembec has built an extraordinary team at Spruce Falls, and the mill has expanded twice since the change in ownership. Employment is now back over 1,000.

Algoma

In December of 1990, on a Sunday, I got a call at home from Bob Sweenor, who was president of Algoma Steel in Sault Ste. Marie. Bob had been appointed by Dofasco, who had become the majority shareholder in the Sault in 1988. I could tell from his voice that he was under real stress.

"Premier, I've been asked to convey to you some news which has to be kept completely confidential."

"Fine, what is it exactly?"

"The Board meeting of the Algoma Steel Company is coming up on Monday, and it is Dofasco's intention to advise them at that point that Dofasco will not be putting any further money into this company."

"What does that mean?"

"That means Dofasco is stopping its liability. We've lost $750 million and we're not losing any more."

"Have you told the union?"

"No, and we don't intend to until we have to."

"I know Lynn Williams and Leo Gerard well and they'll be glad to do whatever they can to help. There are too many jobs at stake for everybody to just walk away."

"All I know is that Dofasco has to stop the bleeding. This company is losing money every day we keep operating."

"There's got to be some creative ways to keep us together and keep the Sault working on making steel. We're not going to walk away from this."

The conversation ended on this sombre note. I phoned David Agnew and Tim Armstrong right away, and we agreed that Tim would head up our efforts to keep things on track. I also phoned Leo Gerard of the Steelworkers to give him a heads-up. His initial reaction was blind fury at Dofasco and Algoma management. Venting was important in those first days.

Our first task was to jointly engage the banks and the federal government to ensure bridge financing until the company was completely restructured and reorganized. It was almost a bridge too far. The feds were firmly in their neo-con mode. Michael Wilson and I had a difficult conversation, where he made it clear that in his opinion there needed to be a shakedown in the steel industry and events should take their course. "Dominion Foundries itself may go under. Stelco's in bad shape. If we both stay out of this we'll end up with a smaller and more competitive industry." I told him I couldn't accept the demise of Algoma, because of what that would do to the Sault and the whole economy of the region.

Ironically, a Quebecker from the Saguenay region was more sympathetic than Minister of Finance Michael Wilson, an Ontarian. Benoit Bouchard, Minister of Industry, seemed to instinctively understand the importance of the company to the whole community. He also understood that the union could be part of the solution. Bouchard agreed to join our efforts to persuade the Royal Bank to stay on as first lender. It took a couple of difficult conversations with Canada's largest bank, but a direct one-on-one with Allan Taylor kept the company alive, with Ontario and Canada playing backstop as partial guarantors.

The next step was to get under the temporary umbrella of the courts. We had to stop anyone forcing the company into receivership, so we applied for relief under the Companies' Creditors Arrangement Act. This was granted by Mr. Justice James Farley, whose wise and ironic counsel was valuable throughout.

The Steelworkers then made the historic decision to become a player themselves. Two things came together to make this happen. The first was the experience of the union itself in the U.S. A dramatic downturn in the American steel industry a decade earlier had forced the union to become partners in business, and sometimes owners, of their own jobs. Employee ownership was not the product of some abstract ideology of worker involvement. It was the result of economic necessity and political will on the part of the union. A new philosophy of unionism and economic partnership followed on from this. A Canadian, Lynn Williams, was at the head of this transformation, and his ideas and experiences shaped the views of the leadership in Canada. The national director of the Steelworkers, Leo Gerard, was on the international executive, and had helped make the decisions that led to changes in ownership in the U.S. He knew the players who made it happen in the banks and investment houses in New York.

This changed political will on the part of the union was critical. It was firmly supported by the spirit of community solidarity in the Sault. The political will of our government was the second critical ingredient in finding a solution. I encouraged Leo Gerard in his efforts to find a worker-led answer every step of the way. The creditors and the economic powers that be were all sceptical, if not outright hostile, to these ideas. When I called a meeting of the banks, existing management at Algoma and Dofasco, the federal government, city officials, and the Steelworkers both locally and nationally, and brought them all into the cabinet office, it was the first time many had ever met. I told them that the Ontario government was not going to bail them all out, that they had to find a co-operative and market-based solution, and that we would do everything we could to broker a solution.

In addition to Leo Gerard and Tim Armstrong, we had the important leadership of Earl Joudrie, who became chairman of Algoma on a temporary basis. Joudrie's job was to produce a credible business plan for the company, and a realistic way to finance it.

There was always the risk of our being so "hands-on" that the parties would keep looking longingly at us for a solution. In the summer of 1991 we had to bridge finance again. This time Michael Wilson prevailed, and the feds bailed out. The banks and the union—a curious alliance—came to us for more, but I insisted to Leo Gerard that the union members themselves were going to have to show their commitment to a solution. This they did, taking a pay cut and "lending" the difference to the company.

The outlines of a solution were becoming clear. The banks would have to reduce the debt load of the company by converting their debt into equity. The workers would inject capital into the company by swapping part of their wages into shares. The provincial government would make this swap more palatable by encouraging share ownership through the tax system. We would also help retrain laid-off workers, and make sure the burden of environmental liability wouldn't instantly bankrupt the new company.

By December of 1991 we knew what had to be done, but couldn't get everyone to agree. At that point we upped the ante. Tim Armstrong came up with an ingenious solution. We would ask the court to appoint a judge with great experience in labour disputes to get a solution. Tim and I agreed that George Adams would be the ideal choice. So did the Chief Justice of the High Court, Frank Callaghan. The deed was done.

George Adams is another one of those wise souls who understands that life is about finding solutions and not scoring victories. He kept everyone talking, and narrowed the differences. He imposed a news blackout, and by mid-February we were almost there. On Sunday, February 23, 1992, I came to a meeting of all the parties, with their lawyers, in the Park Plaza Hotel in Toronto. There must have been seventy or eighty people in a large conference room, and it was obvious the good judge had kept them there all hours. I told them we couldn't go on indefinitely, and that we couldn't let all these efforts go for naught. I expected that many of the lawyers and accountants in the room had never been to the Sault. I told them a lot of families and communities were depending on them.

I remember the date well, because it is my wedding anniversary. George Adams, Tim Armstrong, and Earl Joudrie asked me if I would cancel plans for dinner and spend the time with Leo Gerard instead. Leo was balking at the size of the Steelworker contribution, the absence of a further sacrifice by Dofasco, and Ontario's reluctance to put even more money into training. It was also clear that the magnitude of the task ahead of him in persuading his own members to go along, in fighting critics within the labour movement, and the risk of the whole enterprise collapsing whatever he did were weighing heavily on his mind.

I cancelled dinner plans with Arlene and spent the night with Leo Gerard and his advisers. It was an evening of unembroidered frankness, matched only by the same degree of candour when I got home. It wasn't the first or last time politics had pre-empted our personal plans. Leo sent flowers. Algoma had taken more than two years.

The Algoma restructuring was approved by the courts and accepted by the parties. A new company was born, with the workers themselves as the major shareholder. They acquired the right to appoint members to the Board of Directors. But the most important changes were still to come, because they involved a change in the culture of the company itself. The organization was completely flattened. Worker training and worker involvement became the order of the day. A new CEO, Al Hopkins, accepted the new mandate with gusto, and became a spokesman for a different way of doing business.

As in the paper business, we also benefited from the change in economic conditions. The lower dollar and stronger growth in the U.S. and Canada combined with lower debt loads and wage costs to make the company profitable in 1994 and 1995. Share values rose steadily, which meant that those Royal Bank executives seething at my hardball tactics in the first bridge-loan discussions should have been carrying me on their shoulders as election day approached. But of course they weren't.

De Havilland

The first day of the election campaign in 1990 was meeting and greeting workers at the plant gate at de Havilland in Downsview. I had long taken an interest in the company, from my time as finance critic in Ottawa years earlier, when it was a federally owned Crown corporation and the short-lived Joe Clark government began musing about privatization. It was finally sold by the Mulroney Tories to Boeing in 1985, a move which I had strongly opposed. The marriage never really "took," and after five years of labour strife and cost overruns the American owners announced their plans to sell the company.

I got an unusually warm reception that bright summer day, a sign of things to come. Reporters asked me then about Boeing's plans to sell. I issued the blanket denunciation of the Tories for having abandoned Ontario, and David Peterson's Liberals for having dropped the ball. Ontario would have to be a player in any discussions about a sale, I said. Public ownership would be preferable to seeing the company disappear or fall into the wrong hands. I was suitably disciplined by my staff for swaying ever so slightly "off-message," although even they were buoyed by the handshakes and the thumbs-up signs all around us.

The fate of the de Havilland Company very quickly became a major preoccupation after the heady days of the summer of 1990. The company was and still is a major player in the Ontario and Canadian economies, the largest industrial employer in Metro Toronto; the largest aerospace company in Ontario. It employed more than three thousand employees directly, and an additional thirty or forty thousand jobs in the whole sector depended on de Havilland's success. At the centre of wartime production, the company's planes of the fifties and sixties, the Beaver and the Otter, were world renowned for their durability and reliability. New Short Take-off and Landing (STOL) technology had been developed by the company, and this led to production of the first DASH plane, the DASH 7, to be followed by the DASH 8.

Technology and product were strong. Management and ownership were another story. It was part of Hawker Siddeley, a British company that eventually sold to the Canadian government in the 1970s. The Crown corporation model guaranteed money but no strong leadership. Boeing had deep pockets, but couldn't turn it around either. Labour-management relationships were notoriously bad. There was a long and bitter strike in the summer of 1988, which sealed Boeing's determination to get rid of the company.

Boeing announced its intention to sell in 1990. This immediately put the company's order book in question, since competitors were quick to say that there was no assurance de Havilland's DASH 8 would even be produced the next year. This in turn significantly devalued the company. By the time we took office, the issue was front and centre. Once again my key co-conspirator was Tim Armstrong.

Our first step was to signal to the world that we were not going to sit back and merely watch events unfold. Ontario had not been a player in the changes of the seventies and eighties. The

Mulroney Tories were not about to admit that they had made a mistake in choosing Boeing five years earlier.

I asked Armstrong to get a group of people from the industry together, which included Gerry Dias from the Canadian Auto Workers Union, as well as business people like Gil Bennett, Bill Blundell, David Pecaut, and Bill Corcoran. Our problem was that Boeing owned the company outright, and could sell to whomever they wanted, subject only to approval from Investment Canada if it was a foreign investor. At that point the federal government would have to ask us for our opinion, but nothing more.

Boeing decided early on that "the only option" was to sell to the French-led European consortium that produced the main competition to the DASH 8. This made the union furious, since they rightly feared that the long-term objective of the consortium would be to wind down production of the DASH plane. Buying a competitor in order to build it up at your own potential expense is not usual business behaviour: far more likely that de Havilland would be the ugly stepsister.

For all our work and interest, I was reluctant to buy the company for the province on our own. I was not impressed by the federal experience of the 1970s. The idea of an open-ended subsidy was anathema. We suggested another route: a partnership between ourselves, Aerospatiale (the French consortium), and Bombardier, the Canadian company which had been so successful in its purchase of Canadair in Montreal.

The Canadair privatization was the beautiful twin when the Mulroney government got out of the airplane business in 1986. For reasons that I still don't understand, at that time there had been no effort to build one strong Canadian aerospace company out of the wreckage of the 1970s. Bombardier had grown from its origins as an inventive snowmobile and snow-grooming equipment company to expand into mass transit. The company had then purchased the British Crown corporation Short's from the Thatcher government, which was its first venture in aerospace, followed quickly by Canadair, which manufactured water-bombers and corporate jets. The company flourished.

I first met Laurent Beaudoin, the chairman of Bombardier, and Raymond Royer, president of the company, on April 29, 1991. Our meeting was not about de Havilland at all, but about another provincial undertaking in distress, the Urban Transit Development Corporation. UTDC, which made subway and rail cars in Thunder Bay and designed and built light rapid-transit systems in Kingston, had been sold to the Quebec-based company, Lavalin, by the Peterson government. Lavalin fell on hard times, and we were left holding the bag, with good technology but virtually empty factories in both cities. A few years later Lavalin was to become part of a larger group, SNC Lavalin, which is now very successful.

I told them that any sale of a provincial asset like UTDC would be on a competitive basis. We had been approached by a couple of other potential buyers, and wanted to get the best deal for the province. I invited them to submit their bid on that basis. I had a similar meeting with the principals of the German company AEG. In the end, Bombardier submitted the best bid. Bombardier UTDC is now employing more than 800 people in Thunder Bay, in a completely remodelled factory, selling subway cars around the world. Kingston has more than 300 workers, and is fully engaged making the LRT system for Kuala Lumpur, Malaysia, as well as other centres.

As a result of our first meetings over UTDC, I got to know and like Laurent Beaudoin, Raymond Royer, and other members of the team at Bombardier. As our options were steadily narrowed by Boeing over de Havilland, I sought Bombardier's interest as a key private-sector partner. Boeing's exclusive talks with Aerospatiale kept everyone else at bay, but I tried to persuade the chairman of Aerospatiale that it would be prudent for him to seek a strong private-sector Canadian partner, and that Bombardier was the logical choice.

We were treated by the French with considered condescension. Who was this provincial upstart telling the chairman of one of the jewels in the crown of France how to do business? Didn't he understand that the Canadian government, the "senior government," had expressed no such concerns? I subsequently learned that Bombardier received the same treatment. Laurent Beaudoin made it clear in the summer of 1991 that the three-way partnership I was searching for just couldn't happen. The French wouldn't accept Canadians having a majority share, or anything like equality in the management of the company. A junior role was of no interest to Bombardier.

The federal government then made it clear that they were not about to stand up to either Boeing or Aerospatiale. They refused to insist on a Canadian partnership. Bombardier backed away. It looked as if the stage was set for a French takeover of de Havilland. The best we could do was take a minority share as a province in order to have a continuing presence at the table. Better than nothing, but not much.

At that point the fairy godmother appeared in the unlikely manifestation of Sir Leon Brittan, a Thatcher Tory who had been appointed as European Community Commissioner with responsibility for competition policy. Sir Leon was at once an ardent free marketer and an Englishman who must have known how British Aerospace felt about being squeezed out by the French. His ideology and his nationality conveniently combined. When he paid a perfunctory protocol visit to my office on September 20, 1991, I had the strongest sense that the fix was in.

As indeed it was. The European Commission killed the Aerospatiale takeover of de Havilland, saying that it would give the French company too big a market share. This meant that the full year and a half's discussions between Aerospatiale and Boeing were down the drain.

We were thus faced with both a crisis and an opportunity. A crisis, because Boeing was now in full-blown shutdown mode. Thanks to wasted time and wasted opportunity, the company's order book was almost empty. So much for the genius of private enterprise. An opportunity, because the chance to do what had not been done in the 1970s and 1980s—to create an integrated Canadian aerospace company building on our strengths in both Quebec and Ontario—was now clearly with us.

Laurent Beaudoin and Bombardier saw their main chance and took it. I met with the company and senior officials from the government and we agreed to keep talking, to work closely together, and to make our own deal before going to either the federal government or Boeing.

The feds were furious when they realized what was happening, but I knew they would have to play. The aerospace industry in Montreal had been handsomely funded by Ottawa. I was not about to let them off the hook when we were in trouble in Ontario. They could not afford to be seen to be publicly critical, however they might be seething privately. As a result of our strategy, we got a 49 per cent share of the company for our investment, and the right to name three people to the board. For a similar investment, Michael Wilson got to come to the signing ceremony. Laurent Beaudoin and I met regularly to go over broad plans for the company, and Ontario's interest was well protected. We were constantly involved in the company's marketing efforts, its vision for new product development. We purchased the company from Boeing for much less than offered by Aerospatiale, leaving Bombardier to do the hard bargaining and assume full responsibility for managing the company.

January 22, 1992, was a great day. All the employees were brought together to witness the signing of the transfer of ownership to Bombardier and the government of Ontario. I had quietly wondered what the reaction would be in a workforce with more than a trace of Orange to a takeover by a Quebec-based company. Laurent Beaudoin got the answer when he rose to speak. Cheers all round.

Employment at de Havilland now stands at more than 4,000, compared to fewer than 3,000 in 1992. The order book is full. In June of 1995, the company announced its plans to proceed with the design and to build a new DASH 8 plane, the 400, which will seat seventy passengers. Above all, the company is now an integrated part of a major international company with an overall revenue of more than $6 billion. Sir Leon Brittan helped us more than he could possibly have guessed.

⟵ ⟶

I have described these negotiations in some detail. There were countless others, an inevitable response to the practical crises of the recession. That, and not question period and who put their foot in their mouth, was my major preoccupation. Someone asked me why I spent so much time putting out fires in the first couple of years of our government. My answer was simple. "Because we had so many fires." There were the lighter moments as well.

When I was told of the official visit of the Prince and Princess of Wales, scheduled for October 1991, I suggested we try something a little different.

"Why not greet them officially in Sudbury?"

"In Sudbury, Premier?!? I'm not sure that's ever been done before."

"The province doesn't stop at Eglinton Avenue. They can visit Science North, the Cancer Centre. They'll get a tremendous reception from the people. What else has been suggested?"

"They're expected to preside at a fund-raiser for Lester Pearson College. Galen and Hilary Weston have organized the whole thing."

"That's fine, but we should try and expand the dinner to include other groups in education—perhaps literacy more broadly."

Thus started a negotiation with "The Palace," Ottawa, the lieutenant-governor's office and our own protocol group, each with its own wish list and non-wish list. I was naïve about the amount of attention that would be aroused by the visit. There would not simply be dozens of journalists, but hundreds, even thousands.

The Toronto Sun decided to declare on its always thoughtful front page that inviting the royal couple to Sudbury was a "Royal Snub." This in turn was rightly interpreted in Sudbury as the Toronto media snubbing Ontario's north.

In the end the visit came off without any serious problems. School kids lined the streets of the cavalcade as we headed toward Science North, one of the great children's science museums in North America. Hundreds of cameras clicked incessantly at all of us on stage. Princess Diana, who is as drop-dead gorgeous in person, close up, as she is on camera, whispered, "They're waiting for the wind to catch my skirt."

"No, ma'am. I'm sure they're focused on my tie."

As Princess Diana and Arlene headed off to the Cancer Centre and a home for battered women, Prince Charles and I went to the Inco smelter, where he was opening a new processor. Thoughtful, well read, he had clearly studied his briefing notes about Canada and Ontario. We had a great chat in the car where he passed with flying colours what I call my "long-ride-in-the-car celebrity test." Most famous people that I have met flunk the "celebrity test." To stay interested and focused, aware and alert in the face of the hundreds of Mr. and Mrs. Publics is no mean feat. Their days are an endless stream of people, usually less important and famous than they are. Appointments flash before them like so many trains through a station. Sitting next to Edward Kennedy once at a dinner, I had the distinct impression that the good Senator was scarcely aware of the city he was in, let alone the identity of the chirpy spectacled fellow at his elbow. The key is the ability to remain human and curious. The simple ability to ask a question and listen for the answer.

Prince Charles shook hands with the miners coming in, joking and even accepting pats on the back without flinching. Inside the smelter was a brand-new prefab building, complete with carpets, furniture, and pictures of horses and hunts. I asked one of the workers exactly what this structure was for.

"That's where you and the Prince will go on your break. We put it up yesterday, and we're taking it down tomorrow. We call it the Royal Flush."

The royal couple went from Sudbury to Toronto to Kingston to Ottawa, meeting people from all walks of life. The province went predictably gaga for Princess Diana and the "little Princes," who fidgeted and picked their noses in church and seemed quite normal.

The gala evening put me at the same table as the Princess. After dinner most of the table left for one reason or another.

"Premier, it would appear you and I are the only ones at the table without a prostate problem."

"Yes, ma'am, for the moment that would appear to be the case."

I managed to steal two dances, but for better or for worse no cameras were permitted to record this event. The Princess asked me to be careful not to knock off her tiara. No dancing partner before or since has given me a similar warning.

I have no profound thoughts on the future of the monarchy as a result of this visit. It is hard to know how any two people, or indeed institution, could withstand the relentless scouting and endlessly lit publicity that accompanies their every moment. It was not so much monarchy that attracted the crowds as celebrity, a celebrity that would only become harder to bear in the years to come.

← →

Out of the blue in late November 1992 I got a call at home from someone whose identity I think I should still protect. The PEN Benefit was being held in a week, and he was calling on behalf of Salman Rushdie.

"You sure? Salman Rushdie?"

"You heard right. He's been invited to the PEN Benefit in Toronto. He's accepted. The problem is that every airline we've asked has turned him down. They just won't take him. Can you think of something?"

Together with a great many others, I worked on the problem for a couple of days. Again, the details should probably not be disclosed, but a great public-private partnership was put together which brought Rushdie to Toronto.

Ed Broadbent, Stephen Lewis, Arlene and I had a fascinating two hours with Rushdie on a Sunday afternoon at a safe house arranged by PEN. He was funny, warm, passionate. He played down the weird life he was forced to live, focusing the discussion instead on what could be done to get the Iranian authorities to lift the *fatwah*. He mentioned that he hadn't yet met publicly with any head of government.

"I'm not a head of state, but I'd be glad to see you in public."

157

"Really?"

"But it would have to be a surprise."

The result was that while my security and political staff knew I was going to the PEN benefit, and knew I was going to make a speech, none of them knew I was going to embrace Rushdie on stage.

I quoted Orwell on fighting political orthodoxy and some of Rushdie's earlier work. When Salman crossed the stage, the startled and excited audience erupted into a sustained ovation for him. It was a great evening.

Chapter Eleven

OUR HOME AND NATIVE LAND

Just as it was an essential truth of our government that we took office during a difficult recession, it was equally true that we took office in the shadow of the defeat of the Meech Lake Accord. I know that many in the public, and indeed in my own office, felt that I was too worried about national unity. It was a preoccupation I could not avoid.

To borrow a phrase, all of my life I have had a certain idea of Canada. The partnership between French and English is an abiding, permanent, and constant part of my own identity as a Canadian. It is hard to imagine Canada without it.

My kids go to our local school in French immersion. I learned the language as a teenager, and have made a point of learning as much as I can about Quebec and French-Canadian history, literature, and culture. I can remember growing up in Ottawa and having mock battles with a gang of kids known on our street as "the Frenchies." When Mom and Dad got wind of this, we were all given stern lectures about Canada and who we all are. The lessons stuck.

I came to the premier's office as an internationalist and a strong believer in a federal Canada. I also recognized the need for change, and that some of my fellow Ontarians might be less interested in this than I. Patriation came in 1981 with a price: the legislature of Quebec did not assent to it, nor to its terms. This was not surprising with a majority separatist government. But it was equally true when the Liberals returned to power in Quebec in 1985.

For Pierre Trudeau this was unimportant. The Quebec caucus in Ottawa had strongly supported patriation with the Charter of Rights. Lévesque had been mortally wounded at his own convention. Separatism was in complete disarray after Bourassa's return to power and the collapse of the PQ in 1984. In Trudeau's view, there was nothing more for federalists to do except to stay the course.

Mulroney and Bourassa disagreed. From their perspective, a generous response from Canada and the nine provinces to Quebec would end the sense of conquest which had tainted patriation and the Charter of Rights. Separatism was not dead, and would revive again, strengthened by the mythology of the Night of the Long Knives and the Kitchen Deal. Thus was born the Meech Lake Accord.

The arguments against Meech have always struck me as quite bogus. That Quebec is distinct in that it has a French-speaking majority and that its laws stem from the legal tradition of the Napoleonic Code rather than the English Common Law strikes me as self-evident. The other clauses in Meech that recognized Quebec's joint jurisdiction over immigration and assured Quebec of its position on the Supreme Court simply confirmed what was already there (and what had already been conceded by Trudeau).

Yet Pierre Trudeau was a root-and-branch opponent, and decided that he would not go quietly into the night. He created a curious coalition, one that succeeded in defeating both Meech and, later, Charlottetown.

I say a "curious coalition," because in English Canada it represented both those high-minded individuals who could not abide what they saw as an erosion of a strong federal government and believed in the immaculate symmetry of ten identical provinces with equal (and insignificant) powers, as well as those less high-minded folks who wanted to "stick it to the Frenchies." Trudeau made anti-French bigotry respectable, both over Meech and over Charlottetown. There is no greater irony in his political career.

❦ ❧

Trudeau, Clyde Wells, and Elijah Harper got their way. All the compromises and asterisks couldn't hold the Meech Lake Accord together, and despite Brian Mulroney's and David Peterson's efforts it all collapsed in late June of 1990.

The reaction in Quebec was swift and brutal: Bourassa made an emotional and ambiguous speech about Quebec always having been a distinct society. As a result Parizeau came over to shake his hand. It was a symbolic gesture that changed the chemistry in Quebec in ways Bourassa, I am sure, never fully intended. David Peterson went quickly to Quebec to provide symbolic assurances of Ontario's continuing partnership, and then began planning for his own re-election. A public poll showed him with more than 50 per cent support, which was confirmed by our own surveys. Our first overnight poll after he called the election on July 30, 1990, showed us at 17 per cent.

I badly underestimated how the Ontario public was assessing David Peterson's role in Meech, and what their real views were about the Accord. If Meech had, in the end, been passed by Manitoba and Newfoundland, David Peterson would have received a real boost for his role. As it turned out, he shared the blame for its failure, and was increasingly seen as someone who was prepared to give away the store, and seen as too friendly to Quebec. The equal irony was that I was the one to benefit from this reaction, even though my position on all these questions was not dramatically different from his. I was only a bit player, which in this instance played to my advantage.

❦ ❧

On Friday, September 7, 1990, I arrived at Queen's Park, slightly shell-shocked, but as happy as I had ever been. We had done what everyone said was impossible, won a majority victory for the NDP in Ontario.

My first call that morning was from Brian Mulroney. I had met him once, at my brother John's wedding fifteen years before, when

I was still a law student and he was working in Montreal. When David died in 1989, Mulroney had phoned me at home early the next day, something I deeply appreciated at the time. He spent some time giving me real encouragement. While the cynic can say that he just went through his Rolodex and made the ritual gesture, it was a gesture that meant much to me.

Mulroney's real charm and intimacy in private is hard to square with the plummy, starched formality that became his public style. In private he is funny, profane, and direct. In public he is remote, relying on a kind of bogus eloquence which creates an immediate distrust from his listeners. His French style is more of a piece, which I think accounts in part for his success in Quebec and his greater credibility there than in the rest of the country.

I found it impossible to dislike him personally. This used to drive many in my party quite crazy, since they were always able to translate political differences into personal antagonism. I have always found this more difficult, and in fact can't do it.

"Bob, I have one word for you."

"What's that, Prime Minister?"

"Vindication, Bob, vindication. You don't have to take any crap from all those people who said you could never get there any more. You're there. You've made it to the mountain top and nobody can take that away from you."

"Well it was certainly a long struggle and a big surprise."

"Enjoy yourself today, because it won't get any better than it was last night and is today. Those bastards in the civil service are going to start coming at you with paper and you'll be fighting just to get to Sunday."

"It's very good of you to call."

"My pleasure. Mila and I are looking forward to seeing you soon."

As it turned out, there was no political or personal interest on his part in a meeting until ten months later.

No premier from any province called to offer congratulations when I was first elected. It was a curious welcome to the club. I finally started picking up the phone myself after the swearing-in on October 1, and had my first conversation with Robert Bourassa on that very day. Frank McKenna later explained that everyone was completely burned out by Meech, but I think part of the explanation has to be the sense among them (no other New Democrats yet!) that there was something singularly strange and odd about the election, and about an NDP premier in Ontario.

My first conversation with Bourassa was friendly, if more formal than the first exchange with Mulroney. He and I had spoken during the last months of Meech, and he knew of my support. He had been close to Peterson, and was still in touch with him. Preoccupied with the aftermath to Oka and (unbeknownst to me at the time) facing his own illness, he emphasized that Quebec was embarked on a process "that I don't entirely control" because of the rejection of Meech. We agreed to meet soon.

↤ ↦

I kept the intergovernmental affairs portfolio for myself in the cabinet-making process. I felt that the issues were going to be so much a part of being premier that I should do it myself, and didn't want the potential problem of having one of my colleagues taking a different tack. As things turned out, this was wise. I had the enormously able advice of Bud Wildman in the native affairs portfolio to provide in-depth support as the issues became more complex and time-consuming.

Wildman was an extraordinarily effective minister, first of Natural Resources, and later in Environment and Energy. Bud was born and raised in the Ottawa Valley and moved to the Sault in his twenties. He was a school teacher and became active in the OSSTF, and was elected in the NDP mini-sweep of 1975. He was an effective critic in the House, and an incredible constituency man: on one of my frequent trips to his riding while in opposition we went for a day to Dubreuilville, an almost entirely French-speaking lumber town north of Wawa. I have never seen a man know more people and share such an obvious affection with his electors. It transcended any language barrier.

Bud was a passionate supporter of native rights, and had wavered on Meech precisely because of that. I wanted him to take

163

on the native affairs portfolio. I needed to take it away from the domination of the lawyers in the attorney general's ministry. I also wanted a northerner to deal with it, because Bud would keep his ear to the ground politically and let us know how far we could go.

It so happened that the days after the swearing-in gave me an opportunity to signal a clear direction for the province in our dealings with native people. A conference was being held on aboriginal rights across Canada. I had been asked to speak.

Stephen Lewis, the head of the transition team, urged me to go, and I did. Stephen had led the way in the 1970s when as NDP leader he raised the issue of mercury poisoning in north-western Ontario in the legislature. More than any other mainstream political leader in the country, he brought the issue of native rights to the forefront. He kept it there even when it proved politically difficult and indeed unpopular in many parts of the province.

I was very aware of the importance of that contribution when I became leader of the party in 1982. I travelled extensively across northern Ontario and met with chiefs every summer. Jack Stokes, who was our member from Lake Nipigon at that time, and had served as Speaker of the House from 1975 to 1981, accompanied me to my first meeting with the northwestern chiefs in 1983 in Kenora, and when it was over he was appalled. Jack, a legend for candour, took me aside and said, "That was terrible. You talked. You didn't listen. You didn't give it time. You were too blunt. Migawd you were awful."

It was an object lesson. The point I had tried to make in the meeting was that the native leadership had to take provincial politics more seriously, because of education, resources, and social services, and all the other practical ways we had to deal with each other. So a specifically provincial and Ontario focus would be a good idea for both of us.

This was not a welcome message in 1983. The chiefs believed their essential relationship was with the Crown, and with Ottawa. We were interlopers. But I had also failed to understand the differences in culture and style that are all important in every conversation. As Arlene has had to point out to me a few times, I am one of those people for whom the opposite to talking is waiting—rather than listening!—and patience and silence have never been among my greatest virtues. It was something I would have to learn. The next summer, Jack took me on a tour of the northern part of his constituency, and as we visited Big Trout Lake, Summer Beaver, Fort Hope, Winisk, and Lansdowne House, I listened. I tried to shut up. I spent time just hearing what others had to say.

I went back many times, and in the winter of 1989-90 flew north to the James Bay Coast. To travel north to James Bay is to meet several uncomfortable truths. Up the coast from the Quebec border to the point where James Bay meets Hudson Bay are nestled five communities—Moosonee, Moose Factory, Fort Albany, Kashechewan, and Attawapiskat. Each is very different, with its own unique character, but all share a common reality: a profound and systematic poverty rooted in the encounter between Europeans and our first Canadians.

It was just a two-and-a-half-hour flight, but it was a trip to a very different world. Only Moosonee and part of Moose Factory have running water and sewage treatment: in the other communities these advantages are exclusively confined to those buildings where non-natives live and work. It is a colonial world, where the native people have their own language—Cree—their own culture, their own way of life, and yet are effectively ruled by a white, alien authority.

The meaning of the phrase "self-government" suddenly became very clear, and its historic parallels with the demands of other colonized people around the world are immediate and visceral. It is not just the overwhelming poverty. It is the absurdity of the physical layout of a town like Fort Albany, where all the white institutions are on a hill, across the Albany River from where the natives live. When the ice breaks up in the spring, people have to be flown across the river if they need medical help.

This continuing discrimination creates many moods among the native leadership—resignation, frustration, anger—but above all a sense of separateness, a sense that survival is about keeping distance and integrity. In their experience, politicians come and go, bureaucrats come and go, plans are made and unmade. As they see it, negotiations are literally endless. Their overwhelming experience is that governments are not really interested in "settling" anything. There is no requirement, other than that of vague conscience, that governments should. Courts are hideously expensive, and not particularly receptive. Without them there is no forcing governments to do the right thing.

It is impossible to escape the conclusion that what we are talking about here is racism. In what other Ontario communities would we accept thousands of people, whole communities, doing without basic sewage treatment and running water? To say "that's a federal matter" misses the point entirely. If Ontario goes in and builds a small hospital for the community, and then supplies the nurses' residence with the necessary amenities, doesn't that raise the issue of why white civil servants are getting this and no one else?

Economist John Kenneth Galbraith talks of "private affluence, public squalor." Here it is the other way around. Wealth is associated with the government, with public money. With the exception of the Hudson's Bay store, and the local priest and minister, the white establishment is exclusively a government establishment.

I concluded from these experiences of the 1980s that our forming a government gave us a chance to make a difference. This conclusion was to make life politically difficult for us on numerous occasions, and put us at odds with many in our "natural" political base. The Federation of Anglers and Hunters, for example, was to wage a particularly unconscionable campaign against the concept of native hunting and fishing rights.

But it's fair to say that we started out with a mission, and between 1990 and 1995 this mission put Ontario in a leadership role. Canadians are not alone in having to come to terms with our history. We share with every "settler culture" the need to accept the rights, the history, and the personality of those who were here before European settlement.

We were to learn that this is not an easy course to take. Majority opinion in Ontario is not easily persuaded to accept deep diversity: the Charlottetown debate showed how readily people turned to the simple argument that we have one constitution, one country, and therefore one set of rights for everybody. Pierre Trudeau and Preston Manning both made these arguments with force and simplicity, and for the time being they have won great resonance outside Quebec. The only trouble with this simple ideology is that it will lead to the break-up of Canada.

If it weren't for the Supreme Court of Canada there would be no sense of collective aboriginal rights in Canada worth a damn.

This was not our only difficulty. There is no one "aboriginal nation" and certainly no strong sense of collective mission, organization, or leadership. Individual chiefs and band councils are jealous of their political authority, and loath to concede it to any provincial or national organization. The infighting within aboriginal organizations parallels that of any other group, with the result that it is exceedingly difficult to negotiate agreements which are then ratified.

We had some important successes. In the first year of the mandate, we negotiated a Statement of Political Relationship, which set out the basic truth that relations with band councils and their leadership should be on a "government to government basis." We agreed that we would work to negotiate workable self-government agreements. This agreement was solemnized in a ceremony at the top of Mount McKay near Thunder Bay on August 6, 1991, and was the first of its kind to be struck in Canada.

We also worked hard on a Round Table with the native leadership in Ontario. This in itself was difficult, because among the chiefs there was much suspicion about dealing with a provincial government. There is a deep strain of tradition that the relation between settlers and natives is a relationship between the Crown and first peoples: "settler governments" at the provincial level are deeply suspect in this view, and should just get out of the way.

The practical difficulty with this is that the notion of some personal treaty with the King or Queen is just so much romance. The province has practical authority over policing, family and child welfare, hunting and fishing, private property, resources, education, and health care, just to name a few basic issues. No "self-government" which does not deal with these issues is possible. I have never asked Queen Elizabeth what she thinks about these questions, and she hasn't asked me either.

The federal government has legal authority over native issues as recognized in the British North America Act, but has been reluctant to show any real leadership. With the collapse of the Charlottetown process, they did set up a Royal Commission on Aboriginal Peoples, which will no doubt produce a compelling report and some profound research, but this all amounts to a clearing of the collective throat in the absence of political will—on all sides—to deal with these questions.

I say "on all sides" because the end of dependence is difficult for everyone. The majority culture has to learn that native self-government means conceding real authority and real power in areas that have until now been the monopoly of provincial and federal bureaucracies. Dismantling these bureaucracies, Lord knows, is very difficult.

But native self-government also means responsibility. When Yassir Arafat goes from hobnobbing with potentates to sitting in Jericho and Gaza and deciding where the sewer and water has to go, and has to worry about how to pay for it, it is, to put it mildly, a difficult transition. The same will be true for the native leadership. Gone the endless flights to endless conferences to endless negotiations in endless hotel rooms. Getting rooted in providing real solutions to real problems will be painful.

Consider the issue of taxation, for example. It is a source of great pride to the aboriginal peoples that they do not have to pay income tax to the government of Canada for work done on the reserve. This offends the majority culture. One of the first consequences of self-government will have to be financial responsibility. No self-governing entity in the world can exist without taxing its members.

I became an advocate of self-government not because I saw it as some kind of "giveaway" by governments. Quite the opposite: powerlessness corrupts just as surely as power does. The exaggerated rhetoric, the excessive language, the unrealistic demands were all the product of a pathological relationship, one it is in all our interest to change.

For example, the bands and elders we talked with saw health as an important right, but had almost no access to decisions about where dollars would be spent, what would be given priority, or how the system would work. This was true regardless of the issue: chronic care, user fees, diabetes (of which there is an alarming incidence across the North), ambulances, travel, birthing. You name it, there was no control.

The institutions of economic domination had to be addressed as well. My favourite sign at the entrance to the Hudson's Bay store in each of the communities in the Far North is "Shop and Compare." Compare with what? Starvation? The prices are exorbitant. Frozen hamburger at $8 a kilo. T-shirts for eight-year-old kids at $15. Pampers at twice the cost in any city. There is nothing free, adventuring, enterprising, or ennobling about any of this: it's called extracting whatever you can from the rump of empire and monopoly.

We decided that governments should use their countervailing power on behalf of consumers. We made co-ops possible, and helped limit the power of monopolies in isolated communities. They were nothing but a licence to print money.

For generations Ontario governments said there was nothing they could do. It was one of the ironies of history that on the Quebec side of the border the James Bay Cree are famous for having signed a deal with Quebec Hydro, a provincial institution which was flooding traditional hunting and fishing lands. From that deal came capital, and success for some.

We did not have a project as huge as James Bay to generate the money for a massive capital grant, but we did determine from the earliest days of the government to make the attack on native poverty a priority.

We made sure our work on housing was expanded to include housing on reserves, and projects for urban natives as well. We built child-care centres where none had been before.

On basics like housing, child care, health care, and sewer and water, we made a point of including native communities for loans and grants, even though constitutionally speaking this was the sole responsibility of the federal government. There has always been much debate about federal spending power, and the ways this can and should be exercised. It is a simple fact of constitutional life that a provincial government that can send money for development in Jamaica can do the same for development in its own North. Nothing in the division of powers or the natives' insistence on retaining their direct link with the federal Crown takes away from this simple fact. Ontario could do with its money what it wanted, and for us this included meaningful action for first citizens living north of the fiftieth parallel.

This was, for me, a source of real pride. We deliberately chose to make this a priority for Ontario, which admittedly came with a certain cost. But as events unfolded, this commitment on our part allowed me to play a pivotal role in the next round of constitutional talks.

Chapter Twelve

THE ROAD TO CHARLOTTETOWN

The trick in that first year was to keep working on the constitution without talking about it. Quebec had gone off on its post-Meech lurch, and soon after our initial phone call in October Robert Bourassa went into hospital for treatment of his melanoma. He was out of commission, and the Belanger-Campeau process led Quebeckers into a long dialogue with themselves.

I asked Tony Silipo, an able caucus member, to chair a special committee of the legislature on the constitution. Consultation was the order of the day. Since Quebec was immersed in its own project, it made sense to keep the discussion going in a low-key way. Bourassa was recuperating in Florida in the winter of 1990-91, and I was there as well with Arlene and the girls over the Christmas school break. I went to see him for a long chat in early January 1991. This is my diary note of that conversation:

> *Bourassa was pale from having stayed out of the sun,*
> *thin, but seemed fit. He's in remission...and has*
> *recovered some of his lost energy. The quintessential*
> *fox. Not a lion. Shrewd, like quicksilver. Clearly sees*
> *Europe as the model—which is what makes him a*

*"neo-federalist." Likes to talk in largely theoretical
terms. He is trying to feel me out on a range of possible hypotheses. He claims to have lost control of the
caucus and the party—not the Cabinet. Ryan and
Johnson and Gerard D. OK, in fact Ryan, he
implies, is an even stronger federalist than he is ("a
great Canadian"). He follows opinion, talks much
about what "they" will do. He is supporting a
Canada of regions, in which the regions agree to
devolve or delegate certain powers to the centre—he
is being pressed to make a unilateral declaration of
"sovereignty." Claims to have said no to that, and to
the suggestion from his party that the central parliament be called the "conseil des nations"... But he is
talking about continuing to push for more powers
from Ottawa, and says "if we don't get them by such
and such a date..." I told him this was no good, that
it was no go for us, and that the creation of these
deadlines doesn't work for anybody but the separatists... Objectively we are in a mess. We have no
process to provide a solution. Leadership federally is
weak...the expectation is that I should do something,
but what? Bill Davis wants me to sit tight, which I
think is wise, but subject to much criticism..."*

Bourassa was worried, because he had felt the need to ride the
wave of public sentiment that was whipped up after the collapse
of Meech. But in riding it he also gave it encouragement. He was
not well enough to take charge of events. There was no one minister clearly in command in his absence.

Bourassa is a master of the ambiguous. He enjoys the game of
politics as well as anyone I know, and was satisfied that he had
managed to keep the "sovereignist wave" from completely swamp-
ing the Liberal ship. This ambiguity was to earn Robert much criticism, from both the separatist and from the federalist camp, but
he saw it as an essential way for him to maintain his political base.

This quality became a weakness as well as a strength: the vicious personal attack that came from the separatists can only be explained by the fact they believed that Bourassa had made a conversion after the failure of Meech. To anyone who knows him, or has spent even five minutes talking politics with him, this is absurd. Robert Bourassa believes the Canadian federation has to change, to become more decentralized, to recognize more the position of Quebec and the realities of a changing economy. The idea that he tricked the people of Quebec into thinking that he was some kind of separatist, whose real dream was of an independent Quebec, is nonsense.

Bourassa did create serious problems for himself after the collapse of Meech: it was one thing to announce that, despite what Clyde Wells or anyone else might say, Quebec was a distinct society, free to follow its own destiny. It was quite another to say that henceforth Quebec would not participate in any constitutional discussions *à dix*, and would only negotiate directly with Ottawa.

I warned Bourassa in that early meeting in January 1991 that Ottawa could not speak for Ontario. We would have to reserve the right to speak and negotiate for ourselves. I also tried to explain to him that the opposition to Meech had been real, that it was based on the feeling that people were excluded from the outcome, and that there were other constitutional grievances that were not addressed. Whatever came in the future would have to go beyond Quebec in making reform happen. There could not be a pure and simple Quebec round. If the constitution was still on the agenda, it could only be handled, I believed, in a Canada round. The Quebec political leadership never really accepted this, and to this day does not really accept it.

Bourassa was worried not so much because he had lost control of Quebec opinion: he always expressed a wry confidence in his ability to ride opinion and outsmart his opponents. His real worry was that with the formation of the Allaire Commission within his own party, he had lost the momentum within his cabinet and caucus for a coherent strategy.

← →

It had become clear by the summer of 1991 that I needed an exceptionally strong team to provide the kind of balance and leadership that would be necessary to take us through these discussions. I wanted people I knew well and could trust entirely, people whose strengths would complement the experience and depth of the existing Ontario team. I also needed people whose contacts and views extended beyond the bureaucracy into other parts of our society. I asked Jeff Rose, who had just retired as National President of the Canadian Union of Public Employees, to become the deputy minister of intergovernmental affairs, Murray Coolican to join us as deputy minister in charge of native affairs, and Stephen Bornstein to take over as the Ontario representative in Quebec. They were joined by David Cameron, who had been a deputy in the Peterson government, and had returned to the University of Toronto, and who became a constitutional adviser to me. Marcia Matsui, a lawyer in private practice, joined us as special assistant in constitutional matters. In addition, we had the advice of the Deputy Attorney General, George Thomson, and his able staff.

← →

The summer of 1991 saw my first meeting with Mulroney. It was at Harrington Lake, the summer residence of the Prime Minister, and was to be the scene of many constitutional meetings through that year and the next. Mulroney and I chatted for more than an hour alone on the screened porch overlooking the long, narrow lake, and then were joined by David Agnew and Norman Spector for lunch in the adjoining dining room.

Mulroney was, as he always is in person, funny and direct. He poured on the charm. He claimed to feel no bitterness for what had happened at Meech Lake, but could hardly say the words Clyde Wells or Gary Filmon without going through a recitation of personal betrayal.

"Clyde sat as closely to me as you are now, Bob, and told me to my face that he would have a vote. And now he's the darling of the media... Why? When he broke his word?"

Mulroney's heart and soul had gone into the Meech Lake

Accord. He had spent a full year since then, scarcely seeing anyone, avoiding the media, watching the polls descend, and brooding on how to undo what had been done, to make this thing whole again. Since I had been a supporter of Meech, I could understand his frustration. But since I had not really been there with him and the other premiers, I could not completely share his feeling of ownership and betrayal. I saw mainly the need to start a new process with greater enthusiasm.

I tried to make a couple of things clear: the first was that Ontario would be constructive. The second was that we could not be taken for granted, and that a deal between Ottawa and Quebec which went over our heads would not work. We also talked a good deal about how Ontario had changed, and how a changing economy had created a stronger sense of regionalism in Ontario than I had ever seen before.

Mulroney listened, but I don't think he ever saw this as anything more than the predictable chant of a premier.

Mulroney made a point of driving me down to the scrum at the gates to Harrington and joining me in front of the cameras. This was symbolically important: he could just as well have had me go out alone, and avoided the press as he had been doing all year. He made the point in front of the media that he had heard clearly about the impact of the recession on Ontario, and at the same time said publicly that any constitutional solution had to be arrived at, and would be arrived at, with the co-operation of the government of Ontario.

From my perspective, mission accomplished. When I returned to Toronto, my own troops were less happy. Where were the arguments about free trade? Why have your picture taken with the most unpopular leader in Canada? How could any self-respecting New Democrat possibly co-operate with the man partisan rhetoric had turned into the devil incarnate? Wasn't I making the same mistake as David Peterson in associating myself with this man in the appeasement of Quebec?

This was a dilemma from the beginning. In the end, and with the aftertaste of the defeated referendum in October 1992, my own support in Ontario took a beating. The fact that we had achieved significant victories—more House of Commons seats for Ontario in exchange for a watered-down Senate; the Social Charter which provided some protection for social programmes in what we saw as an inevitable decentralization; and a breakthrough on aboriginal rights—in the end proved less important than the perception by some of the public that I had become part of the "Mulroney élite." Yet I felt I had to do what I did. The alternatives would have been far worse.

On the issue of national unity, Brian Mulroney's instincts and beliefs cannot be faulted. He was right about what needed to be done after patriation. His success in negotiating Meech was remarkable. The country would not now be in a constitutional crisis if it had passed. I disagreed with Brian Mulroney on many things, but on the issue of keeping Canada together I shared much of his vision of needed generosity and change, and admired his courage and his skill as a negotiator. By the same token, the rest of Mulroney's agenda, and his style, ended up infuriating Canadians. The personal mistrust he generated helped sink Charlottetown.

↞ ↠

In the fall of 1991, Joe Clark began his deliberations across the country, and took on the task of co-ordinating the federal government's strategy on the constitution. Mulroney's decision to appoint Clark had some strong arguments in favour: Mulroney could not be seen to be personally immersed in what would become a very complex file; Clark had built up a considerable amount of good-will in the country as a kind of senior statesman in external affairs; other politicians respected Joe as someone who worked hard and had come away from some difficult defeats—first by Trudeau, then by Mulroney himself—with dignity and humour.

I got along well with Clark, despite the fact that I had moved the motion that led to his defeat as prime minister. We used to joke about this a lot in the early days of his appointment, but Joe appeared to bear no deep grudges. He listened, and his skills at listening were instrumental in fashioning a consensus.

Clark's flaw was that he was never able to convey a sense that the federal government had a core negotiating position. Temperamentally, he disliked confrontation. This in turn meant that discussions became more like a smorgasbord than a give and take. Trudeau's epithet that Clark was a "headwaiter to the provinces" was a cruel cartoon. From my experience this was less the issue than Joe Clark's inability to force the mutual concessions that would produce a deal. These were skills that Brian Mulroney had in abundance.

The other difficulty with Clark's appointment was that it meant we were, in effect, dealing with two federal governments. This was Joe's file and Brian's obsession. Joe came to feel and understand that whatever happened it could not simply be another "deal for Quebec." Mulroney was preoccupied with defeating separatism in Quebec, a preoccupation made even more acute by the presence of his former friend Lucien Bouchard in the House of Commons. Mulroney had his own network in Quebec, and in particular his own relationship with Bourassa, which was stronger than his friendship with any other first minister.

As the discussions became more intense, this would become more and more of a problem. Mulroney kept talking about how the objective was to "get another car in the window" on display before the referendum deadline set by Bourassa. Clark knew that the rest of the country resented Bourassa's timetable and Bourassa's deadline, and that whatever happened had to have resonance right across the country. Mulroney was more and more bored by the details, but increasingly determined to make good on the commitment he had made to Quebeckers when he took office and to reverse the failure at Meech.

On the Senate, for example, I got completely mixed signals from Ottawa. Mulroney had no time for Triple-E, that is, an *elected* Senate, with each province having an *equal* number of senators, and the Senate chamber having *effective* power as a governing body. But Clark kept this idea on the table, in part no doubt because of his western constituency. This "lowest common denominator" approach of Clark's made it impossible for him to forge a consensus. He brokered a temporary deal on July 7, 1992, which then had to be reworked to get to Charlottetown.

Bourassa's strategy had problems of its own. The reports of Belanger-Campeau and Allaire, which had each given vent to the separatist wind, had created a momentum which he could not fully control. Bill 150, which set in motion the train for a referendum before the end of 1992, was passed in the late spring of 1991, and at our meeting in June he had expressed the thought that if nothing better came along he would have to be guided by whatever the Quebec people decided in a referendum. He cited the example of Prime Minister Harold Wilson and the British referendum on membership in the European Common Market, when Wilson said he would live with either result, and the British people could make up their own mind.

I was not convinced this made much sense, and told Bourassa at our next meeting in Montreal in June 1991 that whatever arose out of federal-provincial discussions we would have to do more than simply go back to Meech. Harold Wilson had used the ruse of hiding behind the referendum to get a result he wanted at the expense of the little Englanders in the Labour Party. It was not exactly a display of quintessential political courage, and not much of a model.

The "make me a better offer or I'll call a sovereignty referendum" strategy coming from Bourassa, combined with the refusal to participate in any constitutional discussions except on the basis of a direct one-on-one with Ottawa, put all of us, including Bourassa, in a difficult bind. In the end, the two had the effect of reducing Quebec's negotiating leverage.

Ross McClellan, a former MPP, current adviser to the government and great friend, used to point a finger to his head and say "take one more step and I'll shoot" as shorthand for negotiating strategies that didn't make sense. Bourassa made life more complicated for himself and for federalism than he needed. He made his shift after Meech because he needed to express Quebec's public dismay at what had happened, but he also felt that his pipeline to Ottawa would ensure a better offer.

I kept telling him that there was another train in motion in the rest of Canada, and that there would be no "private offers" coming from Ottawa on behalf of the rest of the country. Quebec was disdainful of our approach, and didn't take the broader negotiations seriously until the outlines of the understanding were already set.

Ottawa resented our determination to create a federal-provincial process worthy of the name. They resented our insistence on terms and conditions, and they resented having to admit that they had lost control. This resentment never really left, although there was a grudging acceptance of the new order after the meeting of March 12, 1992.

This was the meeting where Ontario insisted on opening up the process to the native leadership, and having a full-blown discussion with everyone in the room. At first there was resistance from Alberta, as well as the federal government, but this eventually broke down. That day it was clear that we were going to have a real Canada round that went well beyond simply making an offer to Quebec.

There were mutterings about these naïve ideologues from Ontario taking over the process. Certainly Clark's position with Mulroney was made more difficult, but I still believe that it was the only way to proceed that would have any credibility with the broader Canadian public.

We had set out our own concerns at earlier meetings and in a presentation I made in Ottawa before Beaudoin-Dobbie in January 1992. I rejected the ideology of Triple-E, and asserted that while the Ontario government had no problem with Quebec's distinctiveness, we could not simply have a Quebec round all over again. I kept urging Quebec, both in public and in private, to find a way to come back to the table. Two other changes were necessary for Ontario: a social charter to protect social programmes in the moves to decentralization that were inevitable; and real progress in addressing the needs of aboriginal people.

The social charter was at first not particularly popular with the other provinces, even our friends in B.C. and Saskatchewan. I saw it—and still see it—as essential to keeping the national glue in a more devolved Canada. There was an important tradition in

Canadian public life, which was particularly vital to the left of the Liberal Party and many in the New Democratic Party, that feared devolution would necessarily mean a dangerous erosion of Canada's social programmes. My own sense was, and still is, that centralization is not always synonymous with social justice. The provinces in fact played a far more important role in the creation of good social programmes than the Fabian and Liberal centralizers have ever been prepared to admit. We needed to find a way to express our common concern about the future of solidarity and social programmes in a new constitution which would include the provinces.

At the same time, I was sceptical of entrenching too much in a constitution, because this offended my sense of the responsibility of democratic governments to deliver programmes paid for by taxpayers. Some, including members of my own caucus and cabinet, wanted us to go further, and spell out in great detail any and all social "rights" in an enforceable constitution, but I didn't think this was either desirable or possible. We should not ask our constitutions to do too much. Something has to be left for the day-to-day give and take of political life.

❦ ❧

As meeting after meeting unfolded in March, April, and May of 1992, we made substantial progress in a number of areas. Quebec was kept informed, and never said never. The federal government's "two track" of Mulroney and Clark made life more confusing. Bourassa's decision to continue the boycott was only comprehensible if he believed that the process could not possibly work. He may have been encouraged in this by Mulroney himself, or he may have reached that conclusion on his own. I kept hearing what a shrewd game was being played. I didn't see anything shrewd about staying away from the table where decisions were being made.

We made good progress through the spring on every issue except the Senate. The notion of a Triple-E Senate was beloved by the Western provinces and by Newfoundland, which was ably represented by Ed Roberts at all these early sessions. Their arguments were forceful, emotional, and persistent, and while I was sceptical about them I knew enough to realize that for the Western provinces, as well as for Clyde Wells, this was a huge make-or-break issue.

We were at loggerheads on the Senate for months. The notion that Ontario with its eleven million people would have the same number of Senators as Prince Edward Island with its one hundred and thirty thousand people was hard to accept, to put it mildly. It was equally clear that the other provinces not theologically wedded to Triple-E were prepared to hide behind Ontario's opposition. And, naturally, the Triple-Eers were only too happy to bash a province which combined size, power, and an NDP government.

I kept an active dialogue going with my good friends Roy Romanow and Bob Mitchell from Saskatchewan. Mitchell attended all the sessions of the "Clark roadshow" and was a key player, always wise, ironic, and looking for solutions. I was surprised by his vehemence on behalf of an equal Senate. Romanow came to our house for supper and kept up the arguments. I was sceptical, but I wanted to break the log-jam. The difficulty was how to do it, given the logical opposition from Ontarians and Quebeckers.

As things got down to the crunch in late June 1992, we had a meeting with Mulroney at 24 Sussex Drive, without Bourassa, which was not particularly helpful. Mulroney went off to Germany, telling us to wrap it all up. He left convinced that a solution was not possible, and I agreed with him.

Many things combined to change this mood, and make an agreement among the nine provinces possible. For Ontario, I felt some kind of agreement was better than nothing. We needed to get Bourassa and Mulroney to the table to complete a deal. We also needed to make sure we were all there when the eventual deal was made. An impasse would have produced some kind of Hail Mary pass from Mulroney. I had no idea what that might be.

While Ontario's views on the Senate were based on a clear sense of our self-interest, a compromise might be reached if there was give on one of the famous Triple-E's. At a technical level, we began to hear noises from the other provinces about increasing Ontario's number of seats in the House of Commons, and some real room on making the Senate less all-powerful. In other words, some E's were more important than others.

At one point in the last days I asked Wells if we got agreement on everything would he agree to put back the veto for Quebec, and he said "yes." At that point I felt we would have enough of an agreement to bring Quebec back to the table, provided the others would accept the rest of Ontario's package on the social charter and aboriginal rights. For my part, I could see the advantage of trading off more House of Commons representation for Ontario with a Senate whose powers would be reduced. I had reason to believe that the symbolism of equality in Senate representation was worth a great deal more to the proponents of Triple-E than equal power to the House of Commons.

The initial agreement announced on July 7, 1992, at the Pearson Building was made possible by one last factor: Quebec's absence from the table and the contrasting, elliptical messages we were getting from them began to aggravate us all. Alberta kept saying that Bourassa would not give an unequivocal "no" to the equal Senate idea. Clark reported the same thing, and Quebec obviously thought it could hide behind Ontario, and so didn't need to take a forceful position itself.

I had assumed that Clark was in constant contact with Mulroney in Germany, and that his eventual support for the Pearson deal had the stamp of approval from the Prime Minister. After all, Secretary of the Cabinet Paul Tellier was with us throughout the day and at several points confirmed the statement that Quebec was not unequivocally opposed to the equal Senate idea.

When I spoke with Bourassa that night he was subdued, polite, but clearly surprised at the agreement. Mulroney, on the phone from Germany the next day, was agitated. I then realized that Clark had been acting on his own. Mulroney was convinced that any notion of an equal Senate, combined with the recognition of aboriginal rights, would make the deal very hard to sell in Quebec. I tried to be more upbeat, but he was having nothing of it, and clearly implied that I had let the side down by agreeing to the Senate compromise. I had assumed Clark and Tellier were acting with his full knowledge and approval, and that they were prepared to leave me twisting in the wind alone, taking the full blame for the collapse of the talks, if that were to have happened.

The next few weeks in July and August of 1992 were odd, to say the least. Quebec's position was that it could not come back to the table unless all the conditions of Meech Lake were met. The other provinces and the federal government had reached an agreement, and since Quebec had refused to turn up for the negotiation, the implacable line was that this was the last word.

I was at the cottage, and Mulroney was working the telephones furiously. The federal government had a bad case of buyer's remorse. The Quebec caucus was unhappy and had given Clark a rough reception. Mulroney was convinced that the deal could not be sold in Quebec, and wanted me to announce that I had reconsidered my position. I said I couldn't do that, but that if Quebec were to come back to the table, the plan could be made to work. He pushed again, and I gently pushed back. Other calls confirmed that the Rolodex was working away with the same idea being put to other premiers.

The compromise reached was that Mulroney would invite all the premiers, including Bourassa, to lunch at Harrington Lake, but that this would not be a formal first ministers' meeting on the constitution. This meant that the native delegations were kept away, which they were understandably unhappy about, while the premiers and Mulroney met around the lunch table.

It was an odd experience when we had our first meeting on August 4, 1992. Mulroney sat at one end of the table, Clark at the other. The meeting began with Joe Ghiz giving the speech that Mulroney had wanted me to give. Ghiz had always been a profound sceptic on the subject of the Senate. He had no time for Wells's "theology." While P.E.I. would have benefited enormously, he thought it all a trifle overdone. He started the discussion by setting out his own view that the Triple-E Senate idea was simply not going to work.

It soon became clear that this, the first direct conversation among all the premiers and Mulroney, had to be kept alive, and had to be turned into full-scale negotiations. This could only be done if everyone kept two necessary fictions clear in their heads. Quebec had to be able to say that all the elements of Meech had been obtained. The rest of us had be able to say that we were not abandoning the agreements reached in early July at the Pearson Building. So long as we all kept repeating the mantra, we could move on from private chats at Harrington to real negotiations.

In the end, this is what happened. None of us could afford a breakdown, because Bourassa had boxed himself in with his referendum timetable. With his return to the table, we were in the box with him. He needed "an offer" to put on the table because of his referendum legislation, and whatever he did had to look like "Meech plus." By leaving his return to the table so late, this was difficult to achieve, and in fact his own public servants (who had been the architects of this strategy) sabotaged his significant accomplishments in the negotiations. They denounced them in phone conversations made on cellular telephones, which were conveniently intercepted by the media. No premier was more poorly served by his professional staff than Robert Bourassa. No civil service did more than that in Quebec to achieve its own misguided private agenda at the expense of the public good.

In fact, Bourassa achieved a good deal during the last week of full-blown negotiation. He made the idea of Senate reform palatable by securing a guaranteed representation for Quebec in the House of Commons. At the same time, Ontario increased its Commons representation. Bourassa and I combined arguments to persuade our colleagues of the merits of a less powerful Senate in exchange for our accepting equal numbers.

As it turned out, we may have been trying to square a circle. At the time it was the only argument our Western colleagues and Clyde Wells could accept. In reality, Triple-E is a bumper sticker. In its pure form it will never be acceptable to either Quebec or Ontario. The argument that "all provinces are equal" is true in the sense that each province as a member of the federation has an equal right to participate in the life and times of premiers' conferences, and other such gatherings. Each province is equally entitled to exercise the powers granted to it under the B.N.A. Act. But, as a statement of how a second chamber can in fact function in Canada it is quite unworkable, and the simple repetition of the slogan, however loudly, will not make it true.

Bourassa was equally effective in clarifying the wording around the groups' efforts on native self-government. Here he had the support of a number of premiers who were unhappy with how far Ontario had managed to move the debate. My role here was to keep the native leadership on side, as further "clarifications" were sought to ensure the provinces' continuing responsibilities for civil order. This was especially important to Bourassa after the bridge closures in Montreal, but he was not alone in expressing concern that the process of negotiating self-government had to be practical and orderly.

At one point I was sent off to a corner to draft wording that would meet these concerns. I also had to convince Ovide Mercredi, Grand Chief of the Assembly of First Nations, that this was the best we were going to get. If he couldn't agree, native people would lose all the progress we had made the last several months. I tried to explain to him that the "latecomers" to the negotiations— Bourassa, Mulroney, and most of the premiers—were already enormously sceptical of the process and how far the discussions had already gone. I feared at that point that if Ovide had walked out to get more time, or to increase his leverage, all would have been lost. Just as we were having this discussion, Gil Remillard came in with alternative wording from the Quebec delegation that would have set us all back behind square one. I knew that if I even showed it to Mercredi he would walk, and I said as much to Mulroney, who in turn told Remillard to back off, which he did.

The other stickler in this area, as in virtually every other, was Clyde Wells. Wells had become a hero to many outside Quebec because of his stand on Meech Lake. I did not share this adulation, because I always felt that the Wells/Trudeau view of the Constitution, taken to its extreme, would lead to the break-up of the country. It was too inflexible, and ultimately too ideological, as if somehow the country had to be made to conform to some Cartesian logic. My own view has always been different, starting from facts, from history, from the diversity of our traditions, and what is going to be required to keep us all together. Constitutions don't make countries. Countries make constitutions, and what is done by convention and practice is just as important as what is written down.

Many of Wells's supporters in Ontario used to tell me how much they admire him because he always called a spade a spade. In fact, if presented with a spade, Clyde Wells would say that "this is, and can only be, a gardening instrument that is not a shovel, and not even a trowel, but rather a hand-sized tool that must be of certain dimensions and qualities in order to meet the definition that has been objectively set."

Mulroney's relations with Wells were soured by the fact that he had failed to call the vote on Meech in the Newfoundland House of Assembly in June of 1990. Since I hadn't been at the table at Meech, it often fell to me to try and find words that Wells could live with. It wasn't easy, but I found that once he accepted Charlottetown he campaigned hard for the agreement.

When Mercredi, Wells, and Bourassa decided they could all live with some compromise wording on native self-government, I began to feel that we were actually going to get to an agreement. Bourassa and I had dinner alone together and we agreed the worst was behind us. The final challenge was to get Quebec to accept that bigger changes on the powers of the provinces, much beyond what had already been initialled, was simply not practical at that stage.

Bourassa understood this instinctively better than Remillard and his advisers. It soon became obvious that there was a profound difference of opinion among members of the Quebec delegation. At several points on the very last day of discussions at the Pearson Building, Bourassa would adjourn our "premiers only" sessions to talk to his delegation, who could be seen shouting and arguing about how much more he had to insist on.

What this ignored was that there were real limits on how much further any of the rest of us could go. If we had further decentralized and plucked dry the carcass of federal powers, some Western premiers might have gone along. But this would have jarred public feelings and opinions in the country. This was hard for the Quebec delegation to understand, and in their late-night phone calls they blamed me and the "hardliners" in the Ontario delegation for their problems.

It is of course always easier to suggest that if only so and so on the other side wasn't such an S.O.B., what a wonderful world it would be. But there has to be some appreciation that others have to sell agreements, too. Bargaining positions have to follow from some strong perceived sense of interest. There was no point in Ontario taking positions that couldn't be sold in Ontario: the record of voting in the Charlottetown referendum, a 5,000-vote margin in favour in my own province, showed that we pushed things about as far as we could.

When the final details were set out at Charlottetown on August 28, 1992, we were all in a good mood. We had an agreement. It certainly responded to the need to move beyond Meech without betraying the fundamentals of what Meech meant: the distinct society for Quebec, the veto, and the clear delineation of powers. To this we had added Senate reform, native self-government, and further progress on a new relationship between the provinces and the federal government.

My own feelings at this point were euphoric. A poll was published, on the front page of *The Toronto Star*, showing support for my role in the negotiations in Ontario at 67 per cent. I believed the country "needed a win," and that the fact we were all there together, after such a long and arduous process, could only be good. All the opinion soundings showed that support for the ideas in the Accord were very high, and that we were behind in only one province, Quebec, but this by less than a huge margin. Both Mulroney and Bourassa felt that with a solid campaign this could be readily overcome.

Meech had failed because of a lack of ratification in the provincial legislatures. We couldn't let that happen again. We couldn't let the country spend another three years on the rack, with the Accord dying a death from a thousand tiny cuts. Quebec was boxed in with its own legislation promising a referendum on either "sovereignty" or "offers." Alberta and B.C. had done the same thing, insisting that true democracy meant the people had to have their say not simply in an election, but in a referendum. I had always voiced considerable scepticism about a referendum, but it seemed to me that a national referendum had always been part of Mulroney's strategy.

So it was that after an enormously complex and time-consuming process of give and take on every word and every clause, after endless consultations, open-line radio conversations, the Silipo road show in Ontario, the Belanger-Campeau road show, the Allaire report, the Spicer road show, the Beaudoin-Dobbie road show, the Joe Clark road show, and endless meetings in every corner of the country, one fateful afternoon in Charlottetown, buoyed by polls and quietly jubilant in our self-congratulation, we agreed, with scarcely a dissent, to send this all to the judgment of the people, confident that in the end they would be well pleased with our efforts.

How wrong we were. I thought that there was something in Charlottetown for everybody. I had failed to understand that there was something for somebody else to get mad at. The Accord faced heavy weather from the outset: our timetable was too fast, because of the dates set out in the Quebec legislation, and didn't allow for the kind of strategizing that it required. We lost control of the campaign very quickly. While we all had illusions that we would be selling it together, the reality of the campaign was that the chief salesman was Brian Mulroney, and he always regarded Charlottetown as the bastard child of Meech.

In Quebec, the nationalist press savaged it early on. The publication of the cellular phone conversations of Bourassa's advisers was devastating. That their analysis was inane and self-serving didn't detract from its juiciness to those who were already convinced that perfidious Ontario had done it to Quebec again. The native leadership became ambivalent almost as soon as the document was printed. Western leaders met a barrage of hostility on native rights and on Quebec, to which Preston Manning cynically added gasoline.

For my own part, right after our discussions ended at Charlotte-town I called a meeting of several hundred people who had participated in all the various round-table discussions over the years. I felt on the first few days of the campaign that we were doing well. The dissent from Judy Rebick of the National Action Committee that we had failed to do enough for gender equality I felt was unfair and wrong in law. I was troubled that this view had support from those known as the "Charter community." I had a conversation with Bob White, president of the CLC, in which he expressed a distinct lack of enthusiasm for the result, as well as the process, but I felt too that this would be hard to sustain for long with a public that I felt wanted to get this matter resolved and behind us as a country.

Toronto writer Rick Salutin has made much of the fact that the élites favoured Charlottetown and that the swing against the Accord was a triumph of democracy. I wish I could be as sanguine. For every thoughtful and principled argument that it did not go far enough here or there, or failed to express perfectly what needed to be done, I was overwhelmed, as were our canvassers, with the sense that the opposition in Ontario increasingly came from those who did not want to recognize Quebec's distinctiveness and those who could not accept the need for self-government for native people.

This to me was always the great irony of Pierre Trudeau's speech for the "No" forces at La Maison Eggroll in Montreal. He managed to ally himself with Jacques Parizeau, Preston Manning, and Rafe Mair as the enemy of change. He blamed "others" for opening up the Pandora's Box of the constitution, failing to realize that no one in modern Canada had done more to focus attention on the issue than he had himself. His attacks on both Meech and Charlottetown were scurrilous, inaccurate, demagogic, and sadly persuasive to many looking for an excuse to say an emphatic "no!" to Quebec.

One of my lowest days as premier came on October 21, 1992. I was campaigning for the Accord in Barrie, Midland, and Penetanguishene. At a sparsely attended noon rally at a mall in Barrie I was confronted by a sea of angry and disbelieving faces. "You've given away the country to the Frenchmen and the

Indians," said one old-timer who insisted he had voted for me in 1990. I came home that night with a sinking feeling. The emotional glue holding the country together was coming unstuck.

During the last week of the campaign we desperately pulled out all the stops. My voice was a rasping squeak, speech after speech, from one corner of the province to the other. The night itself was an anti-climax. We barely won in Ontario and in three Atlantic provinces, but lost everywhere else.

My personal dilemma was that while many Liberals and Conservatives accepted the logic of Charlottetown, the populist base of the province had gone the other way. We were hearing arguments about employment equity, about taxes, about leadership, that pointed to real difficulties for me as premier. I wasn't in the best mood to listen to this shifting anger, but it was there for anyone who cared to pay attention.

After it was all over, the staff at the Ministry of Intergovernmental Affairs (or MIA as it is called) held a wake at George Brown House on Beverley Street. I tried to be chipper about what had happened, but I felt the defeat of Charlottetown most deeply and personally. For twenty-four hours I even contemplated resigning, but realized that this would have been an instance of "exaggerated self-reference." Yet I had, for the better part of two years, focused my energies on constitutional success, and had convinced myself by the end of the summer of 1992 that our efforts were going to succeed.

Brian Mulroney would announce his departure a few short months later, and Robert Bourassa would follow later in the year. Together we had failed to resolve the problem Trudeau had left us. On the other hand, we had succeeded in avoiding a complete collapse, something which was a distinct possibility after the failure of Meech.

I also now believe we did something else. The key elements of Charlottetown—recognition of Quebec's distinctiveness, a recasting of rights and responsibilities of the Canadian partnership (including the social charter), a call for native self-government, a reform of federal institutions like the Senate which were clearly ripe for change—are all issues and themes to which Canadians will return.

Even the federal Liberals, who for the most part sat on their hands and regarded all our efforts with a kind of bemused condescension, are now basing their own efforts on a recasting of the formulas of Meech and Charlottetown. If imitation is the sincerest form of flattery, we should all feel flattered. The tragedy is that it is late in the day, and that the failure of needed change post-patriation has further fuelled separatist opinion in Quebec. The next steps will be exceedingly difficult because earlier options were shortsightedly rejected.

Chapter Thirteen

SOCIAL CONTRACT

Early on in the life of the government, it had become clear that the recession was lasting much longer, and to much greater effect, than most had thought possible. Many observers in the media kept talking about how this crazed group of socialists actually believed that it was possible for Ontario to "spend its way out of the recession." I had explicitly rejected just such an idea in my inaugural speech of October 1, 1990. But the impression certainly remained. And political management is to some extent a matter of impressions.

In the first budget in 1991 we felt an overwhelming need to soften the blow of the recession. Mulroney seemed oblivious to the impact of free trade, high interest rates, and the GST. He reduced transfers to Ontario just as our welfare loads began to rise dramatically. You could feel the desperation in the streets in the winter of 1990-91. To sit back and slash—to fall into some neo-conservative trance—would have been a betrayal of our election. We deliberately raised welfare rates that winter to soften the blow. One cabinet official said our decision was the first time she had ever heard a cabinet decide to give the Minister of Community and Social Services more than she was asking to help stimulate the economy and maintain living standards in a recession. It turned out to be an unpopular decision once the recession began to recede.

The projected deficit of $9.7 billion for 1991-92 was a tough tonic for all of us. It was certainly much bigger than we had expected back in September, or even in December of 1990. Both opposition parties were predictably angry in the House. In the case of the Liberals this hypocrisy was hard to stomach. They had misled the public badly in the summer election, leaving Ontario with a structural imbalance of $8 billion projected into 1991. The Tories' Ottawa cousins had fuelled the Ontario deficit by cutting programs like unemployment insurance and singling us out for discriminatory punishment on major transfers.

Michael Wilson phoned me just before the first budget, and said he had heard "on the street" (I think he meant Bay Street) that we were coming in with a big deficit. He let me know that this was unwise.

"From my experience it's a lot harder to get out of the hole than it is to get into the hole. If I had to do it all over again I'd have attacked Lalonde's deficit from the start. I could never get the support I needed in cabinet to get it under control, and I'm sorry for it."

I replied, "We can't take this bloody recession and your cuts at the same time. Somebody has to provide some extra stimulus to this economy."

"Keynes just won't work," Wilson said, to which I answered, "I think a high deficit number will help make my case for balance over the longer term."

We agreed to disagree, which the federal Tories did at every opportunity.

Ironically, the cabinet had already concluded that we had to re-examine programmes, and cut spending on current operations so that we could maintain our long-term investment in capital and keep the jobs programme alive. We started doing just that even in the first set of estimates, and stopped spending in some areas for the first time in years. We knew then that high deficits were not wise or sustainable indefinitely.

THE TORONTO SUN

In our second budget, for example, we ended across-the-board cheques for every senior citizen, replacing them with a more progressive (and less expensive) tax credit. And we managed without incurring the wrath of the seniors' lobby.

This was lost on the public, since the effect of the recession and of our determination to sustain the people in the province hit so hard by unemployment was that the deficit kept rising. That was the bottom line that seized hold of the imagination of the tabloids and the bond-traders alike. We were in a hole. It looked as if our strategy was to keep on digging faster. The fact that we had cut down substantially our spending on day-to-day operations and that every cabinet meeting was dominated by the agenda of even more spending reviews and cuts wasn't matched by any popular perception at all.

This should hardly have come as a surprise, since the budget numbers had been wrong since David Peterson and Bob Nixon told the world that Ontario had a balanced budget on the eve of the 1990 election. Three civil servants from Finance—Bryan Davies, Bob Christie, and Tony Salerno—had come to see me right after September 6, 1990, to let me know that "certain developments" had created a very different outlook for the fall and winter of 1990-91 than the people of Ontario had been led to believe by the Peterson government. Revenues were down in all departments, and were continuing to fall.

Every estimate I received from the experts in Finance was wrong on revenues and wrong on increased spending on welfare and people. In September 1990, for example, they thought that the deficit for the end of the next March would be close to $700 million. This estimate was out by a factor of several hundred per cent by the time of Floyd Laughren's first budget in the spring of 1991: not because of "socialist overspending," or because of bureaucratic incompetence or malevolence, as the myths would have it, but simply because the recession was worse, revenues were collapsing, and the impacts on people and their families were much greater than anyone had thought. Ottawa's neglect only added to the burden.

This experience left us much burned and a bit wiser. It made me resent the false wisdom of economic projections and prognostications. As is always the case it was "the politicians," not the civil servants and their models, that took the rap with the public for the sense that "things were completely out of control."

Floyd's first budget in 1991 had upset the powers that be, and led to the bizarre spectacle of chartered accountants and stockbrokers in their pinstripes and two-tone shirts arriving by taxi at Queen's Park to demonstrate on the front lawn complete with carefully manicured signs. Floyd Laughren had the best answer to the "Fax Floyd" campaign when he said he was more worried about the fate of the vast majority who didn't have fax machines. The National Citizens' Coalition, a shadowy front group with big money, had already rented a billboard just around the corner from Queen's Park, displaying posters worthy of Allende's Chile. The huffing and puffing of right-wing types who could never bring themselves to go to Ottawa to worry about Mulroney and Wilson's deficits (much higher and far more out of control than ours) was set in permanent motion. They now have billboards fawning over Mike Harris.

We made the mistake of believing the experts who predicted a cheerier revenue and spending picture in the year after the first budget. That mistake made it much harder for us to convince anyone—inside or outside the government—that we were serious about getting the province's finances under control. Again, too soon old, too late smart.

I began to present a different vision to the cartoons of far right and far left in speeches before and after the first budget. At our post-government convention in February, I reminded the party that once in government, we had an obligation to govern on behalf of the whole province. It was my most explicit pitch to date that the old myths and stereotypes had to change, that Ontario's economy was being completely restructured, and that this was having a major impact on the whole of our society. The old conflicts between management and labour, between government and business, between the different factions and segments in Ontario were out of date. This meant a change for business, a change for government, a change for all of us.

I was in the unenviable position where the left felt my brain had been captured by Bay Street, and Bay Street thought I was some kind of Maoist. I was trying to move the party closer to the centre, to accept the market as a fact of life, and to understand the need to work out a lasting understanding with business. A government committed to permanent class warfare couldn't survive and couldn't govern.

At the same time, the failure of conventional business opinion to accept the need for strong social policies always struck me as incredibly shortsighted. The wide gap between rich and poor and weak supports for the most vulnerable only make things worse for "our kind of capitalism." We'll never be able to compete with the southern U.S. on wages directly, let alone the Mexicans. Our competitive advantage is in quality of life, good education, strong social investment. That makes us more productive, and attracts new investment.

Everything we did as a government was an effort to reinforce this simple message. Not meaner, but leaner government. When times get tough, everyone pitches in, not just the poor. Make labour a partner, not an outlaw. Make business a partner, not the enemy.

Ontario's costs and abilities to compete should not just be a concern of right-wing businessmen. They are a challenge for everyone, since the productivity and efficiency of the economy are a necessary precondition for growth, for a healthy society. Elements in my own party and a tradition on the left that is longer and stronger than it is healthy had developed a rhetoric of social rights that is at times divorced from the real economy. Levels of public debt are not something that should only concern the political right. I couldn't see how pretending that there wasn't any kind of a limit to the credit card was a prescription for serious policy. Under previous governments Ontario had decided to allow the credit card debt to run up for a long time, hoping that improvements in the economy, and a sensible discipline in public policy, would allow us to climb out of the hole.

Debt matters, because like everything else it has to be paid for. Compound interest, combined with extravagantly high interest rates such as those imposed by the Bank of Canada, makes it even more costly to do so. But at the same time, there is nothing evil in deficits or debts in and of themselves. People buy homes with mortgages, and don't think of themselves as sinners. Businessmen get loans from banks for huge investments, and do not flail themselves with thorny branches as a result. It is a practical, not a theological issue.

Despite its theoretical merits, the first budget was a major political setback. It was praised by John Kenneth Galbraith and got two cheers from a brave economist at the Conference Board, who announced that it had made a bad situation in Ontario better. Given the extent of restraint elsewhere and the cuts in transfers from Ottawa, still determined to ignore the impact of the recession in Ontario, it provided a counterbalance.

But our own constituents were unimpressed, since the recession was still on. As far as many were concerned, the budget should have done even more. The business community was outraged.

Floyd Laughren's statement that he wanted, in this first budget, to fight the recession rather than the deficit drove many commentators over the top. We were not prepared for the onslaught. The die was cast.

In one of his speeches before the 1936 election Franklin Roosevelt told a story that certainly has meaning for me. A silk-hatted businessman walking on the pier is carried out to sea by a freak wave. Drowning, his shouts are heard by a lifeguard, who leaps in and saves his life. Once revived, the businessman looks around and says to the lifeguard, "I had a hat."

The fact that we were expanding the government's investment in affordable housing to levels unmatched in Ontario history and with no parallel anywhere in Canada was never enough to satisfy those who insisted on more. That we maintained income supports for women and men unable to work because of ill health, family circumstances, or unemployment was lost on many of our traditional supporters who chose to concentrate instead on what was missing. Opposition habits of a lifetime proved difficult to lose.

We never went far enough to satisfy child-care advocates, arts organizations, columnists and others who demand the full moon or nothing at all. Now they have their starless sky.

It became conventional wisdom for our friends to say they were "disillusioned" because more wasn't being done. My reaction was one of disillusionment as well, though of a different kind. What we had inherited from the eighties were high expectations, on every side. At a provincial council meeting of the NDP in June of 1991 there were complaints that we weren't doing more, and that people still expected more. The thought that we couldn't spend indefinitely an unlimited amount of money wasn't in the lexicon.

Thus it was that the second half of my message in June of 1991—that the business community should accept the legitimate role of government, the labour movement, and the needs of the whole community—was lost not only on the business community. It was also lost on those very groups, such as labour, who would benefit most directly from this approach.

↤ ↦

The economy stopped falling in the spring of 1992, although a decent recovery didn't kick in for another year. I went on television in the winter of that year, trying to signal that public-sector restraint had to be the order of the day, and that at the same time major public and private investment in jobs was essential. I proposed a national infrastructure programme, an offer that was eventually taken up by Jean Chrétien in the fall of 1993, after his own election. The response to the statement was summed up in *The Toronto Sun* headline "Thanks for Nothing, Bob." Nothing looks pretty good now, but I don't expect *The Sun* to agree.

The economic recovery was slow and painful. Revenues didn't bounce back: the addition of the GST to the visible tax burden of Ontarians was massively unpopular. It caused something the experts called a "secular change" in tax-paying habits. People went underground, put their money in tax shelters, and revenues kept going nowhere. At the same time, the province's welfare costs kept rising.

The right likes to point to a massive growth in fraud and delinquency as the reason for this, but this just isn't true. People were hurting, the feds cut back on unemployment insurance, and so drove more people on provincial welfare. We refused to join the dirge for cuts and punishment. Things would have been much worse if we hadn't done what we did. Not only did we allow people to keep body and soul—and their families—together, but local and small businesses did much better than they otherwise would have because poor people had a little money to spend.

But the province's bottom line was in lousy shape by the fall of 1992. As we started our work on the budget for the next year, I became convinced that something new and bold needed to be tried. I began sharing my ideas with a few close colleagues, starting with Floyd Laughren, and expanding to include all my P&P (Policy & Priorities Committee) colleagues.

At the same time, the business community was enraged because of our labour legislation banning the use of replacement workers during a legal strike, and making it easier for unions to organize. My thanks from the auto workers for this legislation and for saving de Havilland that same autumn of 1992 was a gratuitous speech by Buzz Hargrove dumping on our government at the CAW council meeting in December.

I realize now that my focus on the Charlottetown Accord, unavoidable as it was, took me away from the necessary preparation for what was to come on the Social Contract. The Social Contract was a good idea, but it was a political failure, and I have to take my share of the blame. The speech I gave to the province in January of 1992 should have been followed up by a series of speeches, meetings, and intense wooing of those who needed to be convinced. Charlottetown prevented me from doing that.

I am often better at seeing problems and solutions than persuading others how to get there. Yet this is, after all, what politics is all about. I can give the speeches and the arguments but don't always have the patience to persuade, to cajole, butter up, and jolly along.

I had used my negotiating resources in the year of Charlottetown (summer of 1991 to the summer of 1992), and just didn't have enough left over for what was to follow.

There is a certain sense of privacy in me, a self-contained quality, that makes me a less than perfect politician. I feel I need this to protect myself, to keep part of my life apart, but I know that it's not always a political strength. At too many points in my career, people important to me and to projects that I wanted to complete didn't know what I was thinking, or why I needed them to do something they might not want to do. At no point in my life has this been truer than during the Social Contract discussions that were to be so important in determining the fate of the government.

The Social Contract project would not have been launched had I not insisted it be tried. It might have succeeded better as a political project had I been better at preparing the ground, and spending the time, in persuading others of what I felt could be done. I didn't do that in 1991 and 1992, for reasons that are understandable, but in the end proved fatal.

Perhaps I should have realized that the blunt observation my friend Jack Stokes made about me years before was truer of my shortcomings than I knew. He said that God gave us one mouth and two ears for a reason. I didn't listen well enough.

In fact I did the opposite of listening when a taxi hand-delivered to me a copy of Buzz Hargrove's speech to the Canadian Auto Workers' Council on December 6, 1992. I couldn't believe Hargrove's attitude, and called him from my kitchen telephone on a Friday afternoon, just before Arlene and I were supposed to join him and other trade unionists at a tribute dinner for Bob White, who had left the presidency of the Auto Workers to become head of the CLC. I blew my stack, and let fly a string of four-letter words, not realizing that my nine-year-old daughter Lisa was listening in the next room. To this day she hands me the phone with a big grin saying "It's Buzz," or "Buzz off," remembering how nothing heard in the schoolyard could compare with that kitchen tirade.

Something in me snapped that day. My resentment at the lack of perspective, the lack of solidarity, the absence of any sense of responsibility for the financial (and political) health of the government, the sense of a never-ending series of demands that would always be disappointed welled over. I lost it in that swearing match with Hargrove, where the most he could say was, "You're not listening to what I'm saying and you're not listening to what my members are saying. Don't shoot the messenger."

Nothing I could do, no argument I could make made a difference. People I had assumed would understand something of our difficulties and fully expected to show some leadership and discipline themselves had decided to placate their own unhappy memberships by joining in the general dumping on me and the government. Nobody remembered that companies and jobs were saved. They only remembered their lost hats.

A political lifetime in opposition had meant that I had spent my career raising expectations, demanding more, and criticizing governments for not delivering everything asked for immediately. I could hardly be surprised that Buzz Hargrove, who had a very different job than mine, would not see why he should start changing the habits of a lifetime just because I had become premier. But I was surprised and angry. There was a huge gap between us at that point, in mood, interest, and outlook.

← →

Looking back now, I know that trade union leaders have their bases to cover. Any realistic sense of politics can only take people where they are ultimately prepared to go, and no further. But to understand my own determination (not to say bloody-mindedness) over the Social Contract, I now realize how much my own thinking was not just affected by lousy economic numbers and the clear, compelling policy need for major change. I had reached the conclusion, if unarticulated even to myself, that it was better to do the right thing than placate some powerful interests. My experience had been that those interests would bite me anyway. Not necessarily a politically wise conclusion, but deeply felt.

And so it was in the New Year of 1993 that I began discussing in cabinet the need for us to do something dramatic to deal with the growing gap between revenues and spending. Managing this would be, in our own party, a huge challenge.

Most of what government spends its money on is salaries and income support for doctors, teachers, Hydro workers, nurses, fire-fighters, police and thousands more. Nearly a million people are paid by taxpayers. Given the depth of the recession, and the problem that uncontrolled debt would cause for key social pro-grammes, it only seemed reasonable to ask public-sector workers to share in the solution. If we simply cut and slashed budgets, as many as 40,000 workers, many of whom were women and minorities without the protection of seniority, would be laid off.

The situation seemed to me then, and still does today, to call for creative solutions that went beyond the fragmented bargaining that dominated the existing scene. If we could get some recognition from the public-sector unions that there was a real problem, perhaps it would be possible to fashion some answers that would seem to be fairer.

These ideas had some important parallels elsewhere. Prime Minister James Callaghan, the last Labour Prime Minister before Tory Margaret Thatcher, had tried to reach understandings that went beyond Gompers-style business unionism.

Many European social democratic governments had developed strong partnerships with business and the labour movement. The Australian Labour Party had won election after a long generation in the wilderness. A key stepping stone had been an agreement with the unions on wages, prices, and the need for balance.

My objective was more focused: to get public-sector management and their unions to address the need for savings, and to achieve these savings without big reductions in service to the public or unemployment among public-sector workers.

This is what I meant by the Social Contract. It went beyond fragmented bargaining. It gave unions a chance to remain active in determining how restructuring should happen and where new capital investments could be made. It was an invitation to partnership in the context of fiscal restraint.

I started that year with a major cabinet change, and a dramatic reduction in the number of ministers and deputy ministers. We merged ministries, challenged the public service to get smaller and more efficient. I changed all of my senior ministers with the exception of Floyd Laughren and Elmer Buchanan. This is never easy or pleasant, but what was remarkable was that, despite the unpopularity of the government in the polls, people were prepared to pull together without huge rancour. I had to go back to caucus time after time, armed with charts and slides, showing what would happen if we didn't do something, and listen to the sense of frustration which everyone felt. The caucus held together throughout the next difficult years, despite strong criticism and a terrible drop in public support. We also had few defenders in the media, with many detractors from left and right. Under these circumstances caucus solidarity was truly remarkable.

The other numbers we worried about even more, Floyd's economic forecasts, only got worse. I shall long remember the briefing session in February 1993, when his officials gave us the projections for the next fiscal year: they were dismal, and showed the deficit climbing as high as $17 billion. Dramatic action had to be taken.

In addition to preparing the ground with cabinet and caucus, we had to get others ready as well. I asked Allan Blakeney to fly in for dinner, and share time talking informally with people at my house. I needed his support in explaining why endless increases in deficits were simply not possible for a provincial government. Allan's ideas on this subject were firm and clear, and had been followed with determination by Roy Romanow's government in Saskatchewan, elected in 1991. But there were many great sceptics and opponents to this approach within the family in Ontario: many believed that a continuing rise in the deficit was better than the restraint and difficult decisions which deficit reduction would require.

The cabinet and caucus, however, were increasingly of the view that something different had to be done. To allow the deficit to rise at a time of economic recovery, however slow, simply didn't make sense. The costs of allowing it to keep going up would be expensive, and would only handcuff future spending decisions because of rising interest costs. Debts have to be serviced. Unless revenues are rising, or inflation is rampant, this is a painful exercise.

In addition to the Blakeney dinner, senior cabinet ministers and I met with the leadership of the labour movement. We had dinner in a private room at Le Rendezvous restaurant. The key union leaders present were Gord Wilson and Julie Davis of the OFL, Leo Gerard of the Steelworkers, Fred Upshaw from OPSEU, Judy Darcy and Sid Ryan from CUPE, and Buzz Hargrove of the Canadian Autoworkers. It was a difficult meeting. Hargrove couldn't understand why we couldn't just keep pushing ahead on our current fiscal path. Others had great difficulty with the notion that a social democratic party should bother about debts or deficits at all: since Keynes, and certainly since the beginning of widespread deficit financing in Canada in the 1970s, it was simply accepted on the left that to worry about these things was a monopoly of the right, and not something that anyone in the labour movement or the NDP should worry about.

There was one slight glimmer of hope at the meeting. Judy Darcy of CUPE did say that perhaps what we should do was think about some kind of "social contract" that would go beyond traditional collective bargaining, and deal with broader concerns in the public sector about job security and training. Hargrove disagreed, but admitted that if that's what people in the public sector wanted to discuss, then he wouldn't try to stop the discussion. Sid Ryan, a CUPE colleague of Judy Darcy's, even said directly that the leadership realized that in all the changes in health care, and in public administration generally, people would lose their jobs, and that this was accepted as a fact of life.

As we prepared for our cabinet and caucus discussions in February and March, it seemed possible that some consensus might actually emerge.

I had been asked many months before to give a lecture at the University of Toronto, in memory of Larry Sefton, former district director of the United Steelworkers. I used that occasion to lay out my concerns and sense of opportunity for the future. Collective bargaining had shown its strength in dealing with the world of more; the issue was, for both the private and public sectors, how well could collective bargaining respond to a world of less.

That message was well received, and understood, by our union friends in the private sector (who, after all had experienced their own, much more brutal social contract imposed by the market). It was not similarly understood, and certainly not embraced, by the leadership of the public sector. I got a call from Bob White in January of 1993, saying that the CLC executive wanted to have a closed-door session with the three NDP premiers. Mike Harcourt of B.C., Roy Romanow of Saskatchewan, and I chatted on the phone. Romanow had some misgivings, but in the end we all agreed that a meeting might "clear the air." As it turned out, that meeting did the exact opposite.

It was clear that the labour movement itself was seriously divided, as people like Ken Georgetti from B.C. and Leo Gerard from the Steelworkers were determined to defend the record and efforts of the three premiers. Darryl Bean of the Public Service Alliance of Canada opined that he couldn't see any difference between us and the worst of the Conservatives. I'm not sure if this is still his view.

This kind of rhetoric pushed us three NDP premiers over the top. We were taking enormous flak from the business community and the general public over our support for labour. Bill 40, where we outlawed scabs and made organizing easier and which had been the subject of such long and bitter controversy in Ontario, was scarcely mentioned. They all had bloody hats, I thought, and weren't about to express thanks or rally behind the cause to save jobs. When it came to the deficit, White asked, "Why can't Ontario just do like the Reichmanns and declare bankruptcy, maybe pay 50 or 60 cents on the dollar?"

Romanow exploded, "The idea that any government in Canada wouldn't pay its debts is an outrage. We'll never form a government anywhere ever again with that attitude. No self-respecting social democrat would ever take that attitude. I can't believe you said it. Do you believe it?"

"You're god-damn right I believe it," White retorted. "Why the hell should working people see all their benefits and everything we've been fighting for all these years go down the drain because you guys have bought into all this new-conservative economics. You're elected to fight for our people, not to stick your nose up Mulroney's ass."

"What??? It's the Tories in Saskatchewan who got us into this god-forsaken hole and it's my job to get us out of it. That's what Tommy [Douglas] did in 1944 and that's what I'm going to do today. And if I have to do it without you and the labour movement I will."

After that exchange there was nothing more to be said. The gulf was wider than when we went in. White's comment in particular left me with a sinking feeling. For him the discussion on the deficit and the debt was banker talk, and we had bought it all. Ironically, Tommy Douglas's minister of finance, Clarence Fines, always used to ask his cabinet colleagues why they wanted to make bankers rich by paying them more and more interest. This insistence on fiscal responsibility in the name of social democracy was Romanow's tradition, and Allan Blakeney's tradition. It was worlds apart from Bob White's.

The meeting was meant to feel like a kind of show trial for the benefit of the media and the membership: a strong labour movement takes three political stooges to the woodshed. If the meeting was intended to produce a change in direction from us, it ended up having the opposite effect. We all resented the set-up of the meeting, and there was no appreciation or recognition of what governing in a recession is really like.

"Just declare bankruptcy and move on" wasn't a serious effort to join the debate or find a solution, and the result was that the leadership of the labour movement lost some of its leverage. They weren't prepared to admit there was a problem, and they weren't really prepared to help. I hoped that the trade union leaders would think again and get the message. They obviously hoped I would do the same, but face-to-face contact was at a minimum as we entered the Social Contract Tunnel of Doom in April of 1993.

I asked Michael Decter, former cabinet secretary in Manitoba, and now deputy minister of health in our government, to head up the team which would take on negotiations for the Social Contract. Decter had done a tremendous job, together with Frances Lankin, in the Health Ministry since joining the government in 1991. He was recruited by Peter Barnes, had extensive contacts in the business community, and had a reputation as something of a whiz kid. I liked Michael, admired his ability to see the big picture in the ministry, and had given him and Frances the task of getting the health budget under control.

They had done as I asked. Health budgets were rising by double digits in the 1980s. Our approach brought this down dramatically. The Premier's Council had set out a new approach for a healthy public policy. Frances Lankin came to cabinet asking support for a bold new direction: an emphasis on prevention of illness, health promotion, and building supports in the community for an aging population. This meant closing hospital beds, but she believed intensely in the strategy and brought to it great determination.

So did Decter, who has since written a good book on medicare in Canada based largely on his Ontario experience. They were a strong team, but by the winter of 1993 Michael was looking for new challenges. He agreed to take on the Social Contract negotiations, with the assistance of Ross McClellan, Peter Warrian, Wendy Cuthbertson, and an eventual cast of hundreds.

Michael Decter brought great strengths to the task. He believed in it, and indeed had argued privately that the first budget had created huge credibility problems for the government. He carried on extensive discussions privately before we held our opening meeting at the beginning of April 1993. We knew that to propose a pure and simple roll-back of wages would be a non-starter. At the same time, to suggest a simple trade-off between a wage freeze and job security would be unrealistic, because it wouldn't get us to the fiscal target we needed to achieve. The compromise we suggested was days off without pay—what would become known, almost instantly, as "Rae Days"—and assorted other measures to get to the targets we felt we needed to achieve.

When Decter showed some of these ideas to many in the trade union movement, they were not met with the shock and horror privately that they eventually were to receive publicly. This became, in fact, one of the real features of all the discussions and negotiations that dominated the political life of the province in the spring of 1993. Back-channel chats would produce one set of responses. But the face-to-face discussions, to say nothing of the media confrontations, led to a sense of an irreparable divide. The professional negotiators were keen to reach some kind of solution. The political leadership in the public sector became a prisoner of its own rhetoric, unable to accept the legitimacy or good faith of the whole exercise, and never believing that if the process were to break down, the government would be capable of taking firm action.

The April opening session was remarkable for the simple fact that it was the first time in Ontario's history that all the representatives of the public sector were brought together at one time for a discussion of the province's financial and fiscal situation. My hope was not that there would be a quick and easy solution, but that the government's desire to do things differently would eventually produce a serious effort at negotiation from the public-sector workers themselves.

As events would prove, this hope was not to be realized. Indeed, the failure to bring around the union leadership to the need for a comprehensive and fully bargained solution led to a split with parts of the labour movement that has yet to be healed. I will naturally take my share of the blame for failing in that exercise of persuasion.

But others have to take their share of the responsibility as well. The public-sector leadership, whatever its private views, and unlike the public at large, was quite unwilling to accept the logic of restraint in face of recession, and was unable to see the opportunity being presented. More power-sharing and more job security in exchange for "Rae Days." I learned that the leadership of the public-sector unions were more interested in the "sacredness" of contracts than they were in the importance of jobs, more concerned with protecting the full benefits of the survivors than the fate of the people tossed overboard. They, as does Buzz Hargrove, think this makes them better socialists. I disagree. It puts short-term expediency before long-term solidarity.

This underlines a major difference between life in the private sector and the public sector. The period from 1945 on had been a time of unparalleled growth, and a culture of continuing gains and steady improvements took strong hold in those parts of the economy where trade unions had strength. The idea that the market might contract and would demand different responses from business was almost inconceivable to a generation of workers and their leaders. I can remember when working for the United Steelworkers in the early 1970s and attending conferences in the U.S. and Canada, the union had 1.3 million members and was forcing gains in benefits, pensions, and wages across the continent: employment security was taken for granted, and what counted was making constant improvements in the "private legislation," i.e. contracts and collective agreements, which marked relations between company and union.

The blissful security and forward motion of this world began to crumble in the mid 1970s with the oil crisis and the arrival in North America of the Japanese car: symbol of the new competition and the global economy. Canada bought some time through the late seventies, but a new reality hit home in the early 1980s with the deepest recession since the war. Companies in Canada and the U.S. demanded concessions; they shut plants and moved them to places where unions couldn't organize. They introduced new technologies which made workers redundant, and which put great pressures on those plants which still employed large numbers of people.

The first reaction to this new world from the private-sector trade-union leadership was pure and simple resistance: strikes, fights, confrontation. It was rhetorically satisfying, and what the membership initially demanded. But the grim reality of lost jobs and lost towns and communities forced a different attitude. In the Steelworkers, for example, the early 1980s in the U.S. saw a devastation of the steel economy in the north-eastern and mid-west U.S. To continue to wallow in the rhetoric and tactics of the 1950s was pointless: the union had to become involved in helping to find a solution, even to the point of buying the company.

"Hitting the wall" means something very real in the private sector. It means a lost job, a community devastated, a padlock on the company gate, and a foreclosure sign on the front lawn. During the last fifteen years, these facts have forced changes in the behaviour of most private-sector unions.

Resistance to the need for a different approach has been strongest in the autoworkers: Canadian refusal to go along with concessions to Chrysler accepted by unionists in the U.S. eventually led to the creation of a separate union in Canada. The underlying economics—principally a lower dollar and lower health-care costs—has always favoured Canadian production in the auto business, and this in turn has meant a different attitude could prevail toward concessions between Canada and the U.S. This will continue to be the case until the underlying economics of production in Canada vs. the U.S. and other jurisdictions changes. When that changes and the issue of plant location and Canadian production becomes more problematic, a different response from the union will have to follow. It is also important to distinguish between what people say and what they are prepared to do: local concessions frequently happen despite brave national speeches to the contrary.

Life in the public sector is perceived differently, and this in turn leads to different challenges in managing change. What we went through in 1992 and 1993 has its strong parallels with what happened in Quebec a decade earlier. A major problem in public finances had to be met head on. There is no way to deal with a problem of this dimension without dealing with public-sector wages and compensation. Either large-scale lay-offs or changes in public salaries or both are inevitable.

It's also worth remembering that Roosevelt's New Deal reduced public-sector salaries unilaterally, and that his first piece of legislation was to reduce the size of pensions for veterans from the First World War. He was dealing with different expectations and a different time.

When these issues are raised publicly—what it means to hit the wall and why this can happen as much in the public sector as in the world of private business—the forces of denial are well at work. "That's not a wall, it's a door, or even a window; don't be such a dupe of the right, we can always borrow to meet the deficit; the deficit is not a real problem, it's a manufactured problem that you shouldn't be worrying about."

A padlock on the company gate is not a matter of opinion. A speech by a premier or a finance minister is. Threats of "what might happen" are seen as just that—threats—and therefore unreal. Political choices are everything, and the economic world is what we choose to make it: this is a blissfully attractive siren call, and so far has seduced most of the political left.

It was certainly the message of public-sector trade-union leadership in the spring of 1993. We were quickly denounced as quislings to the cause, as neo-conservative betrayers, as bad as the Liberals and Tories. I was hung in effigy, burned, and called every name in the book. Floyd was pilloried in his own community, Sudbury, and shouted down at local party meetings by some of his long-standing supporters. Bumper stickers, buttons, demonstrations, T-shirts, the whole paraphernalia of popular protest was brought to bear against us by the leadership of teachers, doctors, and the nearly one million Ontarians who are paid by the taxpayer.

Michael Decter and his team tried their level best for eight full weeks at the Royal York Hotel to bring the discussions down to earth. We began to feel we were making some progress when we got some signs and signals in private that were a little different and better than the public declarations. As we approached the deadline at the beginning of June 1993, Michael and Ross McClellan were both reasonably optimistic that wiser heads would prevail. We had found a little more fiscal room because several years of public-sector restraint in wages would lower the requirements on our financial contributions to pension plans.

As it turned out, our even mentioning the issue of pensions in the discussions gave the unions the excuse to go off the rails again. On the eve of the deadline, the leaders of CUPE, the teachers, OPSEU, and the OMA (an unholy alliance if there ever was one) were seen on the evening news chanting "Solidarity Forever" and ripping up our final suggestions for a settlement. I got a call late that Thursday night from a depressed and perplexed Michael Decter, and we agreed to meet to consider the fallout the next day.

Our options were pretty clear: The budget had already been brought down, and showed that a further $2 billion had to be found from the government and its transfer partners. A partial retreat was not possible. We were too far committed to the principle of shared restraint to pull back. The only issue was how it would be done. Either bring in a law, or simply take out the money and let all the transfer partners, the hospitals, universities, cities and towns, and school boards find their own way to save the $2 billion.

There were good arguments for either option, and in the end we arrived at a compromise, a bit of both. I held a press conference at Queen's Park the afternoon after Liz Barkley, president of the Ontario Secondary School Teachers' Federation, and Sid Ryan of CUPE did their singing and ripping up routine. *The Toronto Star* had me "breathless and visibly shaken," but in fact I was calm and serene.

I felt then, and feel today, that the women and men in the public sector in Ontario were poorly served by their leaders who were caught in a time-warp and a rhetorical swamp that they were unable to leave. They were aided and abetted by the usual gang of would-be proletarian anarchists who were only too happy to attack a social democratic government no matter what it did, and by some on the left who could never adjust to the necessary discipline of political responsibility.

Our caucus meeting after the weekend and our cabinet discussions that same week confirmed the course: the vast majority of caucus, with some strong and eloquent dissents, favoured some kind of legislation to protect the lowest-paid, and to ensure a common standard across the public sector. Minister of Labour Bob Mackenzie wanted to go the legislative route. So did Floyd Laughren, whose advice was crucial in these matters. Within cabinet, Frances Lankin, Dave Christopherson, and Anne Swarbrick were the most troubled by legislation. Bud Wildman had been a negotiator for the OSSTF in the early 1970s, and his wife, Anne, was still a teacher. He expressed deep concerns about what we were doing as well, but ultimately accepted the majority view.

The caucus was a better "focus group" than the cabinet, with a broader range of opinion. The fact that such a convincing majority wanted legislation and felt that the intransigence of the public-sector leadership was completely out of keeping with their membership and certainly with the wider public moved me as well. I met with Judy Darcy and let her know of the way feeling was going in the caucus. She was still unmoved: even at this late date there was no revised or compromise position coming from the leadership. Their thinking must have been that we were bluffing, and that an NDP government would never bring in legislation.

In the end, a few members of caucus did vote against the bill, with Karen Haslam resigning as a junior minister. But what was remarkable was that the political will to stay the course was so strong: at an NDP provincial council meeting that June in Gananoque there were emotional speeches on both sides, Steven Langdon in particular denouncing the idea of legislation as contrary to everything a government like ours should be about. There were equally strong views from the floor that the Social Contract route was better than mass lay-offs.

There was a theological feel to the whole discussion. Words like: "the sanctity of collective bargaining," "Contracts are sacred," "This is not about money—this is about the inviolability of collective agreements." The public-sector union leadership was in fact being asked to engage in a serious discussion about job security and change. The premise was that there had to be a trade-off on costs. It was easier for them to blame the government, join hands in chanting, and hope that we would back down. If we didn't back down, they could always just blame the government for any difficulties, and not have to share responsibility for any momentary unpopularity. It was a simple, political calculation on their part, and while we tried for a full half-year to persuade them of the long-term difficulties they would cause for themselves and their members, this was their chosen route.

Had we wanted to simply "teach them a lesson," the simplest route would have been for us to take the money away from their employers and leave them all to the whim of the "sanctity of the market." I have no doubt, especially now, that this might well have been the smarter political route for the government. We knew that in June of 1993. What we couldn't accept was the tens of thousands of unemployed. I can't accept it now as the Tories proudly declare the end of "Rae Days" and the end of thousands of jobs in the service of the public. Better a "Rae Day"—or two or ten—in the context of a long-term job than no job at all.

As the reader can tell, I am unrepentant about the logic of the Social Contract. An economy in recession means those who are paid by the taxpayer have to show some restraint. Our problem in government was in not realizing how quickly inflation was falling, how dramatically revenues were falling, how fast welfare numbers would explode. In this, as in so many other matters, we were the prisoners of our own rhetoric and past conduct. We had, in opposition, been unremitting opponents of wage and price controls in 1975 and again in 1982. Indeed, we had pushed the opposition to public-sector wage controls to extraordinary levels in the early 1980s, delaying the passage of Tory legislation for months.

Every social democratic government in existence across the world has had to learn this lesson, and every trade-union leadership has had to come to terms with the consequences. I am convinced that if we had been able to persuade the leadership of the trade-union movement, and the professions, of the necessity and logic and fairness of what we needed to do, we would still be in government today. The exaggerated and ideological approach of our opponents would be a matter of late-night speechifying in private rather than the grim reality of public policy.

Some kind of broader understanding that transcends the self-interest of the market-place and its contracts is necessary to offset the harshness of private whim. The public sector is too vast to be run out of a central bureaucracy. It is also too important in the services it provides and its role in the modern economy to be left to the machinations of purely private gain.

Canapress Photo Service

"Always leave them laughing…"
Resigning from the House of Commons in 1982.
In the foreground is Ed Broadbent and Ian Deans, and
next to me are Neil Young, Bob Ogle and Bill Blakie.

Honouring Tommy Douglas in
Oshawa, 1983. Ed Broadbent,
Tommy Douglas and me, soon
after my election as leader.

My support team, Michael Lewis and David Agnew, 1985.

A RARE PHOTO.
THE ONLY EXISTING PICTURE OF FIVE LEADERS OF THE CCF/NDP
AT A DINNER HONOURING TED JOLLIFFE.
FROM LEFT: MICHAEL CASSIDY, DONALD MACDONALD,
TED JOLLIFFE, BOB RAE, STEPHEN LEWIS.

The Toronto Star

POTENTIAL PREMIER AS POTENTIAL JAILBIRD.
PROTESTING TEMAGAMI IN SEPTEMBER 1989.

GREETING NELSON MANDELA AS LEADER OF THE OPPOSITION
IN MAY 1990.

A GRAVESTONE AT THE JEWISH CEMETARY
IN ZIDIKAI, LITHUANIA.

ZIDIKAI, LITHUANIA WHICH ARLENE AND I VISITED
IN THE WINTER OF 1990.

Norm Betts/The Toronto Sun

THERE'S NOTHING LIKE THE FEEL OF A SUCCESSFUL CAMPAIGN.
DADDY AND HIS BIGGEST FANS, LATE AUGUST 1990.

"IF ONLY ALL CAUCUS MEETINGS COULD BE THIS CHEERY."
THE FIRST MEETING AFTER THE ELECTION, SEPTEMBER 1990.

Michael Libby

"PREMIER BOB" SWEARING IN AT CONVOCATION HALL, SEPTEMBER
1990, WITH LIEUTENANT-GOVERNOR LINCOLN ALEXANDER.

Tibor Kolley/The Globe and Mail

STEADY AS A ROCK.
WITH DEPUTY PREMIER FLOYD LAUGHREN AT QUEEN'S PARK.

GOING FOR A WALK. WITH SASKATCHEWAN PREMIER ROY ROMANOW
AT THE LESTER PEARSON BUILDING DURING THE CONSTITUTIONAL
DISCUSSIONS OF AUGUST 1992.

Canapress Photo Service

HE'S NOT SMILING. WITH
PRIME MINISTER BRIAN MULRONEY AT
HARRINGTON LAKE, JULY 1991.

HE IS SMILING. WITH LAURENT
BEAUDOIN, CHAIRMAN OF BOMBARDIER
AT THE SIGNING CEREMONY FOR DE
HAVILLAND, FEBRUARY 1992.

BDS Studios

SHARING A LIGHTER MOMENT WITH HRH THE PRINCE OF WALES IN SUDBURY. OCTOBER 1991.

BDS Studios

"NICE WORK IF YOU CAN GET IT."
LIEUTENANT GOVERNOR LINCOLN ALEXANDER ENGROSSED IN CONVERSATION WITH PRINCESS DIANA AND ARLENE.

THE LINE THAT DIDN'T QUITE HAPPEN.
WITH DOUG GILMOUR AND WENDEL CLARK AT QUEEN'S PARK
IN JUNE 1993.

DANIEL JOHNSON AND I IN QUEBEC CITY, SUMMER 1994.

Courtesy of the Government of Quebec

THE CABINET, 1994.

Courtesy of the Government of Ontario

AT THE RHODES SCHOLARS' REUNION IN WASHINGTON D.C.
WITH PRESIDENT BILL CLINTON, JUNE 1993.

The Toronto Star

MY SMARTEST SPEECH.
AT THE BLUE JAYS' VICTORY CELEBRATION IN OCTOBER 1993.

Canapress Photo Service

MEETING WITH PRIME MINISTER YITZHAK RABIN IN OTTAWA JUST
BEFORE MY VISIT TO ISRAEL.

WITH ROSA PARKS AT A HUMAN RIGHTS
CEREMONY JUST OUTSIDE WINDSOR,
AUGUST 1994.

Julien LeBourdais

A HAPPY MOMENT AS PREMIER.
WITH A YOUNG SUPPORTER AND FORTUNATO "LUCKY" RAO,
AN NDP STALWART IN THE ITALIAN COMMUNITY, AUGUST 1994.

Courtesy of the Prime Minister's Office

WITH PRIME MINISTER CHRETIEN AND TEAM CANADA PREMIERS AT THE GREAT WALL OF CHINA, NOVEMBER 1994.

WITH MY TEACHER SIR ISAIAH BERLIN AT A CEREMONY AWARDING HIM AN HONORARY DOCTORATE AT THE UNIVERSITY OF TORONTO.

Ed Regan/The Globe and Mail

"THEN HAPPY I THAT LOVE AND AM BELOVED."
WITH ARLENE ON ELECTION NIGHT, JUNE 8, 1995.

Chapter Fourteen

ANYONE CAN SAIL
IN GOOD WEATHER

The experience of power changed me. I have already described the difficulties we faced with the labour movement over the Social Contract and the challenges of constitutional reform. But business, government bureaucracy, the party, and the media itself were all parts of the rough seas we had to navigate.

In reading this story, the reader knows the end—at least so far. This is not a tale with the simple message that a politician was brought down by a conspiracy of the mighty forces of evil. I made my share of mistakes, and these contributed to the political defeat of the government. But the obstacles to our re-election were not all self-created. The business establishment was appalled at our election, and after catching its breath resolved to bring us down. The government bureaucracy at senior levels was equally determined to wait us out, and in true passive-aggressive fashion resist change. The party, both inside and outside government, had enormous difficulty overcoming the "barking dog catches the car" syndrome. And the media at once exaggerated our problems and ignored our achievements, steadily and systematically.

This is not to lay blame, but simply to describe the force of the hurricane. As the captain of the ship no doubt I could have done a

better job, and been the author of fewer miscalls than I was. I had
fewer friends than I needed and fuelled an unrealistically ambi-
tious agenda at the beginning. I can't now claim to be objective,
but can tell the story as I saw it and lived it. Others have, and will,
tell a different tale. That's life.

↬ ↳

Ironically, car insurance was not a major thrust of the 1990 campaign because of memories of how our election efforts in 1987
had been mixed with huge problems. Every case of an unhappy
customer was met the next day with a detailed list of the errors
and infractions of the wayward driver. We decided not to make it
a major plank in 1990. Populist yes, on first blush. But on closer
examination a dog's breakfast.

Upon our election, the party was determined that we simply
follow in the footsteps of the Western provinces on the car insurance issue. That was also the strong advice of Allan Blakeney and
Howard Pawley and the initial feeling of caucus. I appointed Peter
Kormos to the cabinet because of his tremendous interest in the
issue, put him in charge of the file, and set up a small task force to
get the plan ready. We announced our intentions in the Throne
Speech on November 20, 1990.

Trouble started almost as soon as we began. The first was
Kormos himself. He was an impossible colleague, and an even
more difficult minister. He missed meetings, threw tantrums, and
belittled his colleagues in cabinet committee. I asked him to get
his act together, but it was clear I was just Big Nurse to him, yet
another authority figure whose nose he would find a way to
tweak. And tweak he did, and not just on car insurance.

On his own he had decided to declare war on the beer companies and their advertising, asserting that what they put on TV was
too sexy and exploitative. This became a silly sideshow. Then,
totally inconsistently, he decided to pose as *The Toronto Sun*'s
Sunshine Boy. This was a soap opera that could only run until I
pulled the plug.

I fired him from the cabinet on March 18, 1991, just before the
House came back from spring break. The press story was that I

had fired him for "appearing fully clothed in *The Toronto Sun*." Not true. I fired him because he was a royal pain. I knew I had enough support in the party and caucus to get away with it. I lost no sleep over this decision.

Kormos was sidelined, but the car-insurance issue was not. I gave the responsibility to Brian Charlton, who was an extraordinarily hardworking and dogged minister. As it turned out, he was also a true believer on car insurance, but ready to work as a member of a team. Through the spring of 1991 we engaged Peat Marwick to do a comprehensive study on the job impacts, and sought more advice on our legal liabilities, as well as the practical dimensions of what needed to be done.

The conclusions were very tough. Lower rates were possible, but not guaranteed, and only if we abandoned the right to sue, a touchstone for Kormos. Job losses would be exceptionally high. If we provided some compensation for layoffs, a greater burden would be thrown back on the rates. If we lost the legal battle over expropriation of business and goodwill with the insurance companies, the costs would be greater still.

Cabinet discussions were at once emotional and complex. We kept sending the minister and his team away to come up with something that solved the problem of the day. Meanwhile, the caucus was increasingly uneasy and divided between those who had followed Kormos into the Valley of the Right To Sue, and those who just wanted an issue that was uncomplicated and they could win.

By June of 1991 it was obvious we were in a swamp. The Peat Marwick report showed job losses of up to 15,000. The legal opinions didn't help, pointing to big potential liabilities. The prospect of having to shell out vast sums in a couple of years (just before an election) and increase premiums to pay for it made me unhappy. Above all, I lost faith in our ability to manage an issue of this size and complexity given everything else we had on our agenda. Another day, another time, perhaps, but now seemed impossible.

After David Agnew and I agreed that something dramatic had to be done, the problem then became how to widen the circle.

Key policy staff like Ross McClellan and Chuck Rachlis agreed quickly. Both possessed great humour, and both had been with me for a long time. Chuck came way from a quick session saying, "This is the only thing we've done on car insurance since 1985 that makes any sense."

Ross was even more blunt. "We don't have the horses to get this done. Shut it down now."

I started with my colleagues on P&P, who were reluctant in different degrees, but who knew the difficulties we faced if we didn't change course. Shelley Martel, like almost all the northerners in cabinet and caucus, was resolutely opposed. Her father, Elie, was even more emotional, saying for him it was a fundamental commitment. "You break this and we're sunk."

Floyd Laughren, Dave Cooke, Frances Lankin, and Ruth Grier were more sanguine. All had wrestled with the competing plans and were equally daunted at what it had already done to our agenda. All agreed it should be dropped, with varying degrees of enthusiasm.

After carrying P&P we had a cabinet discussion which was similarly divided, but also leaned to dropping the idea of public auto insurance. Brian Charlton was not a happy camper, but after a long private discussion agreed that he would support whatever course was adopted by the majority of caucus. He was still determined to go ahead with his package of reforms that would increase benefits and improve the lot of accident victims.

This set the stage for our retreat at Honey Harbour at the beginning of September.

Changing our minds about car insurance meant that we had "broken a promise." It is of course better, in life as in politics, to keep your promises. But when I look at the Harris experience, I wonder if this is always the wisest course. If conditions change, if circumstances are different, a rigid and robotlike execution of commitments often made in haste and imperfect judgment is unwise and even a public disservice. Mike Harris has already broken his word on health care. There will be others, because he will have to respond to events over which he has no control.

Which is another way of saying—if you make a dumb promise in politics, it's even dumber to keep it. So make fewer promises. I wish I had.

← →

In the first days after our election, I made a point of reassuring everyone that I wanted to govern in the interests of the whole province, and that this included business. Yet it was clear that for many we were not really a legitimate government. As one elder statesman put it to me, "You have to understand—your becoming premier was never part of my lifescript."

Our first problem was social. Who you know, and who knows you, is an important part of life. The business élite, for the most part, didn't really know us, and we didn't know them. One of my friends from law school who had gone on to a large Bay Street firm was suddenly called in by his senior partners when they heard that he knew me. This gave rise to the "my cleaning lady's in the cabinet" joke that says everything about the continuing social divide in this country.

Arlene used to joke that before we were married she didn't know there was such a gap between Protestants and Catholics—they were all Christians to her. So too with us and the business community. It took time to learn the differences and nuances, the skills and talents, those who were prepared on a personal basis to make a contribution, and those who would stab us in the front as well as in the back. In the first few months of government we were playing a game of "getting to know you," with its inevitable posturing and gamesmanship.

No one was more helpful in this regard than my brother John. We did not share political loyalties, but our personal bond was never stronger. As a vice-president of the Power Corporation he knew well a great many leaders in the business community. Personally, he is discretion and integrity personified. He admires these qualities in others. We continued to agree to disagree on some policies, but at a personal level his advice was invaluable. We could talk a kind of shorthand with each other about issues and people that helped me chart some rocky waters.

I was also forced to get to know some business people better than others, because of the impact of the recession. The leaders of some of Ontario's best-known companies came into my office seeking direct assistance, bridge loans, whatever would do the trick. We created a specific programme—the Manufacturing Recovery Program—to process these requests and deal with the demands and entreaties with some objectivity. We also established a special team under Tim Armstrong, and relied on the able assistance of Bill Corcoran, who had been vice-chair at Scotia McLeod, as an assistant deputy minister. Aiding Armstrong and Corcoran was a talented crew of industry restructuring analysts led by Peter Tanaka.

I've described some of this restructuring earlier in the book. The demands were relentless, because of the severity of the recession. Our responses were not always popular. Some companies could not be helped, which made some businessmen angry. Some could be helped, which often made their competitors angry.

Of course the "story" about our government was that we were bad for business. This in turn drove the media to throw gasoline on any small flame. So it was, for example, that Cyrus Eaton convinced the media that Ontario was singularly unfriendly to business because we wouldn't fall for his scheme to buy Piper Aircraft.

Let me explain. The Piper Aircraft Company of Vero Beach, Florida, had been placed in receivership because it kept getting sued by unhappy passengers and the widows of unsuccessful pilots. Product-liability laws in the U.S. made the company responsible whenever a Piper fell out of the air, which was either frequently or hardly ever, depending on whether you were a plaintiff or a defendant in a law suit.

Enter Cyrus Eaton, Jr., whose father had established a strong affection for Canada. Cyrus Eaton, Jr. is an entrepreneur of sorts who had established some marketing rights for whatever remained of the Piper Aircraft empire. He proceeded to get in touch with every Canadian premier, advising them that their province could be the beneficiary of a huge investment, which could in turn create more than a thousand direct manufacturing jobs, and endless other possibilities.

News of this bonanza was also leaked to the press, who naturally responded in an appropriately Pavlovian way, demanding to know what we were all going to do to get these jobs. I asked our team in the ministry to get whatever information they could from Mr. Eaton, which they did.

Bill Corcoran is a shrewd investment adviser with a great sense of humour. When he and Tim Armstrong came to see me, he just smiled and said, "There's nothing there." I had visions of a plane factory disappearing on me and heading to Saskatchewan or Nova Scotia. I insisted they meet with Eaton to see if anything was possible. This they dutifully did, and apparently Bill Corcoran did what any tough-minded investor would do when meeting with someone with a bright idea and not much else. "Show us the colour of your money, Mr. Eaton, and we'll see what can be done."

Eaton left the meeting in a rage, and called a press conference saying this socialist province didn't seem interested in a major investment from the United States. He was going to go somewhere where he was more welcome. The press lapped it up. It was yet another bad hair day for the premier in a scrum and question period.

Cyrus Eaton never did find a Canadian premier who would buy his story. And it wasn't Ontario socialism that did him in, but Bill Corcoran's business sense. I kept getting calls from people who'd been burned in some other investment scheme involving Eaton, but when I asked them to go public they declined, because "I don't want everyone to know how stupid I was," as one put it. Better that the government look stupid for turning away an entrepreneur.

While I can still make a strong case that business and the province benefited from the approach of the first budget, there is little doubt that the projection of a $10-billion deficit for 1991-92 transformed doubt and ill-will into outright opposition. Yet even this had its ironies and contradictions. Investment dealers and bond traders in Toronto, New York, London, and Tokyo would shake their heads at the same time as they fattened their wallets on large commissions, and complained to the skies if they didn't get their share of the deals. And we were probably the only government they'd ever dealt with that didn't send a political bagman around the day after a bond float to collect money for the party.

In my first meeting with one leading investment banker, he spent sixty minutes with me, equally divided between warning me about the deficit, worrying about a sluggish economy, wanting to make sure I understood that if the government was going to borrow money his company should get a fair share of the commissions, and closing with a plea not to reduce funding for the hospital with which he was involved. I don't think for a moment he saw anything hypocritical or contradictory in what he was saying.

I quickly got used to the fact that everyone wanted access, and everyone wanted something. It's simply human nature and the reality of politics. It took me some time to distinguish between a real need and a constant complaint. Ontario did need to make changes in the relations between business and government. Government intrinsically tends to over-regulation, empire building, and unnecessary interference. This is true of all governments, at all levels, of whatever stripe: indeed, it is true of all large, bureaucratic organizations.

Ontario did have a competitiveness problem, but this was not the product of any one government. The Canadian dollar had gone too high for our exports. Interest rates were too punishing for all our businesses, and everyone suffered. Some public-sector and private-sector wages had risen higher and faster than our economic competitors, and were helping to drive costs higher than the cost of living. Ontario was not seen as hungry enough for new business and new investment. Bureaucracy was too big and inefficient. We were lousy marketers. American states were much better at being aggressive and attracting new jobs. We were over-taxed and over-regulated.

This has always been the business mantra. It reached a fever pitch after the election of 1990. There is a kernel of truth in all of it. These were not things that New Democrats liked to admit to ourselves, though they were increasingly obvious to most people.

What we tried to do was to address these issues without abandoning our commitment to social justice. We ended up satisfying too few people to get the credit we needed for another term.

Our approach to environmental and planning regulation, for example, was to largely follow John Sewell's advice in his commission report. We devolved more power to the municipalities, and gave them the power to integrate the "green" agenda and the need for development. We reduced the time for environmental approvals from 180 days to 30 days. We passed the Environmental Bill of Rights in 1993 after a long period of consultation with the private sector and the environmental community. Ruth Grier's efforts at bringing all sections of the community together was a remarkable achievement. We took the same thrust in our resource policy, where at one and the same time we increased the number of parks and protected spaces, and also expanded forest production with new technologies using more waste products. The economy of northern Ontario was on the edge of disaster when we took office. When we left, it was stronger and more diverse than it had ever been. Both Bud Wildman and Howard Hampton were strong ministers with a keen sense of the needs of the North. Their efforts produced the province's second largest park, Wabakimi Provincial Park, 2.2 million acres (900,000 hectares), as well as eight new lumber mills. Wabakimi is bigger than Prince Edward Island. We also established the largest urban park in North America and through David Crombie's good offices created the Waterfront Trail, which reconnected the communities along Lake Ontario with the natural wonder on their doorstep.

Both the Planning and Municipal Statute Law Amendment Act (1994) and the Crown Forest Sustainability Act (1994) were passed at the end of our government's mandate, and both reflected a more mature relationship between business and government than the hysterical opposition we faced to Bill 40, the labour-relations bill.

There was something almost inevitable and ritualistic about the *sturm and drang* of the business lobby over changes to the Labour Relations Act. The first businessman to come and see me after my election was not an Ontarian, but the chairman of Mitsubishi Canada, Arthur Hara from British Columbia. Hara phoned me before my swearing in, explaining that he was a good friend of Mike Harcourt's. I invited him to drop in as soon as possible, which he did.

Hara explained to me that he was not a New Democrat, but like many Japanese Canadians felt a strong bond with our party because of the stand against internment and political discrimination that had been taken during the Second World War by leading members of the old C.C.F. He then urged me to bring labour and business together, and get them to see what was in their common interest. He said that ironically I was probably in a better position to do this than any other Ontario leader. He also said that Japanese investors would be watching closely to see how successful we were.

Distrust between business and labour was high, but not because of provincial politics. The business community had become a deeply politicized supporter of the free-trade agreement, the GST, and the overall agenda of the Mulroney government. At the same time, the labour movement was adamantly opposed to all these initiatives, to put it mildly. As business figures became bolder in their support for the political agenda of the Business Council on National Issues and the C.D. Howe Institute, labour's own "anti-corporate agenda" line became more extreme as well. Rhetoric put people at opposite extremes. There were hardly any opportunities for common ground or mutual respect. Quite the contrary: the discourse was rude, crude, and intemperate, on both sides.

The debate around changes to the Labour Relations Act quickly deteriorated into a slanging match, which has never really ended to this day. We started with the simple proposition that it is a good thing for employees to seek to join trade unions. This was rejected outright by most employer groups because they said it made it look as if the government was "favouring" unions. This signalled to me that the employer world of the nineties was very different from the earlier Ontario version where the sense of legitimacy of both sides gave rise to the quiet, corporatist spirit of the Davis years.

Anti-union sentiment and non-union companies are clearly on the rise in North America. Union organizing activity has fallen to an all-time low in the U.S., and in many sectors in Ontario American-owned companies were clearly hoping to follow the lead of their parents in remaining clear of the "union virus." Some observers have suggested that our efforts at reform were not consensual enough, and that this was a break from previous tradition. This assumes that a consensus for a reasonable number of reforms was ever possible, an assumption that neglects the political and social dynamics of our time.

We certainly consulted, both formally and informally, to the nth degree. I set up broader Premier's Councils to deal with both economic and social issues and had a couple of informal dinners of union and management leaders within weeks of becoming premier. They were not pleasant occasions, with a lot of swearing and finger-pointing. Nothing productive came out of them. Labour and management lawyers then produced papers which showed—as if it needed showing—how far apart everyone was. We then decided to push ahead with our own draft proposals.

This was followed by the introduction of Bill 40, which made it easier for employees to unionize, and harder for an employer to break a union. It brought cases to the labour board faster, allowed for the reinstatement of workers found to be unfairly harassed by an employer, and prevented the use of replacement workers during the course of a legal strike. It was, without question, progressive labour legislation, although it didn't go as far as the unions had asked us to. We were to amend it several times, but didn't touch the core provisions of the bill.

Business and editorial response was sweeping. My favourite was a polite, but blunt private exchange with the major newspaper publishers of the province, who made it clear that their business and editorial views were one and the same, and this would continue with a vengeance. Something of the power structure of the province's media became only too clear. I had, after all, walked on the picket lines at CFTO and *The Toronto Star* as opposition leader, and picket-line violence in both instances had strengthened my view that the law needed to be changed. Now the publishers were only reminding me that newspapers were, above all, a business, and that they didn't like what we were doing.

Did these views affect their coverage and view of the government? Of course, absolutely. It would be absurd to pretend otherwise. The government is a democratically elected body and the people have the right to know a great deal about it. The problem is the only place to find out anything is through business-owned media with its own political agenda or preference while pretending to be an objective witness to events. Hogwash.

There was one attempt to reach a compromise, but this never really went anywhere. I got a forthright, provocative letter from a well-known Toronto lawyer, Bill "Whammy" Macdonald. He said he was speaking for a number of business leaders in wanting to find a way out. I invited him and Peter Barnes to a meeting to see what this might be. I indicated that if some middle ground could be found, I would be only too pleased to help make it happen. The initiative evaporated almost as quickly as it started. Something Macdonald said in that one conversation may help explain. "A number of us believe that if you succeed here we could be insuring your re-election." It was clear to me that this was not something Bill Macdonald's friends would want to see.

Any successful partnership makes all the partners look good. While there was eventually a group of business people who developed a strong enough regard for me and what we were trying to do to actually want to see me re-elected, it would be naïve to think that this was ever more than a distinguished and clear-seeing minority. Business as a class wanted our government to fail, and was prepared to do whatever it could to make sure we did fail.

The furor over the labour bill died down almost as soon as it passed, in the fall of 1992, despite claims to the contrary. Investment in Ontario grew rapidly in 1993 and 1994, which must have meant we were "open for business." The fundamentals of our competitiveness improved dramatically. Labour productivity increased. Manufacturing exports were never stronger than in the years immediately following the labour legislation, and we attracted more foreign and domestic capital investment than ever before. Our success in controlling health-care costs, as well as the lower dollar and lower payroll costs, put us at a huge competitive advantage to the United States. This was part of the real Ontario story from 1990 to 1995, and now that Mike Harris is elected, business can shout it to the rooftops without being afraid that they'll make the NDP look good.

In fact, on the ground in the private sector labour-management relations improved. The recession on its own did a lot to focus everyone's attention. Demands were down, and the passage of Bill 40 meant that in a unionized environment management didn't want a strike. The result was the longest period of labour peace, and the strongest improvement in labour productivity, since the war.

Art Hara's idea happened without either side really being able to admit that they were partners. Japanese investors and many others drove up values on the stock market and, more important, demonstrated their confidence by creating thousands of new jobs.

← →

In the litany of bad news that came to me in my first days after the election of 1990, Ontario Hydro's saga stood out. The Peterson Liberals had, despite their earlier opposition, been persuaded to go ahead with the Darlington nuclear project. This was completed in the spring of 1990 at a total cost of well over 12 billion dollars, an overrun of at least 5 billion dollars from the earliest estimates. Under Hydro's accounting rules, this capital cost would now have to be paid for in new rates, which could mean annual increases in double-digit numbers.

In addition, Hydro had produced a report in 1989 which called for new nuclear expansion in the future, as well as huge increases in other generating stations. The projected capital costs were simply enormous, and all this was set to be added to the cost of living, and the cost of doing business in Ontario.

My meetings with the chairman of Ontario Hydro, Bob Franklin, were cordial enough, but neither of us was happy. The Hydro board had many senior people on it who clearly regarded the government of the day as an inconvenience. One of my favourite encounters was with the executive committee of the Hydro board, where two notables, Gordon Bell of the Bank of Nova Scotia and Alex Mackintosh of the old Toronto law firm of Blake Cassels, made it very clear that they were running things and the sooner I learned that the better off everyone would be.

All this reminded me once again of Floyd Laughren's line that the first thing an NDP government should do was to nationalize Ontario Hydro. Like all good lines, it points to an important truth. A large organization like Hydro develops its own personality, its own style, and a stubborn sense of its independence. This was true in Adam Beck's day, and is true today. Making a Crown entity of Hydro's size responsive to any elected government is never easy.

Bob Franklin served as both chairman and president of Hydro, and wasn't happy with the proposition that the government wanted to appoint its own chairman. He decided not to accept a reappointment as president. The Board responded to my appointment of Marc Eliesen, the deputy minister of energy and a former chair of Manitoba Hydro, as chairman by unilaterally appointing a veteran of the nuclear-power expansion, Al Holt, as president. They sent me a long letter with the news.

I didn't know Al Holt, but I recognized a power play. I made it clear that Marc Eliesen was in charge, and that there would be a changing of the guard at the Board. There were angry squawks. These were less important than the dilemma facing us all: Hydro was too big, too rigid, too bureaucratic, too costly. It had amassed a debt of some $38 billion, for which the province was responsible, and whose financing under then-existing plans presumed a constant increase in rates way over inflation indefinitely into the future.

Marc, to my surprise, soon announced that he was moving to British Columbia. This left me with the challenge of finding a new chair and CEO to take on an unprecedented challenge.

At that point, the summer of 1992, Stephen Lewis phoned with a brilliant idea. Why not ask Maurice Strong to lead Hydro? Maurice was stepping down from his position at the United Nations, where he had served as assistant secretary-general with responsibility for the environment. I had known Maurice Strong since my teenage years in Geneva. A man of truly remarkable energy, he had left school early in Manitoba, worked all over the world, and been a hugely successful entrepreneur at a young age, becoming president of the Power Corporation at thirty-four. He had a lifelong interest in public service, and a fascination with the United Nations, where he worked at several points in his career. Entrepreneur, public servant, environmentalist, agent of change: he seemed the ideal choice.

But how to get him to take it? I invited him to join me and Stephen for dinner in Toronto, which he did. His first reaction was negative. He had already decided to move to Vancouver, and to pursue his own business interests for a while. I urged him to think again, that running a business the size of Hydro would allow him to put some of his ideas into practice. I needed someone with his vision and scope to pursue change with energy and determination. He would have my full support in any difficult decision he had to make.

Maurice Strong talked it over with his wife, Hanna, and in September of 1992 agreed to take on the role as full-time chairman of Ontario Hydro. There were some eyebrows raised. To some New Democrats he was too partisan a Liberal, since he had nearly run for the Liberal Party in the late seventies. Strong also had his detractors in the business community, who felt that he moved too quickly through the ranks and couldn't necessarily be counted on to see the task through. He would travel too much they alleged, and wouldn't focus enough on the task at hand.

Maurice Strong's was the smartest single appointment I made as premier. His detractors, from my experience, were quite wrong. He got me into hot water a couple of times because of his enthusiasm for foreign projects, but in this he had my support. I wanted Hydro to take a broader view of its mission.

Above all, Maurice Strong made effective change happen at Hydro. Having made the appointment, I wasn't about to second guess every daily decision. On the broad mandate I told him the province needed rate relief, and a better relationship with the consumer and business. If that meant doing less, and doing it differently, and meant fewer employees in the long run, he would have my support. When the Hydro board made its announcement of big changes in the spring of 1993, I called Maurice a "man of courage." This drove the union nuts, and I got a very angry phone call from John Murphy, president of the Power Workers Union. Murphy had been making a series of incendiary statements about both Maurice Strong and me, and I told him that the province couldn't afford rate increases. Other, positive changes for the union could be made, but Maurice Strong and his management team had my full support.

In fact Strong's changes impacted more dramatically on management itself than anyone else. The executive team was strengthened, rates were frozen, and the capital budget that flowed from the extravagant expectations of the 1980s was slashed. At the same time, Hydro invested in research, and expanded its international horizon. During our mandate, and without massive involuntary lay-offs, the total staff complement at Hydro went from 35,000 to just over 20,000.

Maurice Strong took Hydro from a net drain on the province to a substantial contributor to its industrial turn-around. The only slight strain in our relationship came in 1994 when I insisted that management go back to the table with the union and try harder to reach a voluntary settlement in contract negotiations. In his heart I'm sure Maurice would have preferred a legislated solution. I didn't, because it would have been messy and from what I was hearing from the union a negotiated answer seemed possible, if not universally popular with management.

Strong also had his own views on preparing Hydro for a more commercial approach as a company. He and I reached an understanding on this as well: we agreed that work and studies would be done, covering a broad range of issues, but that no decisions would be made by the Board or the government before the election in 1995. I knew the party couldn't handle any more sharp ideological struggles after the Social Contract, and that this was not an issue the people of the province were burning to deal with.

The public and business and commerce are concerned above all with rates. Any government ignores this at their peril. There is also a sense that Hydro is a key public asset, which should not be sold at bargain-basement prices.

Huge transaction fees would be made by the brokerage houses and the law firms which service them if Hydro were to be privatized. It is not clear that the public would be similarly well served. At the same time, Hydro is still too big and bureaucratic, and I'm sure could be made more efficient by injecting market principles deeper into the bowels of its organization. How to do that without imperilling quality, reliability, and public accountability is a great challenge. Simplistic, ideological solutions are to be avoided at all costs.

Maurice Strong's departure after the election in 1995 deprived the province of someone with a unique sense of how to balance the values of the private and public sector. Ironically, soon after my own departure for the private sector I was visited by John Murphy, replete with charts on the achievements of the period from 1992-95, and the extraordinary advances we had made in creating a more efficient organization. He was, in effect, praising the work and ideas he had denounced with such force two years before. Once more, too late smart, too soon old. Now he and his union are fighting a tougher battle—for survival.

↞ ↠

The theory of modern government is that elected politicians decide on a broad range of policies after receiving the best possible advice from a highly skilled, politically neutral civil service, which then is given responsibility for implementing the policy.

Life is not quite this simple. The senior bureaucracy in the government of Ontario has many talented and public-spirited people. It also has its share of time-servers and careerists. A newly elected government and premier have to spend a considerable period of time sorting out who are good and talented and who aren't, and recognize the inevitable fact that people who have been working in a given area have expertise and a vested interest in having their advice accepted.

One of the best descriptions I ever heard of a ministerial briefing was that of the "Goldilocks theory of government." Each briefing on a difficult issue comes with three options. The first turns out to be much too hot. The second is much too cold. The third is, magic of magics, just right. Ministers thus eat their porridge dutifully as their masters had always intended.

Large organizations develop cultures and rules, and a power and authority structure all their own. This is very much the case in the government of Ontario. While the Tories were in power for their forty-two-year uninterrupted stint, there was no real line dividing partisan politics from public service. This was also very much the case in that extraordinary federal Liberal run from 1935 to 1957, and again in the years from 1963-1984.

David Peterson effected some changes at the top of the senior public service, and also created the Premier's Councils in an effort to make an end-run around the bureaucracy. The communications staffs of a number of ministries had a number of Liberals appointed to them, just as the Tories had put in their people before them.

I had two major managerial problems. The first was that the caucus and the cabinet were new to the world of governing. We had very few political staff with any direct government experience. This made mistakes inevitable, and we made our share. The second was ultimately more important, and we could only make a beginning of dealing with it in our term of government: the management of the Ontario public service was too inward looking and too stuck in routine, with power and authority structures that dated back decades. Information systems were outdated. There was little sense of entrepreneurship and innovation. Just getting things done was difficult, particularly when some senior bureaucrats didn't want to do it.

There were clearly many senior officials who saw their role after September 6, 1990, as representing a kind of permanent government, which would always be there long after we had gone. Much is made of political patronage and how wrong it is to have "political interference with the civil service." This is at best naïve, because it ignores the political reality that there is cronyism and patronage within the civil service itself: deputy ministers promoting their favourites, and being promoted themselves on the say of the cabinet secretary.

Peter Barnes, the cabinet secretary appointed by David Peterson, clearly saw himself as the leader of the permanent government. He would present lists of candidates for various jobs to me, and after a while I realized that the same names kept coming back again and again. I wanted new people and wanted to go outside the civil service. I also wanted to promote people from within who I felt would make a difference. At times these were people I knew; others I had never met, but I wanted people who could effect change.

The cabinet secretary approves the salaries of all the deputy ministers, and establishes the committees that appoint assistant deputy ministers. It is the key position of power and authority within the government bureaucracy. As I became more familiar with the ways of the world, I decided that I would not reappoint Peter Barnes when his term expired in September of 1992, and appoint David Agnew instead.

This decision was naturally denounced as a gross politicization of the "neutral civil service." I shifted Peter Barnes over to the Industry Ministry, with Tim Armstrong continuing to serve as a direct consultant to me on special files. My relations with Barnes remained overtly cordial, a tribute to our upbringing as the sons of public servants. He went on to make some fundamental changes in the work of his ministry, and introduced a new investor service and a much more effective approach to marketing the province. I would continue to hear rumours of his unhappiness with the government, but he always spoke directly to me of his determination to work professionally with our government. I took him at his word.

David Agnew's appointment was not an easy one, but not for the reasons the media and others might have expected. I was reluctant to lose him as a political adviser, where his calm, tough judgment was essential. He was succeeded as principal secretary by Melody Morrison, who was to prove an outstanding mediator between all the interests seeking my ear. The irony of David's appointment was that he quickly became a strong cabinet secretary in his own right. The office of the cabinet secretary was at that time across the street from the premier's office at Queen's Park—in newly renovated offices in the Whitney Block. I used to joke that the job quickly becomes the man, and it was a simple fact that as a consequence of that appointment our focus on administration improved dramatically; conversely political readiness for the next election had to start from scratch.

We didn't waste any time after the appointment in September of 1992. David and I agreed that we needed to plan for a dramatic change in organization and personnel for the new year in 1993, as well as a cabinet shuffle. We shared the view that we were trying to do too much, and that ministers and caucus members were having great difficulty giving up their role as advocates for their particular hobby horses.

"Focus, focus, focus." I couldn't blame my colleagues alone. Throughout my political career I have driven all to distraction by my reluctance to pick just one or two things to do or worry about. In opposition we would go through agonizing sessions before each new political season, and produce short-lists of special topics that would allow us to set the agenda for question period and political activity. There would then follow the inevitable improvisation by yours truly in the daily back and forth. Eyes would roll.

Halfway through the life of the government in the winter of 1993, we were still doing far too much. Every minister had a pet project, which she or he wouldn't, and couldn't, abandon. In addition, every ministry had its own policy shop determined to solve every conceivable problem with legislation, legislation, legislation. There was an unfortunate synergy between the advocacy and Fabian tendencies of many ministers and their political staffs and an irrepressible policy fixation of the middle-level civil service. The result was an agenda that was huge and almost impossible to manage.

Every NDP convention I have ever attended has added yet another ton of resolutions with legislative answers to every conceivable problem. Policy wonkishness is endemic to the New

Democratic Party, and so too to its first government in Ontario. The flip side was a persistent inability to get our message across to the public. The same culture which sees policy as everything and legislation as the answer to any question also sees communication as secondary and advertising as demeaning. We never fully grasped their importance. It is a continuation of the thought that if you only do the right thing that is enough and the truth will win out.

Successful governments have a simple agenda, relatively few items of legislation, and a communications and advertising budget to beat the band. Unsuccessful governments try to do too much, get immersed in the details of laws, and think that advertising is sinful. David Agnew and I agreed thoroughly on these verities, but were not always successful in persuading others.

We started by carrying out a real changing of the guard in the civil service and cabinet in January of 1993. It was a double trauma for me, since it meant letting go a number of able and decent people, and demoting colleagues I liked. We reduced the number of government ministries, giving strong, clear mandates to the new ministers and their deputies.

These changes were followed by the Social Contract initiative as well as the dramatic shift in culture at Ontario Hydro. We finally got the Jobs Ontario initiative up and running, and for all its growing pains it did make a difference. The plan was simple: increase investment in child care and training, and give private employers more incentives to hire people who have been on welfare or seen their unemployment insurance run out. We boosted the plan in 1994 by eliminating payroll taxes on any new employee hired. It provided real training, and real jobs, for well over 50,000 people, and was widely imitated after its introduction. The Tories were foolish to cancel the programme, since it is far more practical than so-called "workfare," which, if implemented as proposed, will prove to be both bureaucratic and punitive.

Ontario led the way in growth in Canada in 1993 and 1994. The capital programme finally started having a cumulative effect as well: Highway 407 was being built as a toll road in a fraction of the time it would have taken under the old Tory/Liberal system; we broke ground on two subway lines, and were ready with two more; the capital budget was held steady and in the end we created jobs. At the same time, we reduced the size of the management of the civil service, and through attrition and early retirement cut the overall size of the public service by more than 5,000 employees.

We also set firmly in motion reforms in three key areas: education, welfare, and the governance of the Greater Toronto Area. Dave Cooke and Charles Pascal were a formidable duo at the combined Ministry of Education and Training. Soon after they were appointed minister and deputy minister, we established a Royal Commission on Learning under the leadership of Monique Bégin and Gerry Caplan.

The Commission did a superb job and pointed to the need for a thorough overhaul of public education. The cabinet, at Cooke's urging, had a number of detailed debates and discussions prior to the Royal Commission's final report, and we responded quickly when the recommendations for early childhood education, better teacher training, a stronger role for parents, and a deeper acceptance of the need to assess students' progress all came out in December of 1994. These reforms were announced by us in a series of speeches and statements in the winter of 1995. Some have been reannounced by the Tories as their own. The difficulty is that the fiscal climate of dramatic cuts in which they are being introduced makes them less possible.

Similarly, in welfare, the success of the Jobs Ontario programme set the stage for a whole new approach. Focus on the needs of all children who live in poverty, regardless of whether their parents are working or not. We expanded the child-care budget by well over 200 per cent. Our approach was to take the disincentives to work out of the welfare system by supporting all lower-income families. The Trillium Drug Plan, which ensured for the first time that every citizen would have affordable access to therapeutic drugs, and the holiday on the employer health tax were an important beginning to an affordable, sensible approach. We ensured that people who couldn't work because of age or disability were strongly supported with a guaranteed benefit, the highest in Canada. Our next plan was to ensure that adults who could work would get a training allowance, payable provided they were enrolled in an upgrading programme and that all children whose parents were below a certain income would receive financial support.

We tried to negotiate this major change with the federal government, without success. A combined federal/provincial enriched child tax credit, and real devolution of labour market training to the province will now make it possible. Both these changes are on the agenda of the first ministers. We can only hope they really happen. Both Saskatchewan and British Columbia are taking steps in this direction.

We provided incentives rather than punishment. Our approach clashed with the Republican ideology which triumphed with Harris's bumper-sticker slogan of "workfare." Harris has, since the election, slashed the incomes of Ontario's poorest citizens, and created a climate where blaming the victim is once again in vogue. Creating work to end enforced idleness, providing education and training, all are good and necessary. We did them. Berating the poor and giving stupid and condescending advice about the price of tuna are neither good nor necessary. They are now key features of government policy.

One of my wiser appointments was giving David Crombie a role in developing ideas for the future governance of Metropolitan Toronto. I had known him since I was a student and he was a young teacher and administrator at Ryerson in the late 1960s. We were both elected to Parliament on the same day, and while I could never really understand his deep loyalty for the Tory party, I always saw him as a gifted mediator and wise soul. He accepted a provincial appointment as chair of the Waterfront Regeneration Trust and used that as a base, among other things, to provide me with advice on changing government within the Greater Toronto area.

The tax structure was a mess. There was too much government. Metro made less and less sense. But seeing the problems did not lead to easy solutions. Municipal politicians loved to hate Queen's Park but could never agree on positive change. I asked a bright municipal thinker, Joe Berridge, for his advice as well. We eventually asked Anne Golden, the head of the United Way, to lead a task force that would produce a set of recommendations for the new government after 1995.

Critics said we were just passing the buck, but in fact we were building an agenda for the second term. Change was necessary, but rather than force-feed the Ontario public, we wanted solutions that had some base in public opinion. We had learned how to govern. All told, our efforts saved and helped to create hundreds of thousands of jobs, jobs that would either have been lost or never created if we had not done what we did. The social contract saved at least forty thousand jobs. Our initiatives with individual companies did even more in the private sector. If we'd followed free-market ideology in Sault Ste. Marie or in the aerospace industry we would have lost tens of thousands of highly skilled, well-paid jobs.

In addition to the turnaround of Ontario Hydro, we could point with pride to cost-saving measures at the Workers Compensation Board, which we did with the hard-won agreement of the Ontario Federation of Labour. The province was in better shape than we found it in the recession of 1990. Our industries were competitive once again. We were attracting substantial private investment. Every indicator which had been heading below the floor in 1990 was pointing in a positive direction by 1994.

One of the best illustrations of the turnaround was the Barnes exhibit at the Art Gallery of Ontario. There had been a classically unfruitful conflict between the government and the board of the AGO early in our term, which confirmed the government's view that the Toronto elite didn't understand that the '80s were over and the elite's view that the NDP were hopeless boors.

Luckily for Ontario, Joe Rotman became the new chairman of the Art Gallery. An aggressively successful entrepreneur, Joe Rotman is also an exceedingly generous benefactor of good causes and a wise soul. He came to see me soon after his appointment in 1992 and said he wanted a new kind of partnership. We agreed to look together for new opportunities for the Gallery. We soon

found it in the extraordinary collection of an American philan-
thropist, Albert Barnes. Barnes had amassed the best private collection of French impressionist art in the world, and proceeded to
give it all to Lincoln University, a small, black, liberal arts college
in Philadelphia.

The problem was that fifty years later the Barnes Museum in
Philadelphia was in desperate need of repairs. The trustees of the
Museum needed to raise millions, and instead of selling paintings
they decided to apply to a Pennsylvania court to vary the terms of
Barnes's will to allow for an international tour.

Joe Rotman and I agreed this would be a great event for
Toronto. Joe persuaded the investment firm of Gluskin and Sheff
to sponsor the exhibit. I agreed to convince the Cabinet that this
was a great opportunity for investment. Together we put a full
court press on the Barnes trustees to get them to expand their
already approved tour to include Toronto.

The result of all this was a hugely successful exhibit at the
AGO. I certainly hoped that its success would be matched by a
political improvement.

Chapter Fifteen

HARD CHOICES

Things should have begun to turn around for us, but this didn't happen. Working in support of NDP candidates in the federal election of the fall of 1993 was very tough. Being premier can be isolating, but there was no protection from public derision. Canvassing in my own riding, with no media present, I was jeered on too many doorsteps for me to shrug it off as something happening on the surface.

Of course we had make mistakes, and the media and our opponents understandably took advantage of them. There was much chatter about "scandals" and mishaps, which left an impression with the voters. No one benefited personally; no one ran off with any money or advanced their family interest improperly; nothing that anywhere else in the Western world would have been regarded as a real scandal happened. But we were quickly nailed as a government of incompetents.

I was, in part, the author of my own misfortune, because I insisted on bringing out my own guidelines for the conduct of ministers and parliamentary assistants to supplement the existing law while the old law was being revised. This did two things. It established a standard that Mother Teresa would have found difficulty living up to all the time. It also put me in the middle of every question about ministerial conduct. We eventually solved the problem by drafting a better law, and learning from our mistakes, but by that time the political damage had been done.

So it was that the opposition and media would have a field day with me having to fend off and answer every question, instead of being able to refer any question of substance to the Conflicts Commissioner (now the Integrity Commissioner). Since I had spent some time in opposition making Liberals and Tories feel uncomfortable about their own ministers, there was understandably much joy in Mudville when pious New Democrats fell prey to the inevitable.

Evelyn Gigantes paid a heavy price for blurting out in the House the name of a mental patient, and others were raked over the coals for writing letters on the wrong stationery, or for having their staff sign letters on their behalf. Shelley Martel lost her cool in a conversation with a controversial municipal politician in Thunder Bay, Evelyn Dodds (later a Conservative candidate), and made some inaccurate statements about her having seen information about the billing practices of a Sudbury doctor. This created a controversy that dogged her for months, and eventually led to her decision to leave the cabinet when she faced the prospect of yet another cross-examination in the House on a citizen complaint about the way her ministry had handled his tax problem.

The combination of an allegation, misjudgment, and a lengthy hearing gave rise to talk of "the Martel affair." Nothing could have been more exaggerated or unfair, but politics is about impressions and perceptions. Shelley Martel was an outstanding Minister of Northern Affairs. She had great support from northern mayors and community leaders. No one did more to rebuild the economy of the North. This counted for much with me, and ultimately with her constituents. The press was hardly so fair.

In November 1992 I was coming back from a trip to Asia when I got an urgent call from David Agnew at the Vancouver Airport. I was dumbfounded to learn that John Piper, my senior media adviser, had decided to pass on information about someone's criminal record to a reporter for *The Toronto Sun*. Since this also involved an ongoing investigation at the Grandview Correctional Facility, where one of our caucus members, Will Ferguson, had been a summer worker some twenty-five years before, the opposition and the press smelled blood.

There are two theories to explain human conduct of this kind: conspiracy theories, which are most beloved by the press and the opposition, and the "screw-up" theory, which from my experience is far and away the most reliable explanation for human error. John Piper resigned the morning of November 20, 1992, before my first chat with David Agnew, and there was nothing more I could do. The opposition, of course, assumed a vast conspiracy, which was then followed by the equally predictable charge of "cover-up."

There is precious little point in worrying about "fairness" in all this: an allegation becomes an established fact. The more lurid and juicy the story, the more coverage it will receive. The press moves in a pack, and has to drive the story to higher and higher fever pitch, in a kind of comic imitation of Woodward and Bernstein. The difference is that in Watergate the press were dealing with a major matter of substance.

Political coverage in the age of television is a branch of entertainment. The forum is the scrum, question period, and the live event. Politicians play the game, along with their advisers, of trying to create the events and impressions that will make them look good on television. They use the medium, as best they can, to convey information, but more important, to convey feelings and attitudes which will prove ultimately persuasive.

Television is key. Indeed television is god. Network television in the United States, which is the centre of this universe, is increasingly driven by the ethics and tone of "Hard Copy" and Geraldo. That tone sets the mark for network news, which in turn drives the coverage, layout, and style of the modern newspaper and commercial radio. While our political culture in Canada is different from the U.S., it is less different than it was: the gap between public and private becomes blurred in a general wash about celebrity and its discontents. What someone is wearing, how they deal with a demonstrator, how they respond to the charge of personal scandal is all grist to the political mill.

By the beginning of 1994 we were on the ropes and had been all but counted out by the experts. Our poll numbers were appallingly low. I would add one more theme to the symphony of unhappiness: our commitment to a genuine agenda of equity and inclusiveness and the contrary emotions this aroused.

Relations between black and other immigrant communities and the police in the Toronto area had long been difficult, and the subject of endless reviews and commissions. Bill Davis had asked Arthur Maloney to bring forward legislation on the review of police conduct in the 1970s; Cardinal Carter and countless others had been asked for recommendations on race; some new legislation had come forward in the Peterson years. But there were still real problems.

The black community felt isolated and vulnerable, even more so as the recession began to tear deeply at the social fabric of Toronto. The police felt beleaguered by endless reviews and a bureaucracy that was becoming more complicated.

In the spring of 1992 after a major civil disturbance in Los Angeles after the acquittal of police officers who were seen to have beaten Rodney King, there was a large gathering in downtown Toronto. This eventually led to violence, and then to charges of excessive use of force. We know now that much of the violence and destruction of property on Yonge Street was caused by *agents provocateurs*. I asked Stephen Lewis to study the problem of race relations, with regard to the police and the justice system, and bring forward recommendations. This he did, and the report was tough: we had to move more quickly on the equity agenda, and had to push ahead with changes in policing to deal with the problem of racism.

Stephen Lewis's report was, in fact, very much in the Ontario tradition. Like Cardinal Carter and Clare Lewis, it pointed to a significant problem and urged public policy to lead the way. Yet for the police community, particularly in Toronto, the Lewis report and the government's response to it were the excuse for a confrontation that was long growing.

Toronto was the issue. Stephen Lewis told me that off-the-record conversations with a number of policemen had convinced him that younger, more progressive officers were afraid to speak up because of the famous "blue line." I had met Chief William McCormack a few times, and found him to have the shortest fuse and the thinnest skin of anyone I'd seen in a position of authority. He hated the report, disliked our government and let that show in all subsequent meetings.

The conflict was joined when the government accepted a long-standing recommendation that police officers report whenever they draw their gun. To this we added a determination to give officers far more training in the use of force. The use-of-force regulation was rejected completely by the Police Association of Metropolitan Toronto, especially after it was recommended by the Police Services Board chaired by Susan Eng. We were in for a struggle, with all those "supporting the police" asked to wear blue ribbons.

The blue-ribbon campaign created a climate where we were seen as being unfriendly to the police and soft on crime. The racial subtext was even uglier: we were a government that cared more for black hoodlums than upstanding, white police officers. It was an argument we couldn't win politically.

We felt that we might be able to turn opinion if we could isolate the harder-line extremists in the Metro police association. For me the issue quickly became one of the integrity of the civil authority. If police officers could decide on their own to wear baseball hats, sport blue ribbons, and openly flout the government, then they could also decide which law they would enforce and when and how they would enforce it.

I had been invited months before to speak to the Ontario Police Association on October 5, 1992. By that time the blue-ribbon campaign had started, and we were in the middle of the Quebec referendum. I spent the day getting heckled by anti-French and anti-native demonstrators in the Barrie mall, and then joined more than four hundred officers at their union meeting in Orillia. As soon as I got out of my car, I was handed an envelope by Ken Pidgeon, president of the association. He urged me to read it before I went in.

The letter told me that, contrary to what we had been promised, the Ontario Police Association would be joining with their brothers in Metro against the government. Solicitor General Allan Pilkey was with me, and I asked for a short meeting with the executive. We went into a little room, and they sheepishly told me that while they personally didn't agree with Metro's tactics, "police solidarity" required them to gang up against us. They'd been at the meetings where we went through the regulation changes, and we had promised more discussion and consultation on the wording. They had agreed then to work with us, and not to join the protest. But that was then, and this was now.

"It's politics, Premier. If we want to get re-elected tomorrow we have to ride with Metro."

"But you know what the Metro police association is saying about the regulations is bullshit, and you know no government can give in to this kind of blackmail."

"That may be, but we have to do what we have to do."

I was then escorted into a room of several hundred police officers. I was greeted by complete silence. Not one stood up to shake my hand or so much as nodded.

I said I wasn't going to run away because times were difficult. The line that we didn't care about policing was untrue, and pointed out that we had increased resources for the O.P.P. by 240 officers when we were asked to do so by Chief Commissioner Tom O'Grady, whom I'd invited to cabinet to talk directly about it.

I said we would consider reasonable suggestions on the use-of-force regulation, but that we wouldn't withdraw it in the face of a police protest. And I concluded by saying that the government is the civil authority. Respect for the law is a two-way street.

The response to the speech was as stony as my initial reception. I went through the crowd and left. The O.P.P. officer who was working with me at the time (who I will not embarrass by naming) said, "I was proud of you and ashamed of my fellow officers," which I appreciated, but I have rarely felt more alone.

There was a demonstration of a couple of thousand police officers and their supporters at Queen's Park chanting, "More Fire Power!" I said I wouldn't meet with the police unions until they ended their protest. Police chiefs were reluctant to tackle the civil disobedience issue. When Arlene, the girls, and I walked past a group of police officers, in uniform, on duty, in the SkyDome during the 1992 World Series, and they started booing and one said, "You're through, buddy," in a fairly menacing tone, it was more than just disheartening. This wasn't the peaceable kingdom.

The issue was eventually resolved with a rewording of the regulation with the principle of reporting gun-use maintained. But the damage had been done. We were the biggest losers politically, but we were joined by others: the police chiefs had to be pushed by their civilian police services boards to enforce their own regulations. Chief McCormack in particular played the short-term politics perfectly, but over time lost the respect of many who felt that civilian authority is an important principle. When he finally left office, almost like a latter-day General Douglas MacArthur, that became even clearer.

We ended up firmly on the wrong side of public opinion on the policing issue. It reinforced the view (internalized by many in the party) that we were essentially advocates of the marginalized, unsympathetic to the mainstream concerns of police, their families, and the general public.

Elaine Ziemba, our Minister of Citizenship, spent years working steadily with business, labour, and minority groups on employment equity. It was an issue the Liberals and the NDP had agreed to move forward in the 1985 accord. The Liberals were presented with options again in 1989 and 1990 but declined to act.

We painstakingly consulted. Our purpose was to create a framework of public policy that would steadily reduce systemic discrimination against women, visible minorities, and the disabled. We firmly rejected the idea of quotas. We limited the law, which was to have been introduced gradually, to the largest employers. The law was eventually passed with the broad acceptance of the employer community, most of whom had been steadily introducing equity measures on their own.

We had not counted on the steady undercurrent of opposition, most of which was based on fear-mongering from the right. The Tories exploited this feeling with a vengeance: the recession, and the social tensions it creates in a multiracial society made for fertile ground. I was proud to have sent a strong signal for equity and inclusiveness but chastened by the political reaction, which we would feel full bore in the election campaign.

✦ ✦

Crime and race are issues of raw emotion. So is sexual orientation. Politics notwithstanding, we entered the fray. There is a history here, which I shall try to describe briefly.

The rights of gays and lesbians to live their lives free of discrimination and harassment had been a focus of debate at least twice in the legislature before 1990. In 1980, just before the election in March of 1981 that saw a majority win for William Davis, the legislature had debated the issue of an amendment to the Human Rights Code which would protect gays and lesbians from discrimination. After an arduous internal debate, the NDP caucus at that time decided it would not move the amendment, which naturally caused an uproar in the gay and lesbian community as well as in much of the party.

During the government of our accord with the Liberals, Attorney General Ian Scott opened up the Human Rights Code for some amendments, but once again sexual orientation was not on the list. To her credit, Evelyn Gigantes insisted that our caucus come to terms with the issue, and succeeded in getting an amendment passed in committee which then became part of the government bill. Liberals and New Democrats joined to pass these changes in 1986. The federal Liberals debated a similar issue ten years later.

This was a symbolically important event, but many practical issues remained. The debate in 1986 focused on privacy, on the right of gays and lesbians to be able to live free from interference.

Certainly that is how I saw the issue and couched the argument at that time.

Increasingly the gay and lesbian community insisted that the issue was no longer simply one of privacy. The amendments to the Human Rights Code, and the Charter of Rights and Freedoms itself, were used to challenge dozens of provincial and federal statutes because they failed to recognize the equal validity of gay and lesbian relationships. From pension benefits to marriage itself, the cultural debate shifted from "leave us alone" to "here we are— we demand acceptance."

Our new, expanded caucus after 1990 was not completely ready for the change. Frances Lankin made a quick regulatory amendment to the government's own pension and benefits package soon after our election, but the cabinet asked for a "thorough review" of the issue before we would deal with legislation. Howard Hampton, Attorney General until early 1993, read the lack of enquiring signals from most of his cabinet colleagues to mean that we wanted the study to continue. He was right. My own hope was that enough cases would work their way through the courts that opinion in the caucus and the province would move.

We paid a political price for the delay in calling a by-election in the riding of St. George–St. David, to fill the vacancy left by the resignation of Ian Scott. By the time we announced a date, we were well behind everybody in the polls.

During the by-election, Lyn McLeod wrote me a letter demanding to know why we hadn't changed the laws of the province, and promising her support if we did move forward. I kept this letter carefully, because I maintained the fond hope that when the time came to move, the Liberal caucus could be persuaded to support us.

The Liberals won in St. George–St. David, but lost in Victoria–Haliburton to the Tories, where the local candidate made "family values" a central issue. So it was that Lyn McLeod's letter was dead almost as soon as it was written.

Marion Boyd's appointment as Attorney General in January 1993 meant that an advocate for change replaced a competent and savvy political manager, Howard Hampton. Marion was a determined, hard-working minister who had taken on both Education and Community and Social Services. She had run a women's shelter in London before defeating David Peterson personally in 1990. I came to admire her humour and her dedication. Unfortunately these were not enough to chart the stormy waters of the issue of recognition of gay and lesbian partnerships.

Both Marion and her deputy, George Thomson, believed the legal issues would never go away and needed to be faced head on. I agreed personally, but knew we would face a hard political battle, both inside the caucus and in the province.

We met as a caucus in the winter of 1994 to chart the next session. We all agreed we needed to focus on jobs and the economy, but the advocates among us insisted we couldn't betray our commitments to doing the "right thing." That argument won the day, but only with extraordinary resentment from those who simply didn't see this as a priority, particularly with an election year looming.

Marion insisted that the vote be free, because there would be those with religious objections to the government's official sanctioning of gay and lesbian partnerships. That mollified some, but again created problems because it ended up allowing a bitter and divisive public debate.

It is possible we could have passed a smaller package of changes to some legislation if we had left adoption out of the bill. Why didn't this more "political" approach work? My own feeling now is that it was due to a reluctance to see this as an issue that required accommodation and compromise. The gay and lesbian community certainly never saw things in this light and demanded the whole loaf, or nothing.

As everyone knows, nothing is what we got. I had hoped that a public process of bargaining would bring Lyn McLeod and a few supporters on board, but this was not to be. Lyn McLeod couldn't live up to what she had promised to do in the St. George by-election, and the bill was defeated on second reading. The irony is that political gamesmanship produced a result that was less than what the province could really accept. Any published poll that I have seen always indicated a majority in favour of ending discrimination against gay and lesbian couples. One day that will be reflected in our provincial and federal statutes.

Some commentators said my approach was part of a shrewd political strategy to put Lyn McLeod in a corner and make her look bad. Not so. I genuinely believed she and a good number of her colleagues would live up to her promises, even to the last day. She paid a heavy price for her many changes on this issue, far beyond the gay community. It left an impression of her leadership that eventually proved fatal to her ambitions to be premier.

The government fared a little better, because at least we tried. But no loss in the House is good, and I was genuinely perplexed by those who thought honourable defeat going for the perfect package was better than incremental progress.

Each of these initiatives and challenges fed a stereotype that was more damaging to the government than I fully appreciated at the time. The media certainly fed the line that we were too busy worrying about "minorities" and "special interests." It is a sad commentary that to be concerned about civilian control of the police is to be "soft on crime"; to believe in employment equity is to believe in "reverse discrimination" and "quotas"; to support respect for gay and lesbian relationships is to be "anti-family." That none of this is true is irrelevant in the management of the politics of the day. We lost touch with much of our working and middle class base on these issues, more in the style of how they were addressed than in the substance of what we tried to do. The next progressive government will need to learn some lessons from this rocky experience.

Chapter Sixteen

LOSING & LEAVING

Jean Chrétien's election in November of 1993 opened up new possibilities. I knew Chrétien as a loyal member of Pierre Trudeau's team, and of course as a strong personal friend of my brother John, who was his executive assistant from 1963 to 1971. I had admired his run for the leadership in 1984 but disagreed strongly with his stand on Meech Lake in 1990. While I was politically troubled by the size of his win at the expense of the NDP in Ontario in 1993, I still hoped for a new relationship between Ottawa and Toronto.

Apart from the national infrastructure programme, which many of us had been proposing since the beginning of the recession, he did not make the bigger changes I had hoped for. Jean Chrétien was, and is, a fierce partisan. It was impossible to penetrate the triumphalist armour around him. When he needed me, he would call. But there was no great desire to negotiate change. I envisioned a package where Ontario would get some recognition of the depth of Ottawa's fiscal discrimination, and where we in turn would negotiate tax reform and tax harmony. Nothing doing. No deals.

Paul Martin came to see me in the spring of 1994, accompanied

by David Dodge, his deputy minister. Since Dodge was the architect of both the GST and moves against Ontario under Mulroney,
it seemed implausible to me that he would be an ally of change.
In fact, quite the contrary. His defence of his achievements, combined with a healthy dose of Liberal arrogance, made any serious
negotiations a non-starter. Ottawa will deal when it has to deal,
and not before.

I also wanted to move ahead on the agenda the federal government and the provinces had agreed to even before Charlottetown.
This meant making the country work better, ending duplication
in areas like manpower training. I saw Jean Chrétien for another
long meeting, in the summer of 1994. It was a very relaxed occasion. We played golf at the Royal Ottawa, joined by my brother
John. The Prime Minister was in a good mood, relaxed, jovial. He
let me take a few dollars off him, and then invited us both to
Harrington Lake for a swim and dinner.

He was preoccupied with Quebec, but was curiously ambivalent
about Johnson's re-election. "From one point of view it would be
better to deal with an unpopular Parizeau now than a popular
Bouchard later on. We can beat Parizeau in a referendum. But of
course I want Johnson to win." I pushed him again on the manpower file, and simultaneously so did Jeff Rose, along with Eddie
Goldenberg, his special adviser. The Prime Minister was blunt,
"We've offered them a deal on manpower, but they want more,
and we're not going to give them more. The federal manpower
office in Shawinigan does a better job than the province." The
mindset had not really changed.

← →

Daniel Johnson fought the election in the fall of 1994 very much
on his own. I am convinced that if Jean Chrétien had demonstrated a greater capacity for change, Johnson could have won.
This was never the official line in Ottawa, which had essentially
written Daniel Johnson off. I visited Johnson in June of 1994, and
he came to the premiers' meeting in Toronto in August of the
same year. We also signed an agreement ensuring more open
labour markets between the two provinces, ably negotiated by

Frances Lankin and Gerard Tremblay.

The next big move—the federal government getting the message on the need for simpler delivery of training and manpower, and to devolve the management of this issue to Quebec and other provinces—didn't happen when it needed to happen and when it could have happened. So too on other files. Lloyd Axworthy and Paul Martin continued to cut transfers and compound the fiscal discrimination against Ontario. Axworthy would then announce "new" money for training and day care which proceeded to evaporate as soon as we would begin negotiations. Paul Martin kept insisting he wanted to get rid of the GST but could never really negotiate. When he came to Toronto in the spring of 1994, I offered to negotiate on consumption taxes if he would show some flexibility on transfers. Nothing doing. When Jean Chrétien pressed me again on "Team Canada's" trip to China, and again at a private meeting at Sussex Drive over Christmas 1994-95, I made the same offer.

"You're bargaining," he said.

"Of course I am."

"The federal government can't do business this way."

"Then we can't do business."

The Liberal governments in Atlantic Canada fared better in their own discussions this past year.

Having listened to him on Daniel Johnson, I knew full well that for Jean Chrétien there is no sentimentality in politics. He looked at our anemic poll numbers and his own robust position, and decided he didn't need to bargain, and he didn't need me. He would wait me out, and deal with a more malleable Liberal government. Or so he thought.

The year 1994 began for us on a more auspicious note. When Yitzhak Rabin and Yassir Arafat signed the peace accord in September 1993, I used the occasion as an opportunity to bring Arab and Jewish communities together in Toronto. This was a moving occasion attended by more than five hundred at the legislature, and only slightly marred by my getting caught in a cross argument between B'nai B'rith and the Canadian Jewish

Congress. God forbid a trivial thing like Arab-Israeli peace be allowed to overshadow a really important question of who gets to speak where and when on a podium.

This initiative led to an invitation from the Israeli and Jordanian governments for the Rae family to visit in December and early January. I asked several leading Canadian business people with ties in both communities to join us, which they did. It was a remarkable occasion. Arlene had been to Israel as a student in 1968. I had been there once before, as a guest of Histadrut, the Israeli labour movement, in the late 1970s.

The changes we saw were remarkable. Israeli society was markedly more urban, and more affluent. The courage shown by Rabin and Peres had shifted the context of the whole debate. But these sets of changes had provoked a more radical response from the orthodox right who opposed both secularization and the strategy of land for peace.

One of my favourite moments during this trip was crossing the Jordan River by the Allenby Bridge on foot with Arlene, Judith, Lisa, and Eleanor, and meeting my old Ecolint friend Rami Khouri with his family—we had been writing and chatting on the phone for years. I later sat with his mother and reminded her of the "chicken pizzas" she used to make for us as famished teenagers. Rami and I had conquered the Aletsch Glacier together, and thirty years later in 1994 we explored the ruins of Petra with our children. His wife is learning Hebrew so she can take tours from Israel. Rami's father was born in what is now Haifa, and used to shout at me about how Canada had helped to take his land away from his family and turned Palestine into California.

Israel now represents a significant new potential market for Canada. That she has a free-trade agreement with both Europe and the U.S. prompted me to urge negotiations with Canada, which only makes sense. Reporters had a bit of fun with my "conversion" on free trade.

The visit also allowed me to spend an hour each with Rabin, Peres, and King Hussein of Jordan. Their personalities were quite different. Rabin blunt, direct, giving one the sense that he was doing what had to be done, but the real choices in politics were between different modes of worse. Peres was eloquent, a little rhetorical, but the most optimistic. King Hussein was deferential, polite, practical. All were prepared to take risks for peace. But it was Yitzhak Rabin who was to pay the ultimate price. To borrow a phrase, he left the vivid air signed with his honour.

This trip to the Middle East was also successful as a trade mission. It was followed by a mission to Malaysia and China later in the spring of 1994 and by the Team Canada mission to China and Hong Kong in the fall of the same year. Invariably these trips, and those to the World Economic Forum in Davos each February, would give rise to a penetrating analysis of hotel bills and taxi fares by the Ontario media. At the press conference following the trip to Israel and Jordan, the business members of the delegation were astounded at the trivial and thoroughly parochial nature of the questions, which had nothing to do with the value of the trips themselves, or the contracts we had won.

It would be a pity if this attitude, which is invariably shared by opposition parties, were allowed to stop Ontario looking outward. Travel is not evil. There is no substitute for personal contact. Many on my staff rolled their eyes at the thought of yet another trade mission. But they are part of working in the global economy.

The "Team Canada" initiative was something proposed by a number of premiers to a newly elected Jean Chrétien at our first encounter in December 1993. He was initially sceptical, but eventually embraced the idea. Mike Harcourt of B.C., Gary Filmon of Manitoba, and I had all been to China many times; to us it was the next economic frontier for Canada. The November 1994 mission, which took all the premiers except Parizeau on an extended official visit to China and Hong Kong, re-established the importance of the Asian economy in Canadian public policy. Since it is the fastest growing part of the world, it only makes sense.

Helping to sell a train system in Kuala Lumpur or a power project in Jiangsu is just as much part of a modern premier's job as deciding how many new schools we can afford for the next construction year. Resistance to this view is widespread, which means the politics aren't always great, but opening up the partnerships with business that make it happen is essential if we're going to take advantage of our strengths in the world economy.

← →

Ontario's economy improved substantially in 1994. The job creation numbers were dramatic. The premiers' conference in Toronto that summer was a success. Legislatively we were far more focused. Important reforms in forestry, worker's compensation, and planning legislation were completed by the fall of 1994. All of this should have pointed to more success in the polls, but it did not. This persistent unpopularity led, in turn, to a kind of fatalism on our part, which made life more bearable but didn't make for enough renewed political energy.

Paul Martin's federal budget in early 1995 tightened the financial squeeze on Ontario—to the tune of another $2.5 billion—and we knew full well that a detailed programme to deal with the full impact of it would be, to borrow a phrase from an ill-fated Labour Party campaign in the U.K., "the longest suicide note in history." Ontario's interests were badly served by the Martin budget, but try as we might there was not as much political currency in saying so as we had hoped.

To make matters more difficult, the splendid job numbers of 1994 were not being matched by any monthly figures in 1995. This in turn meant that the welfare numbers, which had declined since 1994, hardened again through the winter.

When David Agnew moved away from the political side of government, he left a large gap. A group of advisers—David Mackenzie from the Steelworkers, Dennis Young, Melody Morrison, and Ross McClellan—came together to help prepare our final budget in 1995 and a programme to take to the electorate.

← →

Elections take months to prepare. Our preference initially was to call the House back in early March 1995, and then see from the budget and other legislation whether our star would rise. I wanted the option of waiting for the fall, but this met with universal opposition, since it would look too much like hanging on.

The premise of my idea was that we would bring in a detailed plan of the steps that would have to be taken to deal with the Martin cuts, and our own deficit targets, and let this be voted up or down by the electorate. The consensus was this would be a huge target for our opponents to shoot at, and make our defeat inevitable. Let them each bring out their own detailed and unrealistic plans. We would run on jobs, fighting for Ontario, and the capacity we'd shown for making difficult decisions.

A significant dissenter from the strategy was Arlene, who felt that a "no promises" campaign left the voters with the sense that we had run out of steam and had nothing more to offer. I got very annoyed at this suggestion, saying nothing McLeod or Harris was offering had any integrity. "Your approach has tons of integrity and no politics." She was right.

The die, however, was cast. Unlike some, I can't really blame anyone else for the approach we took. If I had absolutely insisted, I could have called the House back and brought forward a detailed programme, and legislation. But there was no enthusiasm from those around me, and I succumbed to the prevailing wisdom. This view was widely shared in the caucus. When I raised the possibility of postponing the election into the fall at a caucus meeting in February, there were loud groans. The troops were getting ready.

The polls showed only marginal improvement: we were somewhere in the high teens, the Tories ten points ahead of us, and the Liberals into the stratosphere, where they had been parked for three years. Even at this point I saw victory as an outside possibility. My strategy was to focus hard on the Liberals at first, and force their numbers down. Then the battle would be joined with the Tories. I did not believe the public would fall for Harris's approach.

I called a press conference on Friday, April 28, 1995. The election would be held on June 8, 1995.

The first part of our strategy, to bring down the Liberals, worked. Lyn McLeod's campaign became the subject of more media scrutiny than she had received for three years, and her numbers started falling. Our own began to improve, and on leadership we began to make steady progress. Harris in the first week didn't look too impressive, and our crowds were enthusiastic. The ghastly hostility of 1993 was gone. On the Victoria Day weekend I walked the entire length of a parade in Woodstock with our member, Kimble Sutherland, and our popular Minister of Agriculture, Elmer Buchanan. The response was more than friendly. It was enthusiastic, and I allowed myself to believe all things were possible. It was a necessary illusion. Staying "up" is the key to keeping others up as well. My mood swings on the bus were saved by the reports from our overnights of a steady Liberal decline as we headed into the leaders' debate.

I was never particularly close to either Mike Harris or Lyn McLeod. I have a visceral dislike of Harris's political agenda. McLeod was more personally unpleasant in opposition, but I always felt she had to steel herself to say nasty things because she was being advised to be tough. I felt no great animosity to either of them. My task in the debate was to keep pressure on Lyn McLeod, whose Liberals were still in the lead two weeks into the election.

I was under strict instructions not to be too angry or confrontational, and to watch my body language. The trick in these debates in my experience is to be well prepared, but at some point to thank all your pugilistic advisers (who have never been in a real debate in their lives for the most part), and to clear your head to just do your best.

Mike Harris did well in the debate, and while Lyn McLeod did not do badly, she apparently left many voters cold. Coupled with a series of disastrous days with the media heading after her full bore, her numbers started to slip badly. At first, we took comfort from this, because our own overnights showed some real improvement for us. This didn't last, however, and by the middle of the next week it was obvious something dramatic was happening with the Tory numbers.

Was it the debate? I think not. Rather it was the thoroughly dishonest but effective ads the Tories ran. They ran hard against what they called the "quota bill" (employment equity) and hard against people on welfare. There never was a quota bill, but the Tories said loud and often that there was, and together with the assault on the unemployed poor, the campaign was nasty, brutish, and short on honesty, but long on results. Those who do not learn from history are doomed to repeat it. The demagogic Big Lie often wins in the short run. We underestimated the Tories' willingness to run a vicious campaign that appealed to public fear and emotion.

We turned all our guns on the Tories at that point, but by then it was too late. They had done what all successful campaigns must do, defined the issues and defined their opponents. We railed against the Tories, pointing out their 30 per cent tax cut would mean huge cuts in health care, insisting that classroom education and human services would suffer, decrying their latent appeal to resentment and prejudice. None of the Tory numbers made any sense. Nothing added up. But our canvassers in my ridings were telling us that it did add up, that many NDP supporters liked what they saw of Harris's populism, and that we didn't have a chance.

Many months before, I had prepared the girls for just such a possibility.

"We might just lose the next election, girls, and I want you to be ready for it."

Lisa said, "Dad, you're toast. *You* better get ready for it."

I was, but that never makes it any easier. Sharon Vance, who was on the bus with me in each of four campaigns, said she'd never seen me more relaxed or more effective on the hustings, which may well have been true. But the long and short of it is that it doesn't make any difference when the tide has gone out.

I had spoken with Bob White about ten days before election day and told him that Harris was going to win. He said he knew that, and that he would see what kind of statement he could get from the CLC executive. The result was a half-baked endorsement of the NDP in both Saskatchewan and Ontario, which blew in and out of the air in thirty seconds. Julie Davis's opposition to the Social Contract kept her away from the centre of the campaign where she rightly belonged. These estrangements saddened me deeply.

Irony of ironies, OPSEU in its wisdom decided to have regular
hecklers sent to all our events, which prompted me to phone Leah
Casselman in the middle of the campaign and ask what she
thought would happen under a Tory government.

"You're the government now and we want to get you to the
table to negotiate a reasonable agreement."

"I'm not going to negotiate an agreement before the election,
and I'm certainly not going to reach a deal just to keep a couple of
demonstrators off my back."

"Then you'll have to live with the consequences."

"No, actually, Leah, you will."

Could it have gone differently? Only if we had been able to take
a very different approach to governing, and responded to the insecurity of the electorate from another angle completely. I have read
others' accounts of elections, and of governments, and blame is a
cop-out. An NDP government could have been elected to a
second term, but it would have had to govern differently and campaign differently. The fact that it didn't is ultimately more my
responsibility than anyone else's.

I watched the election with Arlene, Jennifer, John, Ginny, and a
few close friends from the campaign. We watched it in the same
room as in 1990. There were no tears that night, since we all knew
pretty much what was coming. I first phoned my parents in
Ottawa, who, troopers as they are, had only words of praise. I
then spoke with Lyn McLeod and Mike Harris, whom I congratulated and promised a good transition. I also spoke with Jean
Chrétien and a few friends who could not be in the room, and
prepared to go to the hall to meet my York South supporters, and
the press who had come with us on the entire campaign. Some
great supporters were there—like Leo Gerard, Fred Pomeroy, and
Gord Wilson—but I couldn't help reflecting on those who had
been with us in 1990 but were not there in 1995—like Stephen
Lewis, Julie Davis, and Bob White. Stephen was working with the
U.N. in New York. Julie Davis had left over the Social Contract.
Bob White was in Brussels.

Back in the hall, I was determined to get on and off the stage with as much grace as I could muster. I thanked my supporters, the people of York South, and wished Harris and McLeod well. I then went on:

> *We never stopped fighting for jobs and work. We refused to single out the poor and the needy for punishment. We refused to fire tens of thousands of public servants. We expanded health services, and strengthened the province's commitment to the environment, to equality, and to all its citizens. We insisted on partnership between business, labour, and government. We saved jobs, and tried to build a province ready to celebrate its diversity and tolerance...*
>
> *I am always learning again that life is too short to be bitter or to look back with recrimination or second guesses. The people have spoken, a new government with a very different perspective has been chosen, and we shall all have to live with the results.*

The next day the press suddenly fell back in love with me. *The Globe and Mail* editorialized at what a splendid fellow I was, as did the *Hamilton Spectator*. My public rehabilitation was beginning just as my political influence was spent.

Shortly after the election I got a phone call from Rob Prichard, the president of the University of Toronto. He offered me a job teaching part-time. I leapt at the chance to do something constructive while I debated about my future plans. In an office in Massey College, provided by the new master, John Fraser, I busied myself preparing for lectures in the fall and a seminar in the spring.

✦ ✦

The last cabinet and caucus meetings were emotional events. For all our challenges together, they were a remarkably loyal and solid group. There were no regrets—only speeches stressing how much we had all done and learned together. Shirley Coppen, who was a nursing assistant and union activist in the psychiatric wing of the

265

Welland Hospital, and who had served as Chief Whip and then as Minister of Labour after Bob Mackenzie retired, pulled me aside and said that she couldn't find words to express her thanks and pride. Thanks to me, for giving her a chance, and pride because she saw she had abilities that had never been realized until she went into politics.

The hard part for me was having to say goodbye to so many fine people, who had become such good friends on the voyage, and my sense that as leader things should have gone better. I had too loyal a crew to say so, but as I retreated to Big Rideau for much of the summer I knew it would weigh heavily on my mind.

Five years before, I had promised myself the election of 1990 would be my last, never expecting to win. Now the vast majority of the party was expressing the feeling that I should stay on to fight yet another election in 1999 or 2000. I agreed to stay on through the fall, and to let people know before the build-up to the 1996 leadership convention. I wanted to keep the story out of the news, and pull the group of seventeen re-elected members through the autumn session.

I also wanted to be an active politician for the Quebec referendum. I travelled to Quebec privately many times in the summer, meeting with leaders of the "No" forces, including Daniel Johnson. I had gotten to know Daniel well during our time together as premiers, and had kept in close touch with him after Jacques Parizeau's election in 1994. There was tension between the Quebec Liberals, the federal Liberals, and Jean Charest, which had to be overcome if an effective campaign could be run against the sovereignists.

The common ground struck was what could most charitably be described as a "minimalist" approach. Put nothing forward that will divide the group. Put the sovereignists on the defensive. Focus on Parizeau as the most unpopular spokesman of the cause of Quebec independence.

In the early days of the referendum campaign, this seemed to work. But this didn't last. The fly in the ointment was the lack of spark in the federalist campaign, and the Quebec media's hunger for a "star." This was astutely provided by the decision of the "Yes" forces to dump their chief spokesman, and to replace Parizeau with Lucien Bouchard. His meetings took on the tone of a revivalist hysteria. By contrast, the federalist rallies that I attended shortly after seemed curiously flat. When tides turn, as they most definitely did in Quebec after Bouchard's "coup," it is a lot easier to describe a problem than to know what to do about it.

I was scheduled to join Daniel and Suzanne Johnson on Saturday, October 21, 1995, for a couple of campaign appearances. As I got on the bus for my first warm-up act, I heard Daniel's account of his morning press conference where he had expressed a "preference" that the Prime Minister say something positive about Quebec as a distinct society. This sounded a little off-message to me, since it then raised the prospect of other premiers saying unhelpful things during the last week of the referendum.

"Do you know what the Prime Minister will say?"

"I was only expressing a preference. I'm sure it won't be a big deal."

As it turned out, the media made it a big deal, particularly when Jean Chrétien was surprised at a scrum in New York by a question about distinct society and stuck to the minimalist script, saying this was a campaign about separation. "Chrétien says no to Johnson" screamed the headlines.

With my unerring sense of timing I had joined the "No" campaign in the hours of a mini-crisis. I urged that Daniel Johnson and Jean Chrétien should talk directly, and put out a joint statement on an agreed, common position. This they did on Sunday. I then phoned a number of premiers from the "No" headquarters and asked them all to ensure as little sunshine as possible between their positions and the joint statement. I thought I had convinced them all, but Clyde Wells went back to his constitutional fetal position as soon as he was asked a supplementary question by a reporter the next day. "Wells says no to *Distinct Society*."

The "No" forces then had to really scramble that last week to regain some momentum. Thus the desperate last rallies, the pleas on TV from the Prime Minister, and the huge demonstrations in Montreal and across the country in favour of national unity.

Coming into referendum day, a Monday, there were conflicting reports on what the polls said, or didn't say. Our side seemed reasonably confident, assuming a shift of undecided in favour of stability and "No," and predicted to me a spread of at least six or seven points, possibly wider.

I had agreed to appear on the CBC television that night, commenting on the results. They did not come in as had been expected by the pros on the "No" side. What for me had always been a scenario out of science fiction now appeared a distinct possibility, and yet I had to appear as thoughtful and upbeat as I could. Slowly the numbers started to turn, toward the narrowest of "No" victories.

The networks always like to cover themselves by having a bevy of commentators and panelists, experts, journalists, defeated politicians, then a flurry of "vox pop" interviews from some bar. I was getting more and more agitated when Parizeau came on and unloaded at the end of the evening. I had never liked or trusted him personally, and when I heard him vent his spleen in language worthy of a Munich beer hall in the twenties, I went ballistic. I was even more upset by the namby-pamby response of the commentators, who seemed incapable of voicing honest anger. When my turn finally came, I said what I thought, that Parizeau's was a vicious outburst unworthy of anyone who aspired to be in a position of political responsibility in any part of Canada. He sounded drunk to me, and I said as much, which enraged the sovereignists on the other panels. At that point I was past caring. I simply had to say what I thought. I'm glad I did. If I contributed in only a minor way to Mr. Parizeau's demise, I am a happy man.

← →

In the meantime, Mike Harris was proceeding apace with his revolution in Ontario. As each of his ministers went further down the path of the true believers, I took no great satisfaction in knowing that this is what I had predicted. Every cut, every slash, every anti-welfare taunt, every ritual scapegoating was a manifestation of the right-wing extremism that had taken hold of the Tory caucus after 1990.

While I had no difficulty expressing my opposition to what Harris was doing, and to rallying our caucus to the cause, I did have real problems seeing how I could lead the movement outside the legislature. Many of those who were most vocal in expressing their opposition to Harris's agenda had been equally vocal in their opposition to me, and indeed had contributed to our defeat and Harris's election. I found it hard to be civil and chummy with people who had not seen the necessity and wisdom of fighting Mike Harris before the election. They preferred the placard to political responsibility, and this was a perspective for which I had no respect. For someone who aspires to be a political leader, these are fatal sentiments. Personal feelings have to be set aside, bygones are bygones, and life is supposed to carry on in the best of all political worlds.

My experience with power changed me. I knew that some cuts would have to be made, and that if we had been re-elected the same demonstrators would have been out after my neck. I could no longer feign the permanent indignation that seems to be required of an opposition leader.

I put off any final decision until after Christmas. Arlene and the girls were, of course, thoroughly in favour of my leaving, though Judith had the most second thoughts since she had worked so hard to get me re-elected in York South. I finally told the caucus at the end of January, at an emotional meeting where all my feelings came bursting out. Others joined in, to the point that at the end of the meeting the only dry eyes belonged to Arlene and to Peter Kormos.

↲ ↳

I made my last speech in the legislature on January 29, 1996, the one-day session called to pass the Tory's notorious omnibus legislation on their blanket cuts. I decided not to leave quietly, but to use one last chance to blast the Tories for having lost a sense of balance.

Social justice, economic efficiency, and liberty have always to be balanced. Balanced economies and balanced societies are just as important as balanced budgets. They are not necessarily at odds or at war with each other. They need to be made to work together. There is a role for markets, for companies, for banks, and for business; there is a role for unions, for universities, for non-profit agencies, and for government; there is above all a role for people, not just the wealthy and the well-spoken, but for those whose lives matter just as much, those who don't have big bank accounts and loud-hailers. I also took the opportunity to quote these words by Shakespeare:

> Let those who are in favour with their stars
> Of public honour and proud titles boast,
> Whilst I, whom fortune of such triumph bars,
> Unlookt for joy in that I honour most.
> Great princes' favourites their fair leaves spread
> But as the marigold at the sun's eye;
> And in themselves their pride lies buried,
> For at a frown they in their glory die.
> The painful warrior famoused for fight,
> After a thousand victories once foil'd,
> Is from the book of honour razed quite,
> And all the rest forgot for which he toil'd:
> > Then happy I, that love and am beloved
> > Where I may not remove nor be removed.

Soon after making my decision to leave politics, I spoke with Juli Morrow, a friend from law school, who is a partner at the Canadian international law firm of Goodman Phillips and Vineberg. She urged me to think about joining the firm, and to talk with Dale Lastman, the managing partner. Dale in turn spoke with his colleagues in Toronto and Montreal and invited me to join the partnership. I knew their senior partner, Eddie Goodman, from his long association with Bill Davis, and I liked him very much for his good humour and infectious energy, if misdirected politically on occasion. After many discussions about how I could help in their work in developing an international practice, I accepted and started work the day after I left the leadership of the

THE TORONTO SUN

Ontario New Democratic Party, on February 8, 1996. The firm celebrated my arrival with a breakfast of bagels and coffee, warm and funny speeches, and a large donation to the Leukemia Research Fund. I had moved on.

POSTSCRIPT

> "The web of our life is of a mingled yarn, good and
> ill together: our virtues would be proud if our faults
> whipped them not; and our crimes would despair if
> they were not cherished by our own virtues."
> —William Shakespeare, *All's Well That Ends Well*

We all carry about with us certain pictures in our heads. When I
was a kid, television was in its infancy. We really did gather around
to watch "Leave It to Beaver" and "Father Knows Best." I grew up
in a world where Canada had a national economy and the assumption of strong central government to go with it; steady economic
growth, with rising incomes; low levels of private and public debt;
a Canada firmly based on industry and resources; a labour force
that was largely white, male, and working a traditional forty-hour
week; and a narrowing gap between rich and poor. Surrounding all
this was a world in which people "knew their place." Most women
stayed at home. Single-income, two-parent families were the norm.
Voting patterns were reasonably stable.

I joined the New Democratic Party as a conscious political
choice. Countless people have said to me since then that I would

have had their support if I had joined another political party. My experiences in England left me with a gut mistrust of Tories, where the overwhelming obtuseness of inherited wealth and privilege is a core feature of the Conservative personality. There is a smugness and complacency about the Liberal Party of Canada which has not really changed since my first encounter.

I decided that I would be truest to myself by working for a party whose core mission is to fight unwarranted privilege and improve the lives of the majority of people. It is impossible, of course, to separate that decision from the relative radicalism of the time. The whole political spectrum was very different in the 1960s and early 1970s from what it is today.

Between 1945 and 1975, life improved for everyone in Canada and Ontario, with very few exceptions. The steelworker factories that I used to visit as a young advocate for the United Steelworkers had tens of thousands of workers (as opposed to a few thousand now), who could all point to their own experience as living proof that collective action and positive government policy had in fact improved their lives.

We live in a world of fewer certainties today. The rising tide of economic growth has lifted some boats, but others have capsized and sunk. Both in the U.S. and Canada, more wealth is now owned and controlled by fewer people. Many working people are clinging to life-rafts. People have gone into debt to support a standard of living they feel they need and deserve, and which they clearly see others, no more meritorious than they, enjoying and even flaunting. Governments have done the same thing.

We now live not so much in a national economy as in a series of regional economies increasingly linked to global interdependence. A sovereign national economy is a figment of the political imagination. It does not exist. It cannot be willed into existence.

Since 1975 we have moved to an even faster and more open information economy. The phrase "global village" was invented by Marshall McLuhan in the 1960s. Thirty years later it is closer to a reality. Manufacturing remains critical to our ability to make our way in the world, but even here the key to our success is how we apply new technologies and new techniques to existing processes, how, to use the buzz word, we "add value." The progress of this technological revolution is even more dramatic than the industrial revolution. We are in the middle of it. Its pace is relentless. Its scope is global. We can't stop it. We can only learn better how to manage it, and how to deal with its impact.

Yet the global village is still not a real community. Some do well. Many more do not. The effect of globalization has been to increase both opportunity and inequality.

In this increasingly polarized world, some people are working longer hours, for which they are well rewarded. Others are not so lucky, forced to accept part-time work when they would vastly prefer more. Women have entered the labour force in unprecedented numbers. Families are being transformed. Canada has become a multiracial country in the space of three decades.

For many, their familiar world has become disconnected in a number of important ways. The wealth that accrues to the highly skilled and the already rich has less and less to do with the immediate community around it, and much more to do with the global economy. Not all Canadians do well in the global competitive environment. In addition, people have lost their sense of connection between the taxes they pay and the services they receive. In a non-inflationary world, where pay-cheques are stagnant or declining, tax increases feel like a direct assault on one's security. The tax revolt we see now is genuine. The left has underestimated its importance, and has been slow to learn what is politically possible in a world with no inflation. Tax increases can no longer be buried in a tide of ever-rising prices and incomes.

The key theory of the right is that inequality is a good thing, because it reflects the natural and healthy range of abilities and appetites in life. In this view, no one should be concerned if the gap between rich and poor grows, because all this means is that successful people are doing better than ever before. And wealthy people spend and invest their money, which eventually ends up in the real economy, and in the pockets of the less fortunate. This is often referred to as the trickle-down theory, though John Kenneth

Galbraith refers to it a little less elegantly as the notion that if you feed a horse enough oats eventually something gets through to the sparrows.

The only thing wrong with this theory is that it isn't true. A redistribution of income toward the wealthiest 20 per cent of the population does not automatically produce the best result for everyone else. When this is pointed out, social democrats and their allies are then derided for advocating that everyone live in a commune and receive the same bowl of gruel as the price for our egalitarianism. That is a convenient cartoon, but it too has nothing to do with reality. One can accept the market as an efficient and desirable place without having to accept that all its distributions are just, or that all we want is to live in a market all the time.

Through reasonable and fair taxes and the provision of decent and efficient public services, the community is strengthened. This does not prescribe absolute equality of outcomes, just a willingness to recognize that community and shared services are important ways in which we affirm what we have in common, what we owe each other.

The price of accepting the global economy, we are told, is that government must get smaller. Most of us would accept that governments should become more efficient, but if it means that we owe less of an obligation to one another in this particular community, that is a different matter. We should not make the mistake of believing that economies that are more equal are necessarily less efficient than Canada's or Ontario's. In fact, quite the contrary. There are, in fact, different kinds of capitalism. We are not absolutely bound to follow the model which attributes an insignificant role to community investment, to sound environmental planning, or to any concern for social solidarity. We can only understand the level of unrest and political volatility in the world today, as well as the rise of nationalism, if we also appreciate that most people do not want their communities and their countries to disappear.

The NDP was elected in 1990 at least in part because working people were resentful of their insecurity. They didn't see their lives improving dramatically as a result of the Ontario boom of the 1980s, and they feared losing even more as boom turned to bust in 1990. Free trade was not just an opportunity. It was part of an awesome change, in which hundreds of thousands initially paid with their jobs.

People turned on us because of the very same recession, because we raised taxes, brought in employment equity, froze public-sector pay and poured well-intentioned gasoline on their growing resentment. Harris appealed shrewdly to all this insecurity, just as Margaret Thatcher did in England and Newt Gingrich has done in the U.S.

That we did many good and positive things was drowned out by the noise of protest that the media and business élites were only too happy to amplify. As many of our allies on the left turned up the volume, they sealed our fate and, in turn, their own.

Harris succeeded in a time-tested, right-wing populist way, by touching the buttons of resentment about taxes, welfare, race, and gender. If the condition of the people improves dramatically as a result of his premiership, then no doubt he will be the worthy beneficiary of a grateful public. If he successfully maintains the resentments that divide people, he may also continue to govern.

But it will not be easy. The disappearance of well-paying jobs for working people shows no sign of abating, and the gap between those who are on the Internet and those who are about to be drowned by the wave may well widen, deepening the resentment among those who are left out.

The tax cut that gives the most to those who are the most well-off is the right-wing salve to the wound of declining real incomes. It is short-term, and a non-answer, but it provides momentary relief and satisfaction. Momentary because, as it is understood that the inevitable consequence of this is a reduction in public services, people will realize over time that you can't get something for nothing.

The real challenge is how to create well-paying jobs for most people, and how to maintain social solidarity in the face of incomes that will probably not rise for most people nearly as much as they did after 1945. When people see that the rising tide isn't lifting their boat, they get mad at the world, at whoever built the boat, at who didn't tie it up properly, and at whose boat seems to be doing better. Suffering in silence isn't in the lexicon any more, nor should it be.

Abraham Lincoln said good politics should always appeal to the "better angels of our nature." Unfortunately, that appeal doesn't always work. Even in wartime, which is when solidarity is at its peak, experience shows that people's sense of short-term advantage will lead coal miners to go on strike, and others to thrive on the black market. Collective self-interest, then, doesn't always prevail. But we have to find ways to link a healthy sense of self-interest with an appeal to community. If our politics only appeals to sacrifice, it will fail.

← →

There has been much nonsense spouted about the issue of public deficits and public debt, from all sides. This is a practical and not a theological question. The public airwaves are dominated by ideological theorists from the left and the right. Many on the left are not prepared to admit that too much public debt is ever a problem. For the right, who are now in the ascendancy, any deficit or debt is a sin. Both views are wrong.

The best explanation I have been able to find for what has happened to all our public finances is that we have used the credit card to maintain the standard of living we believe we need and deserve. Once this started in the early 1970s it became hard to stop, and compound interest and excessively high interest rates did the rest. This is as true for individuals as it is for governments.

A problem that has taken twenty-five years to create, in Canada as in most other western economies, cannot be solved overnight. But it must be solved, and cannot be ignored. To deal with it in a balanced way will take determination and judgment. If we overreact, as some governments are clearly doing, more damage will be done by the treatment than by the disease. If we continue to deny the problem, as many on the left still want to do, we are missing a major, changed reality.

The Hippocratic oath reminds doctors to avoid causing unnecessary pain. Governments need to be reminded of this. Governments need, from time to time, like individuals, families, and businesses, to borrow and to invest in the future. There are many circumstances when it is shortsighted not to do so. But just as a family thinks carefully how it will pay down the mortgage or pay off the car loan, governments have to develop a practical sense about how much current income they want to devote to debt-servicing costs. The more that gets eaten up in interest payments, the less there is for everything else, unless economic growth (or lotteries or higher taxes) produces more revenue. Here, again, the absence of inflation reveals the arithmetic in its stark nakedness: ten billion dollars borrowed today is six or seven hundred million dollars required for additional payment tomorrow. That's real money, and it has to come from somewhere.

We also need to distinguish between different kinds of spending. Business accounting makes a distinction between investment and current operations. Governments should do the same. When they fail to make the distinction, for ideological reasons, necessary investments don't happen. This will affect our competitive position in the future. If investments in mass transit, for example, don't get made, we all pay with congested and unliveable cities. Yet liveable and affordable cites are key to Canada's economic prosperity.

The era between 1970 and 1990 was not only a time of increasing deficits and debt. It was also a time of increasing inequality, higher unemployment than anything we had seen since World War II, higher taxes, high inflation, and high real interest rates. Sensible public policy would surely see that these are all connected. High real interest rates, for example, transfer money from poorer people who borrow money to richer people who lend it. They also exaggerate and compound (forgive the pun) the debt problem.

High inflation conceals real transfers in the economy, because it creates the illusion that everyone is getting more money when in reality most people are not. Persistently high unemployment saps morale and trust among those pushed to the margins, and at the same time puts a drain on public finances.

A political programme, such as we now have in Ontario, that singles out just one problem—"the debt"—and becomes obsessed by it is bound to fail. The Tories' ideology stops them from taking a balanced view. Lower interest rates are a necessary contributor to lower public deficits and debts. More well-paying and stable jobs are also a critical part of the solution: more people paying taxes and fewer people relying on social assistance.

Yet social democracy has to change as well. People turned on us in Ontario because they felt we were not paying enough attention to their real plight. It is too easy to blame others for our defeat. The right spoke to issues and concerns that need to be at the centre of our own politics: work, welfare, and taxes.

If social democrats avoid the politics of the single issue; abandon preachy rhetoric; admit that government needs to change; accept the value and contribution of the market and the reality of a more open and global economy, not as a god but as an essential element of a free and productive society; and recognize the limits of politics itself—if all these challenges are met, we can once again succeed. If we persist in the politics of nostalgia, denial, and blame, we shall fail, and deserve to fail.

In opposition it was easy for the party to become allied with groups preoccupied by one issue or another. The television culture of our times has also fostered time and attention for articulate speakers on behalf of a single cause. Yet governing is necessarily about reconciling competing interests. It often means choosing between something you don't want to do and something you *really* don't want to do. A political party has to be more than a rag bag of complaints and grievances if it wants to govern.

The party is often so preoccupied with doing what it thinks is right that it ignores opinion entirely. We eventually did what had to be done on Sunday shopping, but it took a long time and we paid a heavy price for our intransigence. A less ideological approach would have been sounder. A woman once stopped me on the street and said, "I wish you'd stop telling me when I can shop and when I can't." She was right. We were too much in her face.

The answer to a right that has become more narrow and ideological is not for the left to do the same. In the worldwide debate about changing the way governments work, reforming public enterprise, and reinvigorating the market, it would be tragic if the only voice from the progressive side of the spectrum was to defend the status quo. Big state enterprises and monopolies can be inefficient. They can breed arrogance, poor service, and a culture where people are underworked and overpaid. It is better if people who believe in a positive and legitimate role for government lead the changes necessary than leave it to those who have a visceral commitment to throwing the baby out with the bath water.

It is worth recalling that in the winter of 1978–79 the Callaghan government in the United Kingdom was pummelled by a trade union leadership convinced that talk of a social contract was treachery. The successor to this weakened Labour government was Margaret Thatcher. Nearly twenty years later, a transformed and deeply chastened Labour Party aspires to return to office. Infantile radicalism has never served working people well. We should not have to spend twenty years in the wilderness to learn this lesson.

If bigger government, higher taxes, ending trade agreements, and attacking all business corporations aren't the answer, what is? Social democracy is about enlarging the scope and prospects for freedom and well-being, ensuring that people are treated equally and without discrimination, and reinforcing our sense of solidarity and what we owe each other and future generations. This is the basis for a vigorous public agenda. It is different from the Regina Manifesto: it is not the eradication of capitalism that we should be seeking, but the strengthening of our community, and a broader, more democratic economy.

Technology should be freeing more of us from drudgery. Unemployment should be replaced by less forced working time. "Rae Days" were a way of distributing work differently than firing younger employees. I say to my union friends: change the name if you like, but keep the idea alive. Lifelong education becomes a necessity, and championing fair and affordable access to it is key to a more democratic world. This starts well before grade school, and all the Tory babble about going back to the good old days of babysitting and child-minding misses the point that the children of working parents deserve the best possible education at the earliest age. We are cheating future generations if we fail to ensure it is provided.

These services, or any human service, do not need to be offered directly by the state. But government has to provide the supports and incentives to make sure they are there, and that their quality is of the highest order. We should redefine universality by insisting on better outcomes, not by demanding the same bureaucratic input.

We have made significant progress as Canadians over the past thirty years in reducing poverty among the elderly. That has been achieved not by increasing the amount of the old age pension for everyone over the age of sixty-five, but by targeting increased support to the people who need it most, both provincially and federally.

There is a strong argument for extending this approach. A national income-support programme, carefully tied to the income tax and the Canada Pension Plan, could replace the amazing range of provincial and municipal welfare programmes. Let the provinces assume authority for training, education, and labour market programmes. Let the federal government take on income support, using the tax system to support poorer families more aggressively through an enhanced child benefit. If we do more, across Canada, to help low-income families where parents are working, this is a powerful and practical incentive for people to stay off welfare. We should do most for those who need it most rather than defend all the bureaucratic turf that now exists.

On taxes, we have been bedevilled by the fruitless debate between those who want the tax system to redistribute wealth and those who believe it should only reward success. In fact we want the tax system to do two basic things: to raise revenue fairly, and to

promote growth and national goals like more jobs and more investment in human capital. We need to be more creative about how
this can be done. Taxes on employment are counter-productive. At
the same time, we should be rewarding speculation less and real
investment in people more. I would invite the social partners to
discuss how this can be done. My other criterion would be to say
that lower interest rates are just as important as lower taxes, and
there is no point in keeping deficits and interest rates high at the
same time as we keep lowering taxes in the name of "relief." This is
not relief. This is just trading a headache for an upset stomach.

Lower payroll taxes; more tax credits for job creation, and
investments in training and research and development; taxes on
consumption to be matched by a reduction in income taxes on the
less well-off to ensure fairness and progressivity are maintained.
Continue to provide incentives for employee ownership and
worker participation. Give everyone a stake in the success of the
national enterprise. Keep the whole thing flatter and simpler, and
insist on more co-operation with the provinces. The current duplication and turf warfare are not helping.

One of the greatest, and more pernicious, mythologies of the
neo-conservative era is that of the "self-made man." In real life we
stand on the shoulders of all who have gone before, on the
support of parents and family, of teachers and friends, of community institutions paid for many times over by generations. This is
as true for companies and corporations as it is for individuals:
every school, day-care centre, and hospital we build is a support
and subsidy for successful enterprise. By the same token, Canada,
like all countries, needs globally successful enterprises to sustain
jobs and investment of all kinds, whether that investment is a new
home, a new swimming pool, or a new school.

The new public philosophy we need is this: a vigorous, innova-
tive society where enterprise of all kinds is encouraged, where
every citizen accepts the need for an efficient and productive
economy to produce wealth and a public sector healthy enough to
ensure that everyone has a seat at the table. We should be spending more time building partnerships necessary for this society. We

also need to make sure more workers have access—through direct employee ownership and democratic pension and savings plans—to the success of the enterprises for which they work.

In this democratic economy unions would have a role as partners and not as mere protesters. That requires a culture shift from them as well as from much of what now passes as the corporate élite. The old-boy network is still too strong in Canadian business. A visit to the Toronto clubs at lunch stands in about as great a contrast to the multicultural, multiracial subway underneath as can be humanly imagined. That is not healthy.

Since the beginning of the industrial revolution, national trade union movements have been at the centre of progressive change. The ideas they espoused, over time, became law. This is less true today. There are people in the private-sector trade union movement that have understood and embraced the need for change. I was proud to work closely with them in giving workers a stake and equity in the companies where they have jobs and to pass far-seeing legislation on worker ownership and participation.

Now that dramatic changes are coming, unavoidably, in the public sector, the test will be whether the broader union leadership can also begin to come to grips with the need for a more productive approach. A right-wing, anti-union style coming from management obviously makes it much harder, and makes it easier for the "worse is better" school of trade union leaders to fall back on waving placards and shouting slogans. Business is even more anti-union today than thirty or forty years ago, and as the number of organized workers in the private economy declines, this tendency will only grow. Inevitably, a marginalized trade union movement will act in an even more marginalized fashion.

All Western economies have become less equal in recent years. Workers who in the 1950s and 1960s could look to relatively strong national governments, trade unions, and economic protection to advance their cause are now having to face a rapidly changing and increasingly open world without much help. At the same time, those with globally marketable skills are in a stronger position than ever. The result is the growing gap between the skilled and the unskilled, between those who can successfully ride the Next Wave and those who are being swamped by it.

King Canute sat on his throne and tried ordering the rising waves to stop. Whether Canute's crown is worn by reactionaries from the left or the right won't really matter. The waves will keep coming. Surely a politics that wanted to respond to the changes in the world would aim at providing more and more people with necessary skills. The answers from the theorists sound increasingly anachronistic, because they are.

But they are correct about the pain people are feeling. Real incomes for working families have fallen since the 1970s. The benefits of affluence are less widely shared than at any time since the Second World War. Those who appeal to that pain are going to find ever angrier responses. The right has been more successful in both arousing that pain and in responding to it than the traditional left.

← →

On social and cultural issues like immigration, employment equity, native rights, gun control, and gay rights, as well as the critical social and economic issues like welfare, jobs, and taxes, populist, right-wing politics have changed the style and substance of debate in North America and in Europe. I certainly experienced first hand that these ideas and perceptions have deep resonance in the public. Harris couldn't have been elected without them. The fact that Harris wasn't telling the truth when he said there was something called a "quota bill" in Ontario doesn't matter politically. The fact is he got away with it, and played to a perception I was unable to change.

Similarly on welfare: opinion moved beneath us very quickly. Even Conrad Black joined David Peterson and an apparent solid consensus in making welfare changes that proved enormously expensive when we hit the recession wall. In the matter of a few months, the debate shifted to the classical ground of welfare Cadillacs, single mothers having babies just to stay on the pogie, and every other conceivable right-wing myth. These issues have been with us since the Elizabethan Poor Law of 1601, and the decision to build workhouses in the nineteenth century. Forcing the allegedly lazy, undeserving poor to work for benefits was a central tenet of classical political economy in the nineteenth century. Gradgrind was a Dickensian Victorian figure, and might as well be a senior adviser to Mike Harris. We have rediscovered the roots of what calls itself a "new" conservatism.

So too on taxes. The Tory ideology has played cunningly to a wide audience. No one likes paying taxes, and people no longer see the connection between the taxes they pay and the services they get. This is heightened in the recession, first because low or zero inflation means every tax increase is visible and tangible. Inflation conceals higher taxes, and envelops them in nominally higher wages and incomes. No inflation puts a stop to all that. When we raised taxes in 1993, people felt it right away and saw their incomes shrink before their eyes.

The left-wing take on our government is that we spent all our time cozying up to business, betrayed our principles, lost our base, and failed miserably and abjectly as a government. The right-wing take on our government is that we drove business and investment away with our ideological policies, spent irresponsibly, brought in quotas that prevented young white males from getting work, and encouraged young women to have babies out of wedlock with promises of lifelong income support at handsome and unaffordable levels. And, of course, failed miserably and abjectly as a government.

Both takes are wrong. The government was inexperienced and did make mistakes. But we had virtues as well, and just as it is important to remember and learn from mistakes, it is wise to cherish the virtues. We were right on the need to try to govern for the whole province, and to break down the futile conflict between those who put justice first and those who put efficiency first. We were right to put bankers and brokers and social workers and union leaders in the same room and ask them to work to a common goal. We were right to insist on a major investment in jobs and infrastructure, as well as child care and services to children, right to cut day-to-day spending on salaries when recovery stalled, right to insist on labour peace and a respect for partnership.

We were right on the need for real acceptance of diversity within Ontario, and right on national unity.

I got into a lot of trouble with the left in my own party in Ontario because I reached the conclusion that debts and deficits were not a figment of the imagination of a group of evil bankers, but in fact a matter of great concern to government and public policy. I also reached the conclusion that there were limits to how far people would accept being taxed further, and that the public sector had to show a capacity for restraint and change faced with the decline in the economy. When there is a recession, the operating costs of the public sector, which is for the most part made up of wages, have to be restrained, in order to allow for room for capital investment and stimulus from government. This diminishes the necessity of further taxing the already besieged private sector.

We were not able to convince the public-sector unions of the merits of this approach, and this did much to damage the credibility of the government and its ability to be re-elected. I knew then that if we were not able to win through with our approach, other parties would be elected which would mete out a much harsher punishment, driven by an ideology that included huge tax cuts that would only be achieved by even deeper cuts in service. I take no satisfaction in having been proved right.

Others will have to assess their own actions, and how this contributed to the election of the Harris government. I accept that what I tried to do, and the way I tried to do it, was hardly a political success. In policy terms it was the right thing to do, what Sir Humphrey in "Yes, Prime Minister" would have called a "very courageous thing to do." In political terms, we failed, though there were many good things done along the way.

The right's enthusiasm to dismantle government and the public sector assumes that the economy, left to its own devices, will produce all the jobs and opportunities necessary, and that the outcomes of millions of private decisions will produce the best of possible results. The only thing wrong with this view is several hundreds of years of history, and the fact that people won't accept a world where politics is completely subservient to the private economy, or at least won't accept it without a fight.

The politics of industrial societies has consisted in good measure of people using governments and public policy as a means of overcoming what they have felt to be the unfairness and harshness of the market. That will not change, but the difficulty is that the scope and dimension of the market has become more global, and far more difficult to govern or control.

The nation state will not disappear soon, but there can be little doubt that it will be a less capable instrument of public policy than it was in the nineteenth and twentieth centuries. Issues of governance and regulation will become at once more global and more local and regional. There is a steady growth of international networks on human rights, on the environment, on issues affecting women, on peace and disarmament that will not produce anything like a "world government" overnight, or even in the next century, but a "citizens' politics" on a global scale is imaginable today. On a practical basis, environmental politics and regulation will have to be international to be effective. National and provincial governments will be reluctant to pass policies that their neighbours don't have to.

It is a cliché that we now live in a global economy. The lesson of our first budget, as it was of the first efforts of the French Socialists a decade before, is that no one province can do it on its own. It's not that deficits are bad in and of themselves. It is that no province can strike out entirely on its own. We needed to be part of a national strategy. We were stymied every step of the way because we were alone.

It is clear that on a great many issues Ontario and Canada will have to adjust our policies to take our membership in NAFTA, GATT and the World Trade Organization more fully into account.

We need to create popular continent-wide institutions to match the power of continent-wide capital. This is beginning to happen, but too slowly. The left has lost the battle over NAFTA. We need to adjust our strategy accordingly. It is a hard fact of life that the degree of integration between our two economies is such that if the American Congress were to unilaterally rescind NAFTA and further restrict our access to the American market, we would be devastated. Laments have their place, but they are not the basis for a future politics.

At the same time, the issues that will touch most directly on the creation of wealth will be focused regionally and locally. The most important determinants of wealth and job creation in the next century will be education and training, quality of life, health, and our ability to attract public and private investment. We will not look to Ottawa for solutions in these areas.

At this point you may well ask, why, then, have Canada at all? Is breakup not an inevitable part of this sea-change? My answer is that Canada has always successfully defined itself as a partnership, a group of people who have done great things together in the past and who aspire to do great things together in the future. This is, after all, Ernest Renan's classic definition of a nation. Why break up a partnership if it can show the imagination to change?

Rabbi Hillel, one of the greatest teachers in history, asked these questions: "If I am not for myself, then who is for me? But if I am only for myself, then what am I? And if not now, when?"

None of us should take offence that for generations the French-Canadian majority in Quebec has insisted on finding its own voice. A sense of identity and a demand for recognition are only natural and healthy. But if this self-regard becomes exclusive, we are left with the unhealthiest of politics, the old bugbears of language, race, and religion.

It is simply wrong to assert ethnic or racial identity as the logical basis for the nation. Most countries in the world are plural. And if the sovereignists shift the debate and say, "Our vision for Quebec is plural," surely we are entitled to express our scepticism, and having done that, to say, "Why leave?" By asserting the need for partnership and associations, and going on to describe the common institutions and common partnership necessary to make this new relationship real, sovereignists are revealing that they are really federalists. What must be discussed and negotiated now are the terms and conditions of this renewed partnership. But there will have to be blunt talk: Quebec will not be able to dictate unilaterally the terms of its relationship with the rest of Canada. Nor can the rest of Canada be legitimately expected to accept an abrupt secession on the basis of the 50% plus one vote. There is nothing in the Canadian constitution or partnership that anticipates this kind of action. And Quebecers should be clearly disabused of the fond notion that life will be easier or better outside the Canadian community. Quebec will have little leverage and fewer choices. The sovereignists are kidding themselves and everybody else when they pretend there is a painless way to break up a country. We are already seeing signs of a tragically predictable turmoil within Quebec itself.

I once heard a teacher make what seemed a simple point about the limits of linguistic philosophy. "It's important to have clean eyeglasses, and a good idea to clean them every once in a while. But you don't spend your life cleaning your glasses. You put them on to see the world more clearly, and then you act."

We have been cleaning our constitutional eyeglasses in Canada for a long time. It is an endless process which baffles and annoys most Canadians. It is also entirely inadequate to the task at hand. If we do not recognize Quebec as a distinct society within Canada, Quebec will insist on being treated as a distinct society outside Canada. We must make the structure of a new Confederation generous and flexible enough to include all the partners, all the regions of the country, and all the people of Canada. Above all, we must get on with it. We must not allow the ostrich to replace the beaver as our national symbol.

Leadership sometimes means telling people things they don't want to hear. Politics and economics go together: we can only get our economic house in order, as provinces and as a country, when we can find a deep-seated political stability. So long as the future of Quebec and Canada is constitutionally uncertain, we are just marking time. To borrow a Chinese phrase from a recent speech by Henry Kissinger, "When the heavens are unsettled, small problems become big problems and big problems cannot even be addressed. Hence when there is peace in the heavens, big problems become small problems, and small problems disappear."

We are entitled to ask Mr. Bouchard to bring forward in greater detail the kind of partnership he has in mind for a post-referendum Canada. At the same time, Canadian political leaders should be prepared to at least contemplate what a Canada without Quebec would look like, and what conditions we would really want to attach to continued association and partnership with Quebec.

There are those who say that this amounts to threatening Quebec with dire consequences. Quite the contrary. We have to be clearer among ourselves about what choosing breakup means, and how we would all deal with that world. This kind of effort would also help us to find more creative solutions to the present impasse. We have a right to ask that Mr. Bouchard and his government do the same. The idea that all will be put off for another day, and pretend that nothing is happening, is absurd.

It is not just foreign markets and investors who want answers to difficult questions. We all need them, and delay doesn't necessarily help any of us. It is important to remember that in the European Union, which is a partnership of sovereign states, members are steadily giving up more and more of their powers, agreeing to coordinate activities, share investment in science and research, adopt comparable social policies, deal with disadvantaged areas, and work toward a common monetary and fiscal policy.

On our own continent, NAFTA points toward greater integration and limitation on absolute sovereignty. Quebec was in the forefront for NAFTA. Any partnership with the rest of Canada will involve the establishment of common institutions, the coordination of policies, and the inevitable limitation of sovereignty. It is not too much of a stretch to suggest that this is the reality that federalism itself was designed to address: the need for more devolved, decentralized decision-making; the need for local sovereignties and shared powers where this makes sense. Canada is not a unitary state. Its very creation in 1867 was a coming apart, as well as a coming together, when the straitjacket imposed by Lord Durham after 1837 proved unworkable.

We cannot afford a ten- or fifteen-year divorce proceeding. The world will literally pass us by. Old formulas will not keep us together. The prospect of a renewed confrontation between Mr. Chrétien and Mr. Bouchard as an echo of the old Trudeau-Lévesque debates of the sixties and seventies is appalling: a futile locking of horns, resolving nothing, leaving most Canadians increasingly bewildered and angry.

In the end, we shall accept what stares us in the face: Canada requires the sharing and division of power, of sovereignty. The provinces are sovereign in some areas; federal institutions in others. The world is interdependent. No sovereignty is absolute. We shall relearn these truths and make them our own. We shall have to reinvent and re-create Canada.

We are now a country whose leadership is trapped in a constitutional swamp. Other compelling issues which should preoccupy us—a hungry generation of young children, an environmental crisis, health-care systems stretched to the limit, an economy which longs for leadership, partnership, investment, direction—all take second place. So does the world around us. We are described as "searching for ourselves." Wouldn't "searching for justice" or "searching for others" be more compelling? And wouldn't we be more likely to really find ourselves in that search?

Think of those things we have in common. First there is the land we share. Imagine for a moment the first trip up the Saguenay by Europeans, the first view of Lake Ontario, Superior, Niagara. Go north from the cities huddled along the rivers and lakes near the American border. See the Canada we share. In the embarrassingly self-conscious poetic preamble to the Act Respecting the Future of Quebec (1995), there is talk of "winter" as if this belongs only to Quebec. Not so: we are partners in weather as well as geography. That is why we both go to Florida.

We are not conquerors. There are none among us now. The battle for domination in North America between two European empires is over. Behind us. None of us alive today was there among the foreign troops. Let's stop pretending we were. There is a history to be learned and respected. There is also a mythology from which we must awaken.

The reconciliation must finally include native Canadians as well. For centuries our legal and political systems pretended Canada's first people were invisible. Our culture and folklore pretended they were savages. This too is a history we must now change.

The challenges we face are common challenges. Living and working in a global economy requires teamwork and partnership for us to succeed. A shared challenge of creating good jobs for a new generation, a need to maintain a decent social order, and to keep the sense of our having common obligations for "peace, order, and good government" despite the pressures of the world upon us.

Jacques Parizeau, on his visit to Toronto in December 1994, told Canadians outside Quebec that if Quebeckers voted "yes," the constitutional issue would be over. "The trips to the dentist" would end. I'm surprised he didn't offer us an all-day sucker at the same time. If you don't go to the dentist once in a while, your teeth fall out. Negotiating is not a bother. It is a part of life, part of being Canadian. To try and escape it with one-sided moves is an illusion that will end up hurting everyone. Canada is big enough for all of us. We have shared too much to give up now.

Politics has a lousy name. The word conjures up images of sleaze and corruption, of backroom compromises, of public commitments too glibly made and too easily broken. Sitting with a group of Canadians chosen at random by the CBC, I was confronted with the inevitable "now that you politicians have all failed so badly, what can we ordinary people do to make it better?"

A friend of mine was once describing a dilemma about trouble she was having at work. "So I had a choice. I could either deal with it honestly, or," she said, with a sneer, "I could handle it politically."

There are good and bad people in all walks of life. Politicians are not the only ones among us who change their minds or even break commitments. We can no more avoid politics in our lives than we can avoid breathing. Politics is about values and power, courage and service. It is also about leadership and compromise.

Above all, politics is necessary, necessary to confront the fact that whenever people associate together there will be inevitable questions not only about who gets and does what, but in whose values, and in whose authority, decisions are made. Men on white horses armed with simple solutions are the answer when people decide they've had enough of "politics as usual."

In a simplistic blaming of "politicians" as some kind of lower caste, people are really avoiding the issue of their own responsibility. We are all politicians in our own way and in our own fashion. From family arguments to the politics of the school or the office, there is no getting around the need for participation. Bad things happen when good people sit on their hands. Good things happen when everyone tries to make a difference. These clichés are true.

The world around us is changing at such a pace that we all have to become leaders at the very least for ourselves. The pattern of steady lifelong employment in one job is gone. At every level of society we can't rely on "organizational flow" to get us where we want to go. We have to take stock, make conscious decisions. We can't avoid having to make choices, and the choices we make are in the context of a vision.

Great leaders seem to come by it naturally, but looks are deceiving. The age of television encourages us to be passive, and to assume that leaders are "out there," different from us. Nothing could be further from the truth. The prophet or visionary is not necessarily a good leader, because leadership requires followers. A leader who is so far ahead of the pack that no one else is behind him will not be a leader for very long. The most successful leaders, in any organization, are the people who are constantly testing and refining their ideas in the light of experience, and who know that to be successful they have to strike a balance. People with great visionary ideas that no one seems to understand are not leaders. People who are so rigid that they can't compromise are not likely to be good leaders either. A British politician, commenting on a colleague who was having trouble with the give and take of politics, once said, "If you can't ride two horses at the same time, you've got no business being in the bloody circus."

The trick is to listen to criticism, and take it in, and learn to ignore it as well. That's never easy. Over time, successful leadership needs resonance and followers. Yet to just be popular and test the wind every day with your wet finger won't help you when circumstances change drastically. No one was more popular than Neville Chamberlain when he bought a phony peace with Hitler in 1938. He left office in disgrace a year and a half later, and history has not been kind to his leadership skills, however well he did in the polls while in office.

Polls—and even the stock market—tell us where we've been, not where we're going, or why we're likely to get there. Making opinion, forming it, leading it, is more important than counting it or following it blindly. Things change.

The greatest virtue in all this is courage. As writer and public servant Douglas Le Pan has recently written:

> —*And without a core of courage*
> *how can anything ever be achieved, can anything be*
> *built?*
> *And courage shadowed by weakness may be the most*
> *precious*
> *of all, since it carries sweetness into the heart of the*
> *building,*
> *carries it like honey into the hollows of the honey-*
> *comb.*

← →

I would encourage anyone with a thick skin, a good sense of humour, a love of people and the noise of the arena to take up the torch. I have learned that politics cannot solve all ills, that it is not always to be confused with life itself, but that it is a worthy and necessary pursuit. All in all, I am happy to have done what I did. I helped to take my party from protest to power. Once in power, we were able to do many good things, as well as learn much about what it is possible to do. Our courage may have been shadowed by weakness, but we were also able to carry some sweetness into the heart of the building.

INDEX